83

Cup Magic

Cup Magic

DAVID MILLER

SIDGWICK & JACKSON
LONDON

First published in Great Britain in 1981
by Sidgwick and Jackson Limited

Copyright © 1981 David Miller

I am grateful to the *Daily Telegraph* for permission
to reproduce much of the original material
from 'I was There' for Chapter 8 as well as extracts
from match reports, to Macdonald Futura for
permission to reproduce extracts from *Denis Law :
An Autobiography* by Denis Law (Queen Anne Press),
and to Frances Russell for valuable typing assistance.

ISBN 0 283 98697 2

*Printed in Great Britain by
Biddles Ltd., Guildford, Surrey
for Sidgwick and Jackson Limited
1 Tavistock Chambers, Bloomsbury Way
London WC1A 2SG*

Contents

List of Illustrations

Between pages 96 and 97

England *v* West Germany, World Cup Final, 1966 (*Blick in die Welt*)

Celtic *v* Internazionale, European Cup Final, 1967 (*The Associated Press Ltd*)

England *v* West Germany, World Cup, 1970 (*The Associated Press Ltd*)

England *v* West Germany, World Cup, 1970 (*The Associated Press Ltd*)

Leeds *v* Sunderland, F.A. Cup Final, 1973 (*Keystone Press Agency*)

England *v* Poland, World Cup, 1973 (*The Press Association Ltd*)

England *v* Poland, World Cup, 1973 (*Keystone Press Agency*)

Liverpool *v* Borussia München-Gladbach, European Cup Final, 1977 (*Keystone Press Agency*)

West Germany *v* Holland, World Cup Final, 1974 (*The Associated Press Ltd*)

Arsenal *v* Manchester United, F.A. Cup Final, 1979 (*The Press Association Ltd*)

Arsenal *v* Manchester United, F.A. Cup Final, 1979 (*The Press Association Ltd*)

Dedication

The beauty of soccer is that it means so many different things to different people. I have a friend born within a stone's throw of the Chelsea and Fulham clubs in West London, a life-long, fanatical devotee of both who, every Saturday of the football season, enters a state of animated euphoria at about ten in the morning and ascends towards a crescendo of expectation until, at five to three, he can be said without fear of contradiction to be the happiest man in Britain. It is a measure of his passion for the game, of almost fifty years spent unremittingly hooked on glorious uncertainty, that even the vagaries of Chelsea and Fulham have failed to diminish his ardour. He is, I suppose, the definitive perfect spectator – a man magnanimous enough to appreciate true quality in *any* team, yet blindly partisan enough to believe that the odds are never so great against his own team that they do not have a chance, that fickle fortune will smile upon them – if not today, then next week, next year . . .

His name is Henry Turner, and his infectious enthusiasm is capable of illuminating the bleakest match, for the simple reason that he has come to terms with one of the fundamental truths of life, and football – that, by and large, you have to make your own luck, that you can depend on nothing and that you have to expect that events will constantly steal up and defeat you from behind. These are beliefs without which no football manager can succeed, but which are increasingly rare in the newer generation of soccer spectators, brought up in the 'me' society, encouraged by the endless waterfall of television to believe that we all deserve things for which we do not have the talent, the brains or the perseverance. Henry has all three, and to him this book is dedicated in the memory of many happy moments.

Introduction

Over luncheon sometime early in 1979, I happened to make the point to William Armstrong, managing director of Sidgwick and Jackson, that almost every cup tie down the years was not always what it seemed, that the result was usually dependent on some injury, on the momentary aberration of an individual player, on those imponderables which so dramatically make football a mirror of life itself. In other words, I propounded, it was axiomatic of many of the great cup ties that the 'wrong' team won. Why not make it into a book, suggested my host? And so here we are.

There are two ways in which the 'wrong' team can win. The most obvious is when, as with Leeds against Sunderland in the 1973 Football Association Cup Final, the expectation is universally for a victory by one of the most accomplished of all teams, but the Second Division outsiders achieve the 'impossible' reversal, due partly to the ineptitude of the favourites on the day and partly to such one-in-a-million moments as the save by Jim Montgomery.

There is also the situation in which one team has almost all of the game, yet still loses, as with Bolton against Blackpool in 1953 and England against the United States in 1950, or draws, as with England against Poland in 1973.

And when taking into consideration the matter of luck, I believe that events off the field, such as Gordon Banks' illness in the 1970 World Cup, are as relevant as events on the field, such as Ray Wood's injury in the 1957 F.A. Cup Final, or the aberrations of Barcelona's goalkeeper, Ramallets, in 1961. Yet luck, or bad luck, comes in strange guises. It can be argued, as Rudi Krol does, that Holland's 90-second goal in the 1974 World Cup Final was to West Germany's advantage, while Johan Neeskens' ability to speak Spanish had a strange twist in 1978.

My premise is that football is as much about luck as about ability or application. It is unlikely that you will win anything without some of all three. And the luck factor is especially relevant to cup football, in which the rub of the green and the whimsy of the referee's whistle has no time to even itself out the way it does in league soccer. Professor Peter Sloan, in his perceptive and largely ignored paper *Sport in the Market* published by the Institute of Economic Research (1980), argues that uncertainty of outcome is the key market factor in the merchandising of any profitable professional sport. It is no coincidence that the two single biggest television audiences world-wide for any regular event in any sphere of life are, the Olympic Games apart, the World Cup Final and the F.A. Cup Final.

Many football managers claim that what *really* counts is the league, because that reflects consistency of performance. Yet I believe that their preference is influenced in many instances by the fact that they do not like the element of luck, that many of them would be quite content with something safe, predictable and boring so long as they were on the winning side. I am quite certain that many managers have lost sight of the fact that the fundamental justification for their existence in a professional game is entertainment, an ability to persuade the public to come through the turnstiles. Danny Blanchflower, that most eloquent of all professional footballers, has said, long after his glittering career with Spurs and Northern Ireland and at a time when the game was becoming increasingly functional, that 'football is not *only* about winning, it is about glory'. Of course glory usually goes hand in hand with winning, but not, I believe, necessarily. It is possible to be a glorious loser—because often it is the qualities and endeavours of the loser which actually create the status of the winner. This was so in the 1954 World Cup Final when Hungary lost to West Germany, likewise when Holland lost to West Germany in 1974. It was true of the European Cup Finals of 1960 and 1961, when Eintracht and Barcelona lost to Real Madrid and Benfica respectively, and of the 1962 semi-final in which Spurs agonizingly yielded to Benfica. Sir Alf Ramsey, when he succeeded Walter Winterbottom as England manager in 1963, set about building a team which, among its other qualities, 'would hate to lose'. That is all very well, but it is a short step from hating-to-lose to hating, as we witness continually on the terraces nowadays. Those who consider that hating to lose is synonymous with professionalism should perhaps pause to reflect on the fact that the *Oxford Dictionary* definition of 'glory' does not in any context mention winning.

It talks instead about honourable fame, and that is a condition far more enduring than victory. It is my contention that cup football is, in fact, closer to the ideological objectives of sport, if indeed there are any, than is league football. Too often, in my opinion, league football is a compromise between adventure and expediency. 'The trouble with English soccer,' the famous Yugoslav Miljan Miljanic told me some years ago, 'is that your league clubs play "industrial football"! I see players in September in England who are fresh and adventurous but, by the following April, they are playing like automatons, so it is no surprise that your national team plays without inspiration in the summer.'

Ron Greenwood has been instrumental in producing a swing away from industrial football and back towards a freer, more adventurous game. Like Miljanic, he believes that the role of the international manager is concerned more with a concept of how the game should be played than is a club manager, 'who has to motivate his players at regular, short intervals'. It is perhaps symbolic that Greenwood's success as a club manager with West Ham was primarily in cup football, winning the F.A. Cup in 1964 and the European Cup-Winners Cup the following year, then the F.A. Cup again in 1975 shortly after he had handed over the team management to John Lyall. Subsequently, Greenwood stepped into the breach following Don Revie's shabby defection, and to an extent he has brought to the England team the same freedom of thought and movement which characterized West Ham.

The proof of my contention that cup football is closer to the heart of the matter is provided, I believe, by the West Ham crowd which, in spite of the absence of league success, has suffered the smallest decline of attendance in recent years of any club except Manchester United. This is because they have grown to acknowledge that there is more to the game than winning. Their attitude is epitomized by their adopted theme song—'I'm for ever blowing bubbles, pretty bubbles in the air'. With England, Greenwood is concerned almost exclusively with cup soccer, apart from preparatory friendlies. After England had qualified for the 1980 European Championship finals, in which they were to draw disappointingly with Belgium and lose to Italy, I asked him about his views on the relative values of cup and league. He said:

'Of course you *want* to be successful every week, and there isn't *intentionally* a difference of attitude among players and managers. But I think it may be related to training programmes. Success in league soccer is a matter of consistency, a constant grind. For league soccer you have got to be technically equipped *and* have all the qualities which will stand up to the grind, which may even include being negative to gain points. The sides which do well in cups may be those who relish being in competition over a short period, though that is not to say that clubs successful in the league are not often the ones who reach the semi-final of the cup. But sometimes there are players who are *occasion* players, like Bobby Moore and Franz Beckenbauer . . . They worked really hard when they were building their reputations, but when they had reached the top, you felt they were then waiting for the big occasions. Cup ties *are* more dramatic because, with sudden death, the referee's split-second decision, the defender's error, are so much more critical.

'One of the best things for me about international football is that players are always motivated by the fact that there are half a dozen players waiting to take their place, whereas the league manager, looking for consistency, is largely stuck with the players at his disposal, which may depend on his club's financial resources.'

Greenwood cites the four final matches of the 1976 European Championship as the best group of cup ties he has seen. Czechoslovakia, Yugoslavia and the 1974 World Cup finalists, West Germany and Holland, achieved an intoxicating level of inventive, adventurous challenge, with the Czechs—who had been lucky to eliminate England—ultimately winning the final against Germany on penalties after a game of heroic proportions.

In my selection of matches for this book I set myself several criteria: that they should all have been important before and after they were played, which is not to say that the many I have not selected are unimportant; and that the result should have been achieved by some exceptionally fortuitous turn of events, or that the result hung on an error, or series of errors, or on referees' decisions, which were critical. The product is finally, I accept, an anthology of the matches which fulfil one or more of these conditions *and* which particularly have appealed to me. I personally saw all but three of them, but have included the 1950 defeat of England by the United States of America and West Germany's triumph over Hungary four years later because they were historically significant, and Brazil's narrow win over Wales in 1958 because people overlook the fact that, even without John Charles, the Welsh were so close to halting that remarkable Brazilian side, which included the seventeen-year-old Pele.

I plead guilty to the fact that my view of the game is to some extent romantic, but in that I have been encouraged since I was a schoolboy by several people. My father, an actor, knew nothing of professional football, but instilled in me the value of developing skill and of learning to play with my left, 'wrong' foot. He would come home on leave from the R.A.F.—sometimes only for twenty-four hours, occasionally for a whole weekend—and we would take out my size-four ball and practise trapping on the path across the common, a mere three feet wide and smooth sand, but truer than the goat pasture on either side. The constriction encouraged good control.

The first man to introduce me to the fact that passing was the essence of the game was George Smith, then the Charlton defender and later manager of Crystal Palace and Portsmouth, who visited my junior school and mesmerized me with the sound he made, of leather on leather, when he kicked the ball, and, though I thought about it for a long while, it was only years later that I came to recognize it as *timing*. George, whom I dearly liked for his home-spun philosophies, epitomized the functional manager. 'The trouble with my lot', he used to reflect a trifle morosely when Pompey had slipped into the Third Division, 'is that they all think they are good players.'

I encountered the romance at Charterhouse—whose old boys long ago won the F.A. Cup—in the person of Anthony Wreford Brown, son of a famous chairman of the F.A. His knowledge of the game was primarily amateur, and his tactics tended to owe more to the Dam Busters than to the Hungarians, but I doubt if any 'manager' since Henry V ever gave more inspiring pre-action pep-talks. He was all passion and eloquence and I used to shake physically with expectation as he delivered his battle instructions on the eve of a big match under a bare 60-watt bulb in his class-room.

There then began an association which has lasted some thirty years, when I met Geoffrey Green, the correspondent of *The Times* and doyen of Fleet Street writers. Geoffrey, a former Corinthian centre-half, saw the game as a painter's canvas, an expression of mood and colour, of gaiety and grief, capturing man's better aspirations. When the Queen, investing him with the Order of the British Empire shortly before his retirement, enquired whom he hoped to see contest his last F.A. Cup Final before he settled into his rose-covered cottage by the Thames, he replied: 'As long as it is between fun and laughter, I don't really mind, Ma'am.' After I left university, I joined Geoffrey at *The Times* as a junior sub-editor, where I think I acquired his prerequisite of criticism: that a team should entertain me. Subconsciously entertainment has been another factor conditioning my selection.

The other abiding influence on my 'education' was Arthur Rowe, one of the first, and the most original, of England's breed of manager-coaches. Arthur had been thinking deeply about the game at a time when the coaching by many managers did not extend beyond sending the players out for a run and picking the side on Friday. He had been to Hungary and witnessed the concept of collective play which had already, before the war, surpassed the English. He put his ideas into practice with the illustrious Spurs teams of the early fifties—'make it simple, make it quick'—and only illness prevented him from personally reaping the reward of his signing of Blanchflower. I was fortunate enough to be coached by him when he was with Pegasus, the combined Oxford and Cambridge team, which twice won the Amateur Cup and was the only amateur side to attract a crowd of 100,000 to Wembley. Arthur, with the purity of his ideas, with a concept based on attack, helped to give Pegasus a spirit of crusade, a belief that even on those grotty days in all too earthly surroundings far from Wembley, there was something magical in the game which transcended the business of winning. It is what I learned from Arthur which has made me frown on the negative, the mean and the expedient.

So there is my formula for selecting cup ties down the years —an amalgam of skill, romance and an adventurous spirit, all spiced with that imponderable, luck. For all the matches, I have talked, over the past year, with one or more of the managers and players who were involved, and this has resulted in a new and interesting light being thrown on some of them. Tom Finney and Stan Mortensen recall England's woeful lack of preparation in 1950, while Mortensen blames Bolton for their own defeat in the famous 'Matthews' F.A. Cup Final of 1953. Helmut Schoen reveals the cunning of Sepp Herberger, West Germany's manager, in thwarting the Hungarians. More recently, Rudi Krol, skipper of Holland, discusses how his team had decided they would walk out of the World Cup Final in Argentina because of the hosts' poor gamesmanship but were frustrated . . . because Johan Neeskens could speak Spanish! Luck can indeed take the strangest forms.

CHAPTER ONE

U.S.A.

v

England

WORLD CUP

1950

With negligible tactical planning, an England team containing several legendary names squanders countless chances on a terrible pitch, has a 'goal' scooped out from behind their opponents' goal-line, and suffers a historic World Cup defeat.

The insularity of Britain has been its strength and weakness for over a thousand years: affording protection on the one hand, isolating it on the other from the flow of ideas in the rest of Europe in the arts, professions, industry—and, more latterly, sport. Certainly in football. Throughout the first half of the twentieth century, the English football establishment viewed the rest of the world somewhat patronizingly with a mixture of superiority and suspicion. Having carried the game to the four corners of the globe, with the help of the Scots, it was not so much a matter of whether we considered that the foreigners, with their 'suspect' codes of behaviour, had really overtaken us; but whether we really cared. What more natural, therefore, than that Britain should stand aloof from the first three World Cups before the Second World War.

With persuasion from the secretary of the F.A., Sir Stanley Rous, the British finally condescended to enter the World Cup in 1950. The proposal was that the first two teams in the British Championship should qualify. The Scots, grandly but

perversely, declared that they would only go if they won, lost
to England and finished second—and stayed away. England
went to Brazil, and suffered a historic loss which remains to this
day one of the most notorious reversals of all time, ranking
with Italy's defeat by Korea in 1966, and with Scotland's draw
with Iran in 1978.

Having lost, England promptly returned home, nobody
staying behind to study how these upstarts from Uruguay,
Brazil and Spain were playing the game. If their way were
different from ours, so what. Good luck to them. As the English flew home, there was a gathering in a hotel lounge in Rio de
Janeiro of some of the most eminent football correspondents
from Europe and South America. The British journalists had
left with their team. Those present were addressed by Willy
Meisl, ardent anglophile and younger brother of the legendary
Hugo Meisl who was the inspiration of Austrian football
between the wars. It fell to Willy to explain to the others why
the English, for so long regarded as the world's masters, were
no longer so. He said:

'Britons believe in hard facts and figures. They lack imagination. They will not realize what has happened to their
soccer until they have experienced a string of humiliating
defeats, and home defeats at that. The defeats here in the
World Cup might have a sobering effect, but it's doubtful.
Brazil is a long way from Britain. Only seeing for themselves is, to them, believing. Remember that the British
sports press doesn't tell them what is happening elsewhere—
for the good reason that the journalists themselves are hardly
aware of it. I'd like to remind you that this same lack of
imagination which has caused the decline of British soccer
has often proved itself a national asset. But for their lack of
imagination the British could never have fought on in 1940
against a hundredfold superior foe. They stood alone and had
no earthly chance of victory. But they still went at it, single-
handed, ill-equipped. Their courage, faith and pride as well
as their lack of imagination prevented them from recognizing
how infinitesimal was their chance of success. It was this
which saved them.'

The truth of Meisl's words is reflected by the fact that, on the morning of the match against the U.S.A., the newspapers at home carried a mere four or five paragraphs of preview, even though they had despatched staff writers across the Atlantic. The disaster which followed received perhaps ten paragraphs the following day, and no inquest thereafter. Not then was it a matter of national mourning that a team which contained many of the most illustrious players in English history—Ramsey, Wright, Dickinson, Mortensen, Mannion, Finney—had been up-ended by a bunch of unknown fourth-raters. How did it happen?

The manager in those days was Walter Winterbottom, who combined his duties with those of Director of Coaching—but did not select the team. Selection was in the hands of a committee of selectors, who were influenced almost exclusively by current club form, and by the press. How many times did the famous forward line of Matthews, Carter, Lawton, Mannion and Finney play together? The answer, in fact, is never. On the two occasions when the first four played in 1946-47, the outside left was Mullen against Scotland, and Langton against Switzerland. When Portugal were beaten 10-0 in Lisbon that season, Mortensen was inside-right, scoring four goals, as did Lawton.

By 1950 Lawton, that renowned header of the ball, the famed Frank Swift in goal, and blond, immaculate, peerless Raich Carter had all gone. The selectors switched Matthews, Finney, Mullen, Harris, Langton and Hancock on the wings as frequently and with as little logic as society ladies change their hats. For the World Cup there was no special preparation of the team and, indeed, the F.A. had arranged for a squad to go on tour in Canada simultaneously, Matthews and Jim Taylor of Fulham flying down to join the players in Brazil a couple of days before the opening match against Spain. Tom Finney, whose rivalry with Matthews was a matter of unresolved argument wherever football was discussed, as it is today, still follows the game with interest, taking time off from his family plumbing business in Preston. He says now:

'There wasn't much planning in those days. We met about a week beforehand at Roehampton in London and flew out only two or three days before the start. Frankly, we were way behind everyone else internationally. We were playing at the game like an amateur side. There was no tactical planning for any of the games. Walter was a great theorist, going through the opposition, but discussing them as individuals and not as a team. I cannot remember a single occasion on which he said how we were to play tactically. He would simply give us hints on the technical strengths and weaknesses of our opposite numbers. We played reasonably well in the opening match against Chile, which we won 2-0 with goals by Wilf Mannion and Stan Mortensen, even though we'd only been there in Rio for thirty-six hours. It was steaming hot, and our hotel was right on Copacabana Beach, where life starts at midnight, so you can imagine the noise. It was still the same eight years later for the World Cup in Sweden, when England stayed in the centre of Gothenburg and Brazil quietly out in the country.'

Matthews, whose fitness was in doubt, did not play against Chile; Finney played on the right, Roy Bentley at centre-forward and Mullen on the left wing. There was some talk about changes against the U.S.A., but Winterbottom was overruled by the F.A. chairman, Arthur Drewry, and an unchanged side was named for what seemed no more than a formality— even if the Americans had only succumbed to Spain, in their first match, late in the game.

From Rio the team flew down to Belo Horizonte, where they were accommodated in style by a British gold mining company at Morro Velho, sixteen miles outside Belo. Matthews recalled afterwards: 'It was a fantastic drive from the airport along a red dust road cut out by the mine company, with nearly two hundred hairpin bends and a drop on each side without kerbs. We arrived covered in the red dust which had blown in through the window, but never before have I met such hospitality. If we wanted a car or a mule we had only to ask.'

A possibly critical factor for England, in retrospect, was the loss of Neil Franklin, their centre-half from Stoke, who had played in every game since the end of the war, but shortly before the World Cup had forsaken the £12 maximum-wage environment at home for the lure of peso-rich Santa Fe F.C. in Bogota. Colombia not being members of the Federation of International Football Associations, he was suspended forthwith. Winterbottom, now retired, recalls:

'I tried hard to persuade him not to go, and we certainly missed him very badly. He was one of the best centre-halves I ever saw. For the World Cup we had a choice of the Liverpool pair, Jones and Hughes, but neither had any experience. It was the equivalent of the England team of today losing Kevin Keegan. And, of course, one of the penalties of the selection committee system was that when an important player was injured, and the committee were divided on a replacement, you could finish up with a player whom nobody actually wanted!'

The U.S.A. had one selector, team manager Bill Jeffrey, a Scot now resident at Pennsylvania University. He had a team of novice nationals spiced with a sprinkling of foreigners— Maca, a Belgian left-back, Eddie McIlvenny, a Scottish wing-half given a free transfer by Wrexham the previous year, and Gaetjens, a Haiti-born centre-forward. Borghi, in goal, was an ex-baseball player who was to be a central figure on this bizarre occasion. Billy Wright, then still a muscular, commanding right-half with Wolves before switching to centre-half to complete his 100 international caps, wrote afterwards: 'We flew into Belo and were acclaimed "The Kings of Football". Our World Cup success at that stage was modest, a single victory, but I don't remember any strong protests by members of our party about that all-embracing compliment! When we left, alas, one report was even edged by a black border.'

A crowd of 20,000 jammed into the little ground for the expected slaughter and all seemed serene as England attacked at will. But from the start, things did not go quite right. Jimmy Mullen, the Wolves winger, raced through and, with only the goalkeeper to beat, shot over the bar. At that stage it was a moment to cause the England players no more than a passing smile—a smile which was soon to fade. Winterbottom, who thirty years later still remembers the match as if it were yesterday, and has been reminded of it every time he has set foot in the States, and even though England subsequently had a ten-goal victory, recalls:

'Football wouldn't be the same without these results, but that does not make them any more palatable when you are the victim. And it has to be said that they usually happen on a bad or a small ground. At Belo Horizonte, the grass was that South American kind with tufts every six inches or so, like individual plants, and spaces in between, so that the ball tended to sit up and our forwards repeatedly hit the ball on the rise. We so dominated the game it was impossible to believe we could lose, and it was said that in all we hit the bar and the posts eleven times. Jimmy Mullen had the most chances and, of course, there was the occasion towards the end when a header by Mortensen was almost certainly over the line before it was scooped out, but the referee would not allow it. This is not to make excuses. We missed our chances and paid the penalty. We had no proper preparation the way teams have today, and our players were not used to foreign, unfamiliar conditions the way league players are nowadays, with regular overseas competitions.'

Again and again Mortensen, Finney, Mannion and Mullen had the goal at their mercy, only to shoot too high or to see the ball leap back off the woodwork, or Borghi make incredible saves. The American keeper was afterwards hailed as a world beater.

The goal came in the thirty-seventh minute—and there were conflicting reports of how it happened. The English correspondents and agencies who were there reported that the shot by left-half Bahr from twenty-five to thirty yards struck Gaetjens on the back of the head and was deflected past Bert Williams. But Harry Keough, the American right-back, is quoted as saying years later in the magazine *Soccer America* (an extract from which was sent to my celebrated colleague Geoffrey Green while he was engaged in writing his nostalgic *Soccer in the Fifties*):

'At the time Joe scored we didn't think it had too much significance except maybe to wake up the English team, and they would then rain goals on us. An article needs to be written about that goal because I've never seen it described correctly. First, it was not from a free-kick but from a throw in by McIlvenny in England's half. I was across the halfway line myself when Ed threw to Walter Bahr who had come over from the left. Bahr was in a right-half position when he got the ball, and I was directly in line behind his immediate shot from twenty-five yards. The English centre-half, Hughes, saw it go by at four-foot level, at which time the streaking figure of Gaetjens came into the situation with a headlong, horizontal dive at Bahr's shot. After Joe touched it with his head, the ball veered off its original path, which goalie Williams seemed to have had in control. Joe landed face first in the grass and didn't see the result until he lifted himself up. I couldn't say whether it went over, under, or through Williams.'

Keough also remembers:

'Clarkie Souza, our inside-left and brother to winger Ed Souza, used his ball-carrying skills in the waning minutes to take the ball from outside-left all the way over to the outside-right corner flag where he forced a corner. This took at least forty or fifty seconds and the great Billy Wright was dogging him all the way. But carrying the ball was Clarkie's forte and he could do it against the finest . . . and Wright was the premier defenceman in the world. An unbelievable feat. To this day Clarkie has never been given the credit he deserves.'

The English team, who had changed beforehand a short bus ride away from the ground because the dressing rooms were so inadequate, spent half-time on the pitch discussing what to do. Winterbottom switched Bentley, who was having an ineffective game, to the right wing, Finney to the middle. But the second half produced no relief. Mortensen who, thirty years later, is still the sixth highest post-war English scorer with twenty-three goals in his twenty-five matches, recalls from his home in Blackpool:

'The Americans' defensive tactics were a bit rugged to say the least. Twice in the first half I was clean through on the edge of the area when I was dragged down. I'm not saying I would have scored but I must have had a great chance. The fact is that together with Brazil, the hosts, we were favourites on our reputation to win the competition. When the game finished, we were disgusted with ourselves. I'll never forget it. We threw it away. Tactics then weren't a part of the game, the way they were once the Hungarians had come to Wembley three years later and shown us how to play. We were still playing *totally* attacking football. That was what the crowds at home expected. Walter was very thorough and would tell us the characteristics of our opponents, but he would never attempt to manipulate our players. People wanted attacking football, and that's what they got.'

Billy Wright remembers:

'The harder we tried, the more difficult things became. Over-confidence gave way to overanxiousness, this in turn to desperation. We had enough of the ball after they scored to have won by a cricket score, but the ball was kept far too close on that unreliable surface. We had to contend with a referee, Dattilo of Italy, who seemed determined to let nothing so negligible as the laws of the game come between America and victory.'

Whilst Stanley Matthews recalls: 'Sitting watching, it was agonizing. We could hardly believe it was true and our English friends at the mining camp said it would take years to live this down among the Brazilians who worked with them. We felt we had let everybody down, but these things happen in sport and I don't intend taking the credit away from the Americans.'

In the last eight minutes, the Americans had survived two remarkable moments. Mullen hit a post, from the rebound Mortensen hit the cross-bar, a defender punched the ball clear and no penalty was awarded. Then Mortensen, clean through yet again, was pulled down once more by the ferocious centre-half Colombo inside the penalty area. The free kick was given outside, and Alf Ramsey hit a perfect shot towards the top of the net. But Borghi, in a final moment of defiance, pulled off an incredible save to turn the ball away.

Bill Jeffrey, overwhelmed by the success of his men, claimed afterwards: 'We came to the World Cup to learn, to keep the score down as low as we could. This result is all we needed to make the game a success back home in the United States.' His belief is as yet unfulfilled fifty years later.

Sir Stanley Rous, in what appears to have been a diplomatic

overstatement, suggested that the Americans 'were fitter, faster and better fighters' though, to be fair, Rous realized long before most others the extent to which England had fallen behind their pupils world-wide.

For the game against Spain, which England needed to win to force a play-off, Matthews was recalled, together with Jackie Milburn at centre-forward, with Eddie Baily of Spurs getting his first cap at inside-left and Finney switching to outside-left —to no avail. Spain won by the only goal and Matthews later wrote:

'A pity that Spain, who played some really good old-fashioned first-time football, should spoil their performance with some doubtful tactics. Twice I was pulled back by my shirt when passing a defender, and Mortensen and Milburn were tripped when through. These fouls would have been certain penalties in England. There was also body-checking that was allowed by the Italian referee, Galeati. The Spaniards used their hands freely in the second half and their centre-forward Zarra got the only goal. England, the masters of soccer, had failed even to qualify for the final group. The Brazilian crowd waved their handkerchiefs in the closing minutes chanting "Adios".'

Yet, though referees may have been as erratic then as they are today, though England certainly had their bad luck, it needed another four World Cups before they began to get themselves properly organized.

United States: Borghi; Keough, Maca; McIlvenny, Colombo, Bahr; Wallace, Parini, Gaetjens, Suza J., Suza E.

England: Williams; Ramsey, Aston; Wright, Hughes, Dickinson; Finney, Mortensen, Bentley, Mannion, Mullen

CHAPTER TWO

Blackpool

v

Bolton Wanderers

F.A. CUP FINAL

1953

A tactical blunder by Bolton when reduced to ten men by injury, and a defender moving in the 'wall' at a free kick, made possible this 'Matthews Final' of 1953. Stan Mortensen reveals the moment which gave him a vital goal.

My first experiences of that national institution, the F.A. Cup Final, were lying with my chin in my hands on the lawn under an apple tree listening to the solemn, urgent tones of Raymond Glendenning as he described scenes and events and great names in a way which, to a schoolboy in rural England, had a special, magical quality and left me addicted to this |spring ritual for life. The reality was something even better.

Those now far-off radio tales of Derby County and immortal Peter Doherty and their extra-time victory over Charlton, of Manchester United's suspense-hung win over Blackpool in 1948, were the stuff of dreams. I had no idea then that through the good offices of the Surrey County F.A. I would, as captain of my school side, be privileged to receive a ticket to the hallowed event—under that much maligned system of dispensing tickets for the Final to the grass roots of the game—as early as 1952. Then, I saw Newcastle beat Arsenal by the only goal with Arsenal's right-back, dear, gentlemanly Wally Barnes, badly injured when twisting in the forlorn attempt to halt the quicksilver Bobby Mitchell. That was an indelible baptism and, to my eternal gratitude, I was back again the following year for one of those matches which, then and to this day, it is difficult to describe in a way that truly reflects the drama.

Stanley Matthews was already thirty-eight. I was a school-boy winger and, in the same way that future generations idolized Bobby Charlton and George Best, Matthews was to me—even if at first only in print—the focal point of a game the complexity of which I was still learning to appreciate. I had 'affiliated' myself to him while he was still at Stoke and when, in spite of a public demonstration of protest in the Potteries, he was transferred to Blackpool for a now absurd £11,000, I dutifully transferred my allegiance. It was, therefore, a sad day under the apple tree when Blackpool went down to Manchester United, and even more of one when, three years later, they failed again against Newcastle.

The following year, 1952, I had gone with my father, who had a poor opinion of the professional game, its crowds and its attitudes, to catch my first glimpse of my idol—partnering the sleek, arrowlike Mortensen on a baking August Saturday. They played at Fratton Park and Portsmouth, too, were in their prime. We struggled in at the back of a near 50,000 crowd, my father grumbling that this was no way to spend a fine afternoon, and I was captivated for all time by that marvellous sense of theatre, by the glamour of Blackpool's tangerine shirts, by the hypnotic quality of Matthews' control over both ball and opponent.

Many have tried to describe what his unique quality was exactly. Two things stand out in my mind. Most fundamental, and true of every great player, was that the secret of his game lay not in pace but in change of pace. Matthews was at his most lethal when, arched over the ball like a snake-charmer over his basket, he had reduced his full-back to a standstill. Once Matthews had him a yard away and motionless, the man might as well have been dead. Secondly, and inextricably related to his acceleration, was his exceptional close control, so that he could take the ball round the full-back's tackle as close as a barber removing the soap off your chin. So perfect was the control that he watched not the ball but his opponent's feet.

I don't know about Matthews, for whom the F.A. Cup Final

of 1953 was surely the last chance to gain the winner's medal which everyone in the country but Bolton wanted for him, but I could hardly breathe for anxiety as I made my way to Wembley on that sunny day in May. I went with a school friend, whose father knew a man who knew the physiotherapist of the Blackpool team who had come up with a ticket. I would have been even more prey to nerves had I known, and nobody in that giant bowl of a stadium knew at the time, that my hero was doubtful right up to the last minute. He had a thigh strain, had taken a fitness test on the lawn of the team's hotel that morning and, down in the bowels of the dressing room, was busy having an injection as we all sat high above him, waving our community song sheets.

It was already bad enough, we Blackpool supporters sensed, that the team had lost their fearless goal-scorer, Allan Brown, with a broken leg on the way to the final. Blackpool, finishing seventh in the league, were overwhelming favourites, but there were serious doubts about the quality of their defence. Individual duels were in the offing in which general opinion heavily favoured the redoubtable Bolton. Blackpool's young left-half Cyril Robinson was an inexperienced player in his first cup-tie, who was expected to be exploited by Willie Moir; while veteran England centre-half and Blackpool skipper Harry Johnston could prove vulnerable against belligerent, opportunist Nat Lofthouse, the Footballer of the Year.

There was immediate disaster. With no fewer than nine of the team which had been to Wembley two years before against Newcastle, Blackpool were one down within seventy-five seconds. Their goalkeeper, George Farm, who had not long before played brilliantly at Wembley for Scotland against England, was totally deceived by a low cross-shot from out on the right, the ball screwing through his grasp and off his right shoulder into the net. When that happens in a Final, it is painful for those who are watching, never mind those who have to make it good. Bolton might have gone two up when a shot by Lofthouse struck a post but, just after this, the game took what was to prove a decisive turn when Willie Bell, Bolton's left-half, tore a muscle. In those days there was still no substitution, a factor which repeatedly influenced Cup Finals in the fifties. Bolton, confronted with this serious problem, compounded it by making a grave tactical error. They switched

Bell to outside-left, withdrew Hassall to wing-half and moved Langton inside from the wing. As Stan Mortensen told me many years later:

'That was the biggest blunder of all time. I don't think we would ever have won ultimately but for that. If there was one thing Matthews hated, it was the opposing winger on his flank tackling back. I've even heard him tell wingers to go away and get on with their own job when he was particularly frustrated. By moving Bell to outside-left Bolton had sacrificed one of their means of checking Stan. Frankly, he played only a mediocre part in the game in the first half, and really only came into things later on in the second half.'

Blackpool began to improve against Bolton's rearranged formation and, with ten minutes to go before half time, Mortensen gained a rather lucky equalizer. Bursting through the middle, he hit a left-foot shot and Hassall, coming back fast in an attempt to cover, ran across the line of the shot and deflected it helplessly into his own net. But Farm was again at fault minutes later helping Bolton to regain the lead when he was slow coming off his line to a ball from Langton, and Moir lunged to score with a header. It was anything at this stage but the classic Final which had been expected and when, early in the second half, Bolton's virtual ten-man team went further ahead I and Blackpool's thousands of supporters were in despair. Remarkably, it was the injured Bell who did the damage, somehow getting airborne to head home a cross from right-winger Holden. What price Blackpool now?

Two down with twenty minutes to go, they seemed destined for their third failure in five years. But fate and the sudden ageless brilliance of Matthews were about to strike. Bolton were further handicapped by an injury to left-back Banks, now the man with the responsibility of stemming the flow of a genius. To be sure, Ralph Banks' handicap was only cramp but that, on Wembley's spongy turf, was like a knife in the muscle. Sensing Bolton's predicament, little Ernie Taylor, Blackpool's inside-right, began to feed Matthews with an unending succession of passes, working like some 'powder-monkey' on an eighteenth-century British frigate. Matthews exacted a merciless toll.

There were twenty-two minutes to go when Mortensen made it 3-2, and who better to tell the tale than the men involved? Matthews was now at his most mesmeric against a stricken defence. Out went the ball from Taylor, to the right yet again. If Finney were the more complete player in the matter of scoring goals, and in tenacity and consistency, there is little doubt in the minds of those who played with both that Matthews was Finney's peer in judging the goal-scoring position of his colleagues and deciding when to release the ball. Matthews, still an active player in his adopted home of Malta, and now well into his sixties, recalls:

'Morty had that sense of knowing just where the ball would drop, how it was going to break. All great goal-scorers have it, like Denis Law and Jimmy Greaves. On that second goal I was really just aiming for the far post beyond the goalkeeper, intending to stretch him. Hanson must have taken his eye off the ball for a split second, which was a lucky break for us.'

As the ball came over, 'Morty' was already going like a train for the far post, and he says: 'I think in fact that Stan put the ball a shade too close to the goalkeeper, but Hanson took his eye off it to look at me, and fumbled it. As I slid in behind him with an outstretched foot, I thought the ball was going to go beyond me wide of the post, but I caught it with my studs and it just crept in.' Mortensen collided with the post but was not badly hurt.

Until this moment, even with Matthews beginning to torment the defence, Mortensen had been convinced that Blackpool would lose. 'When we kicked off again at 3-1, I thought to myself: "Well, that's it, three times at Wembley in the Final and three times a loser." ' Now, with the score 3-2, Bolton should have reacted to protect their position. But instead they just stood and took it on the chin like some punch-drunk boxer. By today's cynical standards, what was perhaps most remarkable was that there was never the slightest attempt by Bolton to stop Matthews by illegal tactics. Truly they were in the grip of the snake-charmer.

Ernie Taylor who, five years later, played for the patched-up post-Munich Manchester United team in their emotional ride to the Final, ruthlessly helped turn the screw . . . was scornful of Bolton's tactical paralysis. He claimed: 'They handed it to us. They should have moved Wheeler, who was a good defender, to left-half, and also switched the full-backs. Taking Hassall out of attack disrupted their forwards. Our hero in fact was Morty. The idea that the match was won by one man is nonsense.'

Fellow professionals always recognized the parts played by Taylor, Mortensen and inside-left Jackie Mudie, but the public had eyes for only one player, the stooping, weaving magician on the right wing. He himself was afflicted with none of Mortensen's pessimism. Immediately after the game he claimed, and he still insists on claiming twenty-seven years later, 'I had no feelings at all, my concentration was very good. I knew it was essential not to panic, which is so often what happens and what happened in Belo Horizonte to England. I agree that, from my point of view, the injury to Willie Bell was important, because he was unable to chase back like Langton, and I was freer.'

Yet Bolton tottered towards the final whistle still 3-2 ahead and with the crowd in a frenzy. According to the referee, Mervyn Griffiths, there were only a few seconds of normal time remaining when Blackpool equalized. Mudie was sandwiched three or four yards outside the penalty area. It was now that sad Bolton made yet another mistake. Mortensen recalls quite clearly:

'I put the ball down for the free kick, and I couldn't see the goal as they lined up a wall. Ernie said to me, "There's no gap" but I said to him, "I'm going to have a go." As I turned to walk back, I could see Ernie Shimwell, our big full-back, racing to take up a position on the far post. When I turned round, one of the Bolton players had moved off the right-hand end of the wall and taken up a position on the other end and now I could see the left-hand post. When Shimwell moved up, I'd thought of chipping the ball, but I decided to have a belt and, the moment I'd struck the ball, I knew it was in. I've got a photo in which I've already started to turn round with the ball still on its way!'

Now the game was into injury time, and the noise was like an express train coming out of a tunnel with an infinity of coaches strung out behind it. Out went the ball for one last time, right-half Fenton to Taylor to Matthews; and there was the luckless Banks again facing his torturer. A few yards inside the right-hand corner of the penalty area, Matthews brought Banks to a standstill, then darted past on the outside. Centre-half Malcolm Barrass moved across to cover, too late. While he was still ten yards away, Matthews shaped for his cross, and this is how he remembers it:

'Both Morty and Bill Perry were waiting in the middle. Morty was the nearest, but he was a bit too far forward, almost ahead of me, and there was no angle to put the ball in front of him. But Bill was coming in just right on the penalty spot. When I beat Banks, I hit the ball hard and low. I slipped as I did it, but the ball went straight to Bill . . . and he scored.'

Some people claimed that Matthews mishit the ball. I was sitting on the south side of the stadium, facing him as he crossed, and I doubt it, though of course I could not swear to it at that distance—and, besides, I have to admit that I would not want to believe that he mishit it.

When Joe Smith, the Blackpool manager, who had been a member of the winning West Ham team in the first Wembley final thirty years before, rushed on to the field in jubilation at the finish, Matthews told him: 'Well played Joe, you played a blinder.' In his anxiety, Smith had been chasing up and down the touchline, out-running the ball-boys to return the ball into play, and saving vital seconds. When Bolton kicked off after the 3-3 equalizer, there were only thirty-five seconds of injury time left. The climax to the most famous of all F.A. Cup Finals was that close.

The final, lingering memory of a bewitching afternoon was of Nat Lofthouse and Malcolm Barrass, Matthews' international colleagues, standing back in their losers' shroud and quietly applauding the man whose name was a commonplace around the world—who, whatever the quality and the flaws of his opponents on the day, had so richly earned his medal over a span of twenty-one years. Nor was that the end. The maestro went on to earn another twenty-one England caps, bowing out aged forty-two in the 4-1 World Cup qualifying win over Denmark at Wembley in 1957 when he played alongside the ill-fated Roger Byrne, Tommy Taylor and the prodigious Duncan Edwards of Manchester United. That day they had less than a year to live, but Matthews went on and on, his spartan training throughout his professional life granting him an astonishing return to his home town, Stoke. In October, 1961, he returned at a cost of £3,000, aged forty-six. Stoke were nineteenth in the Second Division, yet a crowd of 36,000— four times the season's average—were there to salute his appearance against Huddersfield. Stoke won 3-0, finished the season eighth and, with Matthews bald and bent but still dancing a merry polka past his full-back, were promoted the following year. We shall never see his like again.

Blackpool: Farm; Shimwell, Garrett; Fenton, Johnston, Robinson; Matthews, Taylor, Mortensen, Mudie, Perry
Bolton: Hanson; Ball, Banks; Wheeler, Barrass, Bell; Holden, Moir, Lofthouse, Hassall, Langton

CHAPTER THREE

West Germany

v

Hungary

WORLD CUP FINAL

1954

Helmut Schoen, one of the most successful managers in international history, pin-points a flaw in Hungary's armour—they were so good they did not want to mark. By having to play West Germany twice, they exposed their tactical weakness.

Hungary, Olympic champions of 1952 and unbeaten during a spell of almost three years, had earned their niche in history by becoming the first foreign side to defeat England at home—if we discount a 2-0 victory by the Republic of Ireland at Goodison Park in 1949. Gustav Sebes and his coach, Gyula Mandi, had produced in Hungary not only a side made up of quite exceptional individuals—by one of those accidents of time which have thrown together almost all great teams—but a co-ordinated unit, whose levels of collective movement and understanding were to provide the blueprint for international coaches for years to come. When they tore England to shreds 6-3 at Wembley in November 1953, it was no more than was expected by those who were aware of the brilliance of the Hungarians, however much of a shock it may have been to those in the birthplace of soccer. To demonstrate that the Wembley result was no fluke, Hungary had repeated the lesson only a few weeks before the World Cup Final by defeating England 7-1 in Budapest. They came to the finals as world champions in all but name, merely requiring the formality of confirmation against whatever other team happened to reach the Final. Presumption can be dangerous.

Geoffrey Green, in his report for *The Times* of that historic evening at Wembley, had written:

'England . . . found themselves strangers in a strange world of flitting red sprites, for such did the Hungarians seem as they moved at devastating pace with superb skill and powerful finish in their cherry-bright shirts. One has talked about the new concept of football as developed by the Continentals and South Americans. Always the main criticism against the style has been its lack of a final punch near the goal. One has thought at times, too, that perhaps the perfection of football was to be found somewhere between the hard-hitting open British method and this other, more subtle, probing infiltration. Yesterday, the Hungarians, with perfect teamwork, demonstrated this midway point to perfection. Theirs was a mixture of exquisite short-passing and the long English game. The whole of it was knit by exact ball control and mounted with a speed of movement and surprise of thought that had an English team ground into Wembley's pitch a long way from the end.'

The team which played West Germany in Berne differed from that at Wembley in only one position, Czibor, the little outside-left at Wembley now on the right in place of Budai, with Toth coming in on the left. It was a team which, amongst Englishmen who care about the game, can be recalled with the same instant familiarity with which we name our own kings and queens. In goal was Grosics, one of the best half-dozen of all time in his specialized position; in defence were Buzansky, Lorant and Lantos, a trio of strength and intelligence; Bozsik, Hidegkuti and Zakarias comprised a midfield trio of quite exceptional vision; and finally, Toth, Kocsis, Puskas and Czibor were the most lethal striking quartet ever assembled, excepting perhaps Brazil's in the sixties.

Of the middle three in a 3-3-4 formation, Zakarias was most defensive, with Bozsik and Hidegkuti the computer brains of the side. The Cambridge University team with whom I was playing at the time went to watch and came away almost

hypnotized by the tactical revelations of Hidegkuti, who wore
the No. 9 shirt and whose scheming from midfield left England
centre-half Billy Wright baffled and bewildered. The running
off-the-ball of Kocsis and Puskas made the conventional WM
formation of England look leaden and amateur and, as Green
so succinctly concluded his report, 'English football can be
proud of its past, but it must awake to a new future.' The WM
formation is a centre-half and two full-backs, two wing-halves,
two inside-forwards, and two wingers either side of a centre-
forward (3-2-2-3).

A year later all was serene in the first round of the finals in
Switzerland as Hungary put nine goals past Korea, thrashed
West Germany 8-3 and then, in a notorious quarter-final in
which three men were sent off, defeated Brazil 4-2. They then
whipped Uruguay, 4-2 quarter-final winners over Finland, by
the same score, and stood on the threshold of the ultimate
triumph as they faced West Germany a second time.

Arrangements had already been made in Budapest for the
Hungarians to be received as national heroes. The team had
received hundreds of cables from their supporters who had
neither the money nor the visas to make the trip to Switzerland,
unlike the tens of thousands of West Germans who came flock-
ing over the border.

Meanwhile the insularity of Britain continued. Their own
team, including Matthews, Lofthouse and Finney and a
disastrous goalkeeper called Merrick, had lost to Uruguay and
the British press now devoted no more than half a dozen
paragraphs to their preview of the Final. Entrenched attitudes
die hard. I remember the 1962 finals in Chile, when England
were eliminated in the quarter-final by Brazil and, requesting
instructions from my newspaper *The Sunday Telegraph* for a
feature on the Final between Brazil and Czechoslovakia,
received the brief and galling reply cable: 'World Cup now
dead, send four hundred words.'

But Germany, entering the competition for the first time in
1952, had a much clearer appreciation of their place in the
world of football. Following that eclipse in the first round, they
had scored fifteen goals in three matches, winning a play-off
against Turkey 7-2, defeating Yugoslavia 2-0 and then, in the
semi-final, Austria by 6-1. One of the few men to have wind
of the fact that the Final might not be the walkover which was

expected was Helmut Schoen. A tall inside-forward who had won seventeen caps before and during the war, he had been team manager of Saarland, which had been a separate state for a time, in the qualifying group which had included the 'new' West Germany and Norway. Subsequently he became Herberger's assistant in the World Cups of 1958 and 1962, succeeding him to guide West Germany to the Final in 1966 and win the trophy in 1974 after a European championship title in 1972. Following the 1978 finals, Schoen retired and it was afterwards that he told me:

'Nobody but Hungary was expected to win in 1954. That was the opinion in Germany, too. Hungary undoubtedly were the best team. But when Germany played them in the first round, Sepp Herberger knew that he could qualify for the quarter-finals even while losing to Hungary, by defeating Turkey in a play-off, so he deliberately did not field his strongest side against the Hungarians. It was a shrewd move, because it meant that, whereas he knew exactly the formation and strengths of the Hungarians, the formation of the German team in the Final would be new to Sebes. Herberger was able to strengthen his side in exactly the right positions, and used a clever mixture in defence of man-for-man marking and zonal marking. When Hungary led by two goals after only eight minutes, everyone naturally supposed that Hungary would beat them, but the Hungarian players were too sure. Herberger had a very good blend in the German team of players who were fighters, such as Morlock, Mai, Liebrich and Posipal, and skilful players such as Fritz Walter and the two wingers, Rahn and Schafer. He also had an excellent goalkeeper in Turek, who was outstanding in the second half when Hungary had further chances to win the match. But from the moment the score became 2-1 after only eleven minutes, the German players knew they had a possibility of winning.'

How history repeats itself! It was to be precisely the same story twenty years later when Holland, with as glittering an array of talent as Hungary, led 1-0 after ninety seconds only to lose to another German side which refused to contemplate the possibility of defeat.

Nevertheless, all Hungary's ambitions for the 1954 final seemed about to be fulfilled when Puskas and Czibor scored in the first eight minutes. This was even better than expected because Puskas ('The Galloping Major' as he was known, on account of his gratuitous service rank) had been injured in an early match and was now less than fit. For the Hungarians, of all people, to be two goals in front and to lose was unthinkable. But that they should win was unthinkable for the Germans. From a hopeless position they played fast, direct, attacking football, bringing the wingers Rahn and Schafer into action wherever possible. For almost the only time in their experience, the magnificent Hungarian side found themselves matched in midfield by the highly intelligent Fritz Walter. Helmut Schoen recalls: 'Fritz was the play-maker and the key to Herberger's plans. If the Hungarians had a flaw it was that, because of their unbroken sequence of success, they only wanted to play, not to mark. Herberger planned to attack their full-backs, which was something they were not used to.'

Remarkably, within nine minutes of going two down, the Germans were level. First Morlock stuck out a foot to deflect a shot by Fritz Walter past Grosics, then Rahn half-volleyed the equalizer following a corner. Hungary, who had begun by playing Czibor out of position on the right wing, were disconcerted, the more so when Turek began to make save after save as they fought to regain the lead. Four saves in particular were memorable: from Hidegkuti and Kocsis, no more than six yards out, before half-time, and twice from Puskas afterwards when the Hungarian captain had broken clear with nobody to beat but the goalkeeper. Kohlmeyer kicked a shot by Toth off the line and Kocsis headed a cross by Czibor against the cross-bar. Both Turek and centre-half Liebrich were playing the games of their lives, and Germany continued to counter attack with skill.

A 58,000 crowd, which had scorned torrential rain to pack into the little ground, was in a frenzy of excitement. On the greasy surface, as the second half slipped by, Germany began to get the upper hand and finally Bozsik was forced into a decisive error. Throughout the match, almost entranced by his own craftsmanship, he had tended to hold on to the ball too long, and now he was robbed out on the left wing by Schafer. The ball was swung into the goal mouth by Fritz Walter, headed out, and Rahn, from fifteen yards, swept the ball wide of Grosics into the net. Only five minutes to go.

A minute later, Puskas had the ball in the net for an equalizer, and English referee Bill Ling pointed to the centre spot. Suddenly he noticed that Welsh referee Mervyn Griffiths, one of his linesmen, had his flag up and the goal was disallowed for offside. Schoen told me: 'From where I was sitting I could not be sure one way or the other, but it was certainly a very close thing.' Desmond Hackett's opinion in the *Daily Express*: 'I thought for once that sandy-haired Griffiths was wrong.'

Still the mighty Hungarians were not finished, revealing character to match their skills. With thirty seconds remaining, little Czibor sank his face into his hands as Turek, for the last time, dived full-length to keep out a ferocious shot. Hungary, a tiny nation of only five million people and with perhaps the greatest team of all time, had been denied the biggest prize in sport. Certainly I have not seen a better team.

Hungary:	Grosics; Buzansky, Lorant, Zakarias, Lantos; Bozsik, Hidegkuti; Czibor, Kocsis, Puskas, Toth
West Germany:	Turek; Posipal, Liebrich, Kohlmeyer; Eckel, Walter F., Mai; Rahn, Morlock, Walter O., Schafer

CHAPTER FOUR

Manchester United
v
Aston Villa
F.A. CUP FINAL
1957

A hideous, controversial injury to Ray Wood, Manchester United's goalkeeper, and a demonstrably offside goal, deny the Busby Babes the Double.

I had a particular affinity with the young Manchester United team, affectionately known as the Busby Babes. Almost all of them were nurtured by Matt Busby from schoolboys into a side which, but for the Munich crash the following year, would have become as great as the legendary Real Madrid of that era. In 1957, at the age of twenty-two, I had only recently given up serious participation in senior amateur football to concentrate on journalism. The United team, with their youth, and their wonderful *élan* which captured the imagination of the entire nation and many beyond, were my exact contemporaries. Warren Bradley, who signed for the club from Bishop Auckland in the crisis following the crash, had been one of my rivals for the right-wing place in the England Amateur XI: he was successful, I was not. When United were robbed of the Double, my heart bled for them. When eight of the squad died the following February, I wept. The style of their football and their collective spirit had a combination of grace and power which together with their youth gave them a unique appeal.

Manchester United arrived at Wembley for the Final against

Aston Villa needing, on the face of it, only to stand up to win. So far as any match can ever be a formality, this was to be it. They were League Champions for the second successive year and, in their first bid for the European Cup, boldly led into that competition by Busby as the first English club and against the wishes of the Football League, they had stormed to the semi-final only to lose narrowly to incomparable Real and Alfredo Di Stefano. On the way, United had played some overpowering football. Losing the first leg of their quarter-final 5-2 away to Bilbao, they crushed the Spaniards 4-0 in the return. Such was the classic style and sportsmanship of the side that, following the visit to Bilbao, the club received the following letter from the Under Secretary of State at the Foreign Office:

'Sir, I am directed by Mr Secretary Lloyd to state that you may be interested to know Her Majesty's Consul at Bilbao has reported on the excellent impression created by the football match held on January 16th between Manchester United and Bilbao Atletico. Her Majesty's Consul remarks on the great cordiality and good feelings on all sides which he believes has made a definite contribution to Anglo-Spanish relations . . . As we all know only too well, international sport can so often engender bad feeling instead of good. I believe on this occasion that we have every reason to be well content at the conclusion of a British team's visit to a foreign country, and for this happy result the Manchester United representatives, players and non-players, who by their bearing and behaviour during an arduous visit proved themselves first class unofficial Ambassadors to Britain, must take their full share of credit. I am, Sir, your obedient servant.'

A very different tale from the contemporary scene, when so many European cup ties create ill will, either because of the destructive behaviour of disruptive 'supporters' or the cynicism of modern defensive tactics. Happily, in 1981, we seem to have passed through the era of English thuggery on the field.

In the preliminary round of the European Cup, United had defeated Anderlecht of Brussels, who were later to become an accomplished European team themselves, by ten goals under the floodlights of Maine Road, those at Old Trafford not being ready yet. Dennis Viollet scored four that night, Taylor three,

Liam Whelan two, and Johnny Berry the other. David Pegg, the only forward not to score, made at least five of the goals in a performance he was never to surpass. Mermans, Anderlecht's captain, said afterwards: 'Why don't they pick the whole of the side for England? The best teams of Hungary have never beaten us like this. Even after Manchester had scored six, they still kept running as hard as at the start. It was fantastic.' Busby's own view in retrospect was that 'it was the finest exhibition of teamwork I have ever seen from any team, club or international. It was as near perfect football as anyone could wish to see.' A crowd of 75,598 at Maine Road saw United beat Borussia Dortmund 3-2 in the next round. On the Monday after United defeated Birmingham City to reach the F.A. Cup Final, Frank Coles, then Sports Editor of *The Daily Telegraph*, wrote:

'The reason for their surge of popularity is quite simple. Under the expert and fatherly guidance of Matt Busby, a happy band of young men have developed a team spirit and comradeship seldom equalled in any of our sports. They give all they have to the club and, in all circumstances, they try to play football. United were superbly served by their three young inside-forwards, Whelan, Viollet and Charlton, not as attackers alone but by the unsparing, willing way they chased back to help whenever their defence was under pressure.'

It could be said, I suppose, that without realizing it, without being given a label, United were playing what in the seventies would be termed Total Football, attacking with at least seven men, defending when necessary with eight or nine. I remember marvelling at their flexibility and seemingly unquenchable energy when they overwhelmed Manchester City, the 1956 F.A. Cup winners, in the Charity Shield.

They went to Wembley themselves the following year in a class of their own. Before the final, Busby said: 'We shall not fail for the want of trying. Now that the strain of this hectic season is almost over, while victory is our crowning ambition, I will be proud of my team come what may.' He had long before acquired the equanimity, when faced by triumph or disaster, in Kipling's words. 'To treat those two impostors just the same'. Little did he know what was in store.

Aston Villa, who had been in danger of relegation earlier in the season, were largely unfancied, with a rough and ready defence strongly inclined to physical intimidation, and an outside-left, Irishman Peter McParland, who could hit lethal goals with both his head and his left foot. United were worried prior to the Final by an injury to Viollet, a sublimely gifted player who, on his day, could catch sunbeams. The alternative was the relatively inexperienced and unknown Charlton, then nineteen. Viollet had a groin strain and, in the circumstances, Busby made the only possible choice in the days before substitutes, and chose the fit player. It was a measure of Busby's paternal attitude to his team that he travelled back overnight from the Football Writers' annual dinner in London to Blackpool to tell Viollet he was not playing, even though the team was travelling down that morning to their London headquarters. 'I was the only man who could tell him' explained Busby. So United fielded the same side which had played in the two games against Real Madrid.

It is ironic that the one player in United's team who was not of international class was their goalkeeper, Ray Wood, around whose injury right at the start the whole game was to hinge. Might there have been some pre-match discussion by Villa on this very factor? From my own experience of F.A. Amateur Cup matches with Pegasus, when coached by both Arthur Rowe and Joe Mercer, I think it is probable. If there was a crack in United's armour, it was probably Wood. Bill Foulkes at right-back was already the veteran of the team, a man of unshakeable resolve, while at left-back, Roger Byrne, the skipper, was an automatic choice for England. At centre-half, Jackie Blanchflower, brother of the Spurs skipper Danny, had gained his inclusion because of an injury to Mark Jones. Less powerful, he was more skilful. The wing-halves, Eddie Colman and Duncan Edwards, were a superbly contrasted pair: Colman small and rubbery, as quick and agile as a squirrel, with tremendous skills—a certain England player had he not perished—and Edwards, an oak of a young man who, but for the crash, might have become an even greater player than John Charles. Edwards played his first game in the First Division at the age of fifteen years and eight months, the youngest player ever, and gained the first of nineteen caps at seventeen years and eight months, also the youngest ever. In 1956–57 he played ninety-five games for Manchester United, England and the British Army. Willy Meisl, internationally respected critic, wrote: 'Duncan was a *nonpareil*. I've never seen a better half-back, a more complete footballer. He could win a match alone, and he won many. For me he was much greater than John Charles because, with all his calmness, there was also a fierce fighting streak . . . the most lovable boy ever to run on to a football field.'

In attack, Berry was a sprightly goal-scoring winger who had been bought from Birmingham; Whelan an inside-forward from the Republic of Ireland, not unlike Gerry Daly a generation later; it was he who had scored an incredible goal, beating four opponents, to turn the match when United were three down in Bilbao. Tommy Taylor, England centre-forward, was the prize of a cloak-and-dagger record £30,000 transfer from Barnsley; Charlton was the pride and joy of United's famous old chief scout Joe Armstrong and had been discovered almost by accident one misty morning in Northumberland. Outside-left David Pegg could run the legs off a deer but, sadly, was destined to play only one game for his country.

When considering the injury to Wood, it is worth noting that the laws of the game on charging the goalkeeper are no different from those for any other player: the charge must be shoulder to shoulder, and the goalkeeper must be in possession of the ball. It is therefore obvious that, to make a fair charge, it must be made from the side. Yet, almost always, a goalkeeper is facing his opponent, making a fair charge impossible unless the opponent moves in a semi-circle to line himself up alongside the goalkeeper—who is hardly going to remain stationary during this time. It is generally claimed by the British that international football has given goalkeepers too much protection, but it is indisputable that the accepted rough-housing of goalkeepers in Britain right up to the sixties was largely illegal. It was, for example, a grossly illegal charge by Nat Lofthouse of Bolton on Harry Gregg in the 1958 F.A. Cup Final which helped defeat United's patched-up post-Munich team.

In 1957 I was not in the press box but standing on the terraces no more than thirty yards from the point at which, in the sixth minute, McParland leapt at Wood head on and broke his cheek-bone. In that instant there was no way in which McParland could make a fair charge. What had happened was that McParland had closed in on a cross from the right and had headed the ball straight towards Wood, who gathered it with both arms, four yards off his line. He and McParland were then face to face and some ten yards apart. But McParland did not check his run, kept going and, as he reached Wood, took off from his right foot and turned his left shoulder in towards Wood's chest. Wood had held his ground, rightly believing himself immune to such a charge, and was now struck by the full force of McParland's airborne weight. At the last moment, Wood turned his head, and his cheek-bone was struck either by McParland's shoulder, or more probably his head, sustaining a depressed fracture. Wood's head jerked back under the impact like a boxer's, his hair standing on end, McParland spinning off to the right. It was one of the worst moments I have ever witnessed on the football field. Suddenly, a great team had been illegally depleted. Wood lay stunned, was carried away to the dressing room, and McParland recovered at least sufficiently to score both Villa goals in the second half.

Desmond Hackett, my predecessor on the *Daily Express*, was emphatic on the Monday morning about where to place the blame. 'I thought McParland was impetuous and angry after missing an easy chance.' This echoed my feelings and those of a million others who considered McParland's action deliberate. Certainly he was booed almost every time he touched the ball thereafter, and the booing continued when Villa went up to receive the Cup, making it a most unsavoury afternoon.

McParland's own account of the incident contained contradictions. Immediately after the match he stated: 'When Wood caught the ball, I went in to shoulder charge him and he turned as I *hit* him [my italics]. The booing was most unfair and made me even more determined to score. I was upset that Ray had been hurt and, at the end, went to shake hands with him.' But McParland subsequently admitted to Hackett: 'I had just missed an easy chance, and I was determined to get the ball again. Wood was there in front of me and I charged him as hard as I could. Certainly I was angry at the time, but only angry with myself.' Frank Coultas, the referee, talking to Roy Peskett of the *Daily Mail*, said: 'Should I have sent McParland off? Personally, I saw nothing vicious. It was clumsy, but with no foul intent. If Wood had not gone down, I would not have given a foul.' This I find quite incredible.

Wood, who came back for the second half to play in a concussed state on the wing for nuisance value, and bravely but in vain went back into goal for the last seven minutes, hazily recollected: 'I had the ball in my hands when the charge came. McParland never had any chance to get it. I think it was a bit unnecessary. The next thing, I found myself lying on the grass covered in water, and I heard somebody saying "I think his jaw is broken".'

It was ironic that, only the previous day, the F.A. Council, with myopic conservatism, had voted not to support a F.I.F.A. resolution to allow substitutes in competitive football, in spite of the evidence of its own Wembley showpiece regularly being marred by injury. United now reorganized their side, Blanchflower going into goal, Edwards switching to centre-half and Whelan dropping back to wing-half, his performance making him for many the man of the match.

During the interval which, thanks to some fine work by Blanchflower, was reached with the score still blank, Wood was taken out on to the strip of grass outside the dressing room by physiotherapist Ted Alton. Wood, unable to judge anything on his right side and still concussed, missed most of the balls which Dalton threw at him. A small boy, not recognizing him or knowing the drama as 100,000 people waited inside to see if Wood would return for the second half, asked him if he would like to join a game with some friends round the corner. Since it was obvious that he was in no state to go back in goal, Busby decided it was just possibly worth his going on the right wing, but he was a sorry, bemused figure.

United were functioning, needless to say, at nowhere near their peak, with four positional changes; after sixty-eight minutes, McParland headed the first of his goals from a cross by Villa's outside-right, Leslie Smith. Five minutes later, he grabbed his controversial second. Villa's inside-left, Dixon, beat Colman inside the penalty area and, moving away from goal, turned and hit a shot from thirteen yards. The shot crashed against the crossbar, at which moment McParland, as was demonstrated conclusively by subsequent film, was at least three yards offside only two yards from the goal-line and close to Blanchflower. As the ball rebounded, McParland moved away from Blanchflower and hooked the ball into the net. Only by the time he shot was he onside.

Coultas claimed afterwards: 'McParland was not interfering with play. The ball had not been passed to him and he was not blocking the goalkeeper's vision. Had he been in line with the goalkeeper and blocking his vision, then he would have been interfering with play while in an offside position. And don't forget, I had a linesman and he did not flag.' Villa's manager Eric Houghton insisted: 'McParland was in an offside position when Dixon hit the crossbar but he was in no way interfering with play. To say that McParland's goal should have been disallowed is simply sour grapes and not worthy of further consideration.'

There were only seven minutes to go when Taylor, who seemed to have suffered more than most from the tactical disruption and who had had a miserably ineffective match up against the formidable Dugdale, gave United renewed hope with a header from a corner. At 2-1, it was perhaps not too late. In a last, desperate gamble, Busby sent Wood back into goal, enabling the team to reform—but the Double, like the Treble, was to prove a mirage, and a superb team had been denied its rightful place in history. Villa had won the Cup for the seventh time, and it was said that McParland got two goals and a goalkeeper. Bill Foulkes admitted to me in later years that for the first and only time in his career, 'I went after an opponent that day with the intention of nailing him.'

I had not even waited for the presentation of the trophy but left the stadium in a mood of total dejection and slowly walked the five or six miles back to our flat in Finchley, reflecting not only on the injustice but the stupidity which barred the way to substitutes. Busby was subsequently criticized by some for not sending Wood back into goal earlier but, as Foulkes recalled: 'Busby always took the long-term view. Winning a Cup Final was not worth jeopardizing a player's career for.' Wood himself admitted that, 'if I had gone into goal earlier I would probably have fallen down between the posts', while Busby said, 'he should never have come out at all for the second half.'

Houghton was notable for both his inaccuracy as well as his indifference to Wood's misfortune when he claimed: 'There was nothing wrong in what McParland did. Wood was holding the ball and there was the chance that he could be charged over the line [Wood was in fact *four yards* from the goal-line at the time, making it impossible]. It was accidental that their faces met. I am proud of him. Two semi-final goals followed by two in the final is grand work.' Sports people can be frighteningly subjective.

It is strange reflecting today that substitutes were then somehow thought to be immoral, and Arthur Oakley, the League president, made the extraordinary statement, 'I'm not sure substitutes are the answer to unfortunate happenings like this; the cure sometimes proves worse than the disease.' Yet Wood's injury was the fifth in six years to mar the Final, following Barnes of Arsenal (1952), Bell of Bolton (1953), Meadows of Manchester City (1955), and Trautmann of Manchester City (1956). In 1959, Dwight of Nottingham Forest broke a leg but, leading at the time against Luton, Forest held out to win, the only team besides Manchester City to do so. In 1960, Blackburn lost Whelan and went down to Wolves. As Busby pointed out, the law is unfairly weighted against the goalkeeper: if he is fouled it is a free kick; if he commits a foul it is a penalty. Ultimately, sense prevailed and substitutes were introduced.

It was at the end of the 1957 season, with its mixture of success and disappointment, that Geoffrey Green, correspondent of *The Times*, asked Busby what he felt he had done for football and for Manchester United. 'The time to judge me is when I'm at the bottom', Busby had replied modestly. How close he was to Munich's pit of despair he had no way of knowing.

Manchester United: Wood; Foulkes, Byrne; Colman, Blanchflower, Edwards; Berry, Whelan, Taylor, Charlton, Pegg

Aston Villa: Sims; Lynn, Aldis; Crowther, Dugdale, Saward; Smith, Sewell, Myerscough, Dixon, McParland

CHAPTER FIVE

Northern Ireland

v

Czechoslovakia

WORLD CUP

1958

*Injuries to both their goalkeepers stop short the
remarkable success of Northern Ireland in the 1958
World Cup.*

Sweden in 1958 saw what might fittingly be described as the
last of the romantic World Cups—a tournament in which the
spirit of adventure and sportsmanship still flowed through most
teams, a tournament in which cynicism, brutality and functionalism had not become an accepted part of every nation's
tactics. It was still a game in which the best, as opposed to the
most expedient, sides were likely to succeed. It was the first
World Cup for which I was there on the spot and, although
I have attended five more since then, and witnessed some
dramatic and indeed historic moments, none has had quite the
same charm.

Part of the appeal, no doubt, can be attributed to the fact
that all four British nations were there. Northern Ireland had
joined their stronger English and Scottish brethren by eliminating Italy. Wales had won a play-off against Israel for a vacant
place. This home game coincided with Manchester United's
European Cup away leg against Red Star of Belgrade, thereby
probably saving the lives of the Wales team manager Jimmy
Murphy, Matt Busby's assistant, and Geoffrey Green of *The*

Times, who would both otherwise have been on the British European Airways Elizabethan aircraft which crashed on take-off at Munich.

Sweden in June is a lovely country, unexplored by the myriads of English holidaymakers who head southwards to the sun. In many ways, in spite of their reputation for being somewhat cool and aloof, the Swedes were among the most hospitable of all the World Cup hosts, and I do not know any journalist from Britain who was there who does not recollect those months as being some of the most pleasurable of his professional life.

Of the four British teams, the Irish, without a doubt, were the least rated. England, in spite of the loss of Roger Byrne, Duncan Edwards and Tommy Taylor at Munich, still possessed a team, including the young Charlton, capable of going all the way to the semi-finals or beyond. Scotland, though without their manager, Matt Busby, who was still recovering from severe injuries, had a team which included such renowned defenders as Caldow of Rangers and Turnbull of Hibernian, plus Leggatt, Collins and Mudie in attack. Wales boasted the best team in their history, with the Charles brothers, John and Mel, and Cliff Jones, a left-winger second in the world only to Gento of Spain. Whom did Ireland have?

First and foremost, there were, as manager and captain, two of the most perceptive men the game has known: Peter Doherty and Danny Blanchflower. Doherty had been one of those players who, though his public image as an inside-forward with Manchester City and then Derby County had not been as conspicuous as those of many of his contemporaries, was revered by fellow professionals. Blanchflower, who had made his way via Barnsley and Aston Villa to become captain of Tottenham, was the most articulate individual, both vocally and in print, that his profession had known. There are many stories about his wit but the best, and one which reveals his exceptional presence of mind when many others would be under stress, relates to the start of the 1961 F.A. Cup Final as the teams were being presented to Princess Alexandra. Halfway down the line of Tottenham players she stopped and said to Danny, who was introducing them: 'I see the Leicester team have their names on their tracksuits.' Replied Danny, quick as a flash: 'Ah, yes, Ma'am, but you see, we *know* each other.'

The Irish squad arrived in Sweden unsung, and settled into their modest headquarters on the south-west coast near the town of Halmstad. But they jolted everyone into taking notice when they beat Czechoslovakia with the only goal, a diving header by Wilbur Cush, in the twenty-first minute. Blanchflower recalls:

'Peter Doherty roused us all. Before him, we all knew that in most of the matches we played we were going to get beaten. When Peter arrived it was different. Without telling us lies, he persuaded us to go out and play with confidence and optimism. He was afraid of nobody. And I suppose he was fortunate that with Jimmy McIlroy, Bertie Peacock and myself, he had players who gave him a bit of a chance. His one handicap was that the officials were still picking the team and, even with all the injuries we suffered, I think we would have done better if Peter had been picking the team. Mind you, there were ways of influencing the officials . . . !'

That opening win against the Czechs was a typical illustration of Doherty's psychological approach to his players. Travelling through Copenhagen on the way to Halmstad, Doherty and Blanchflower saw a poster announcing a warm-up friendly match between the Czechs and Danes. Danny thought they ought to go and watch, but Peter reckoned the officials would never agree to it. When they arrived in Halmstad, they discussed the matter with Billy Drennan, the energetic young secretary of the Northern Ireland F.A. 'Leave it to me', said Drennan. Half an hour later, Doherty was called and told: 'The committee have heard that the Czechs are playing in Copenhagen. The chairman has decided you must go and watch them!'

Back one hundred miles to Copenhagen went the manager and his captain, wondering whether they should have bothered to 'feed' the idea in the first place. The Czechs were vastly superior, and Denmark hardly had a kick all night. Doherty turned to Blanchflower and pronounced: 'The Czechs are a powder-puff team.' Blanchflower, for a moment, could not believe his ears until he realized that this was merely Doherty's way of screening his players from a truth which could only diminish their prospects. They duly beat the Czechs, but then suffered a 3-1 defeat by Argentina. Blanchflower says: 'There's no doubt in my mind that they were the best team we played in the tournament, including France, who beat us in the quarter-final. But they were too busy climbing out of bedroom windows after midnight.'

Ireland forced themselves back into the reckoning with a tremendous 2-2 draw with West Germany, the champions, after being in front twice, thereby earning a play-off with Czecho-slovakia forty-eight hours later. The hero of the match against Germany was Harry Gregg who, a few months earlier, had performed rather different heroics when several times scrambling back into Manchester United's crashed aircraft to rescue survivors. Now, in Malmo, he had a 22,000 crowd repeatedly applauding his superlative and daring saves, even though half the crowd were Germans. He twisted an ankle and hurt a shoulder, yet remained the inspiration of those in front of him. Germany's wingers, Rahn and Schafer, were constantly threatening, but so too were Bingham and McParland for Ireland. It was from a centre from Bingham that McParland scored after fifteen minutes. Soon Rahn equalized but, ten minutes after half time, McParland scored again following a corner. The second equalizer came near the end from young Uwe Seeler and might have been saved, but Gregg was restricted by his injured ankle and could only watch the shot from twenty-two yards flash in off the post. And so to a play-off with Czechoslovakia.

Ireland were faced with a variety of problems, not least that they were unable to find accommodation in Malmo for this unscheduled match, and had to return to Halmstad. Gregg's ankle was severely swollen and, although he bathed it in cold water for hours on end for the next two days, he could not put it right, so Uprichard was called up as deputy. Tommy Casey, Newcastle centre-forward, was also a casualty from the match against Germany and, after considering Derek Dougan of Portsmouth and Fay Coyle of Nottingham Forest, Doherty finally settled on the Grimsby outside-left, Jackie Scott, who was to switch with McParland immediately after the kick off. Ireland had to win against the Czechs because a draw after extra-time would have seen the Czechs through to the quarter-final on goal average after their six-goal win over Argentina.

In mounting tension and in fading light, with a meagre

crowd cheering their every move towards the finish, Ireland pulled off the most dramatic win in their history. The deciding goal was scored by McParland in the first half of extra-time, and there were wild, patriotic scenes on the touchline at the final whistle. At the heart of the battle was Blanchflower, shuffling up and down the whole length of the pitch with his peculiar bent-legged gait, never missing a trick. Czechoslovakia were outplayed most of the second half and, most of all, lacked the guidance of a Blanchflower.

Misfortune had continued to dog the Irish from the beginning of the match. After only ten minutes, Uprichard sprained an ankle, as Gregg had done, and later broke a bone in his left hand. Peacock twisted a knee in the second half and returned after treatment to limp on the left wing, with Wilbur Cush dropping back to left-half. The Czechs at the start had looked the better side: yards faster in defence, superior in physique and in their heading. But the pace of their strikers, Feurizl, Borovicka and Molnar, was soon seen to be mechanical and predictable. The Czechs could be forced into inaccurate passing. Ireland's spirit never flagged, Keith and McMichael were steady at full-back and Cunningham solidly reliable at centre-half. Blanchflower could hardly have improved on his performance and, with the equally intelligent McIlroy, carefully pulled together the slightly frayed strings of the Irish team.

After a quarter of an hour, the Czechs took the lead when Feurizl and Cunningham went for a high cross, missed, and outside-left Zikan nipped in to head the ball past the handicapped Uprichard. Now Czechoslovakia threatened to run away with the game, the dapper Masopust, midfield general of the brilliant Dukla side of Prague, making the most of the early Irish errors. But McParland, playing powerfully through the middle and well prompted by McIlroy, was causing alarm to the Czechs. He had scored all but one of Ireland's goals so far, and now equalized just on half-time after three furious, successive shots by Cush had been blocked.

The second half was mostly Ireland, but they could not exploit their advantage. Bingham headed against the crossbar, Zikan at the other end missed a gaping chance and extra-time arrived. The Irish fell to the ground, knotted with fatigue. Desperately, Doherty tried to rouse his men for another effort, and gallantly even suggested that Uprichard should go to hospital for attention. Equally gallantly, Uprichard refused, suggesting to Blanchflower that he should play out of goal—'but he urged me to stay'.

Blanchflower now turned his attention to the rest of the team and told them with a grin: 'Come on, we have better character than they have . . . well, anyway, we have *more* character. And they're as tired as we are.'

Ten minutes into extra-time, as dusk fell on the stadium, Ireland had a free kick not far outside the penalty area; Blanchflower shaped to take it. He recalls: 'It was vital, so I took my time, thinking "it's got to be right". Fortunately, I managed to find McParland and, when he put it in, it was the greatest moment of my career.' For a man who chooses all his many words carefully, and who had a long and famous career, that is a significant statement.

Tension mounted as the Czechs realized they were on their way out. Their right-half Bubernik complained to the referee, Gigue of France, that he had been fouled, spat at Gigue when his complaint was ignored, and was promptly sent off. The Czechs later protested that, at that stage of a marvellous match, nobody had any spit left. But they still had some fighting reserve, and pushed everyone but goalkeeper Doejsi into Ireland's half. Somehow, Uprichard and his defence hung on for a place in the quarter-final, but it had been a Pyrrhic victory. For the game against France only two days later, Ireland had to travel back yet once more to Halmstad, then another 250 miles across Sweden to Norrköping, with their squad reduced to ten fit men and no goalkeeper. Of the two potential goalkeepers, Gregg was the only possible choice: Uprichard had his hand in plaster. Gregg played with his ankle heavily strapped and could not kick properly, even with his good foot, because of the strain imposed on the other. Peacock's twisted knee meant that he was out of action for several months; Casey gamely returned with several stitches in his leg. Dougan, who throughout his career never had a bite to match his bark, and Coyle were not considered, their form being too questionable. The team, whatever Doherty's permutations, was spent.

France, with their three musketeers at inside-forward, Fontaine (record scorer in the finals with thirteen goals), Kopa and Piantoni, won almost as they pleased, though somehow Gregg held out till half-time. Kopa, running at a dozen different speeds, totally lost Cunningham. In vain did Blanch-flower and Cush, now at left-back, attempt to stem the tide; and in the second half France whipped in four, the marksmen being Wiesnieski, Fontaine, with two, and Piantoni. But, as Doherty claimed: 'It was an achievement even to qualify, let alone finish in the last eight, and we had to contend with impossible injuries. There was still glory in defeat.'

Northern Ireland: Uprichard; Keith, McMichael; Blanch-flower, Cunningham, Peacock; Bingham, Cush, Scott, McIlroy, McParland
Czechoslovakia: Dolejsi; Mraz, Novak; Bubernik, Poplu-har, Masopust; Dvorak, Molnar, Feurizl, Borovicka, Zikan

CHAPTER SIX

Wales

v

Brazil

WORLD CUP

1958

The most feeble goal of the tournament, deflected off a defender's knee, and an injury to John Charles, allow Brazil to stutter towards their first World Cup triumph.

It seems churlish to suggest more than twenty years later that Brazil, three times World Cup winners, might never have won the trophy for the first time in Sweden: but that is a fact. Their remarkable team, with Garrincha on the right wing, Pele at inside-forward, Zito and Didi in midfield, and Nilton and Djalmar Santos at full-back, was still taking shape as the tournament progressed and was really only into its stride by the time it reached the semi-final. England, in the first round, were the only team against whom Brazil failed to score and, in the quarter-final, the exotic South Americans only won by a fluke goal against Wales.

Had John Charles, most assuredly the best player ever to come out of the Principality, been fit to play, it is arguable that Wales and not Brazil could have contested the Final with Sweden. This was the most accomplished of all Welsh teams, every player coming from the First Division and some of them capable of playing for almost any team they wished. Charles, one of the outstanding all-round players of any generation, who today runs a pub in Leeds after once being the toast of Europe, reflects:

'We should have won against Brazil, even though I was forced to watch from the touchline. We looked the better side for much of the match. The Manchester United centre-forward, Webster, who played instead of me, should have scored in the first minute when he was clean through, but he knocked it wide with only the goalkeeper to beat. Jack Kelsey in goal was marvellous, as usual, but although he made several important saves he didn't have as much to do in this match as he did against Mexico.'

Kelsey was the best British goalkeeper of his era, making 327 appearances for Arsenal between 1951 and 1962 and playing forty-one times for his country. Kelsey was in the tradition of so many fine British goalkeepers, quiet and un-demonstrative on the field. He was big, immensely hard, quite fearless and, for a big-boned man, extremely agile. He often needed to be, for both Wales and Arsenal. The most noticeable thing about him was a huge pair of hands, on which he was said to rub chewing gum to get a better grip. Like the Charles brothers, John and Mel, like Ivor Allchurch and Cliff Jones in that same team, he came from Swansea. Gary Sprake, the Leeds goalkeeper who would succeed him in later years, also lived in the same street. It was Kelsey's everlasting complaint that he never had a chance to stop Brazil's goal which beat him, the ball being deflected. Sadly, it was on tour against Brazil shortly before the next World Cup in Chile that his career was effectively ended when Vava, the Brazilian centre-forward, caught him in the back, inflicting a muscle injury from which he never properly recovered. But in the soft sunlight of that summer in Sweden, he had never played better.

John Charles, twenty-seven at the time of the competition, was, in a word, prodigious, capable of playing with equal facility in almost any position on the field, though in fact his career was divided almost equally between centre-forward and centre-half. As a centre-half, standing well over six feet tall and with a sculptor's model of a physique, he was cast in the grand Corinthian mould: a player who would influence events all around him and in both penalty areas. He had joined the ground staff at Swansea but moved to Leeds when he was fifteen, and at eighteen became the youngest player ever to represent Wales. After three years, Leeds switched him to centre-forward; he scored thirty goals in twenty-one matches, and the following season was the leading goal scorer in the League with forty-two.

Two-footed, and phenomenally powerful in the air, he seldom used his huge strength to intimidate. The most illustrious phase of his career was yet to come—in Italy, where he was idolized and affectionately known as Il Buon Gigante, 'The Gentle Giant'. In 1955-56, he scored thirty-eight goals in the First Division and, finally, Leeds had to relent to pressure from abroad, selling him to Juventus for the startling sum, in those days, of £65,000. Italian football was already notorious for its defensiveness yet, in four successive seasons from 1957 to 1961, Charles scored with unprecedented freedom: twenty-eight, nineteen, twenty-three and fifteen goals respectively. Twice Juventus won the championship, and Charles formed a famous partnership with the swarthy, sensuously skilful and occasionally wicked little Argentinian, Enrique Sivori. To this day there has been no player in world football comparable to John Charles in size *and* refinement.

Ivor Allchurch, in 1980 still playing local league football in the Valleys at the age of fifty-one, was the blueprint of the old-fashioned inside-forward, a game-maker if ever there was one, a paragon of footballers. With a perfect temperament, unrelenting stamina and, as it often seemed, eyes in the back of his head, he was as exceptionally gifted as he was modest. Dave Bowen, who played behind him at left-half in Sweden, recalls:

'It was claimed by some that Ivor was the best player in the tournament, and *that* in a competition including Pele, Didi, Kopa, Fontaine, and Blanchflower! He could pull the ball down out of the sky from anywhere. Although he played for most of his career at a lower level with Swansea and Cardiff, he was most of all a wonderful player to play *with*, because he was always there to help you out of a jam. He himself never seemed under pressure.'

I can vouch for that. In 1961, I saw Allchurch play in two World Cup qualifying games against Spain and the legendary Di Stefano. Although the former Argentinian, widely regarded as the greatest player of *any* generation, would always have to be given the edge in the matter of goal-scoring, in these two games, in Cardiff and Madrid, it was Allchurch who exerted the greater influence. In Madrid, with his partner Phil Woosnam injured in training the day before the match, All-church played the Spaniards almost single-handed . . . and nearly won. In twenty years, 1949-68, he scored 251 goals in 694 League matches for Swansea, Newcastle and Cardiff, gaining sixty-eight caps.

Mel Charles, though never in the same class as his brother, moved from Swansea to Arsenal and, in Sweden, played at centre-half behind John. He possessed much of the same natural physical ability and, though not a great player, would have made a much higher impact on the game had he had a more competitive temperament. Cliff Jones, at outside-left, was one of the last of his line in the world game—a tearaway, express train of a winger who could frighten not just full-backs but entire defences out of their wits. Bowen, later to become general manager of Northampton, whom he would steer to the First Division, remembers: 'Cliff had a great tournament, with his electrifying pace. Always, of course, he would run with the ball, run and run until sometimes he infuriated you, but how he could scare the opposition!'

Wales, like Ireland, arrived in Sweden as no more than make-weights, having gained entry via the backdoor in a play-off with Israel. But they had in Jimmy Murphy a manager who, like Peter Doherty with Ireland, could rouse his men with nationalistic passion. Bowen, himself an immensely competitive wing-half with Arsenal, says: 'Jimmy had a lilting voice full of emotion, and he could cry when he wanted to. That's not saying anything against him, simply that his emotion was close to the surface. Big John [Charles] idolized him, and we all respected him for what he had done with Matt at Manchester United, especially his contribution in keeping United going following the crash earlier that year.'

Everybody knew Wales had some players, but nobody supposed they had much of a team until they held Hungary 1-1 in their opening match. Although the famous Hungarian team which had lost in the previous Final had been torn apart in the uprising of 1956, they were still a formidable opposition with three or four of the old guard—Grosics, Bozsik, Hidegkuti—and three brilliant newcomers, inside-right Tichy and wingers Sandor and Fenyvesi. The game was regarded as a formality for the Hungarians, and Sandor gave them the lead. Yet, by 1958, defensive tactics were just beginning to creep in: not enough to mar the tournament, but sufficiently to affect one or two results, including this one. Murphy had done his home-work: Bowen was detailed to shadow Hidegkuti, Allchurch put tremendous pressure on Bozsik, and Hungary were neutralized in midfield. John Charles, climbing high on the far post to meet a corner from Jones, equalized with one of his inimitable headers, and Wales were in business.

Next they drew with Mexico, thanks to Kelsey's brilliance and a fine goal from Allchurch after half an hour. Wales indeed might have won, roared on by a detachment of the Royal Navy on leave in Stockholm, but Mexico equalized three minutes from time. Against the hosts, Sweden, who were improving with every match and whose cheerleaders had to be banned by F.I.F.A., Wales needed to win to qualify or draw for a play-off. They drew. Following the somewhat physical nature of the first encounter, Hungary, desperate to qualify, were obviously determined to intimidate in the play-off. It was a time of extensive political demonstrations again back home in Buda-pest, and the team was in a highly emotional state. John Charles recalls: 'They kicked me to death. They were so deter-mined to qualify because they did not want to fall short of the achievement of their previous side. But even though I didn't play well, I must admit it wasn't a good tournament for me, not what I would have liked. I played okay in the first game against Hungary but not really in the others.'

Tichy put Hungary ahead, Allchurch equalized, and twelve minutes from the end, Terry Medwin cut in past left-back Sarosi to blast the winner. Bowen says: 'That was a good performance—with under 3,000 people watching! Ivor had a superb match; he was poetic that night, really special. He put so much pressure on Boszik that he was never effective. Hidegkuti wasn't playing. The Russian referee Latychev refused us three penalties when John was hacked down in the area.'

And so to the confrontation with Brazil, an elevation Wales had not dreamed of when they set out. Ron Hewitt, the Cardiff inside-forward who had also been injured against Hungary, recovered for the game in Gothenburg, but Webster had to stand in for John Charles. Pele, seventeen and playing only his second game, was not yet the sensation he was to become in the Final against Sweden, and Wales' hopes seemed to rest heavily on the ability of long-legged Spurs left-back, Mel Hopkins, to check Garrincha, the black Matthews from Botafogo. Garrincha, with his bent legs and crouching run, and his blinding speed, was at this stage the most formidable opponent in the tournament but, on the day, Hopkins played him extremely well.

It was a splendidly balanced, elegant, rhythmical Brazilian team. The elegance began in goal with Gylmar who, in the first round of the finals against Spain in 1962, would give the most memorable display by a goalkeeper I have ever seen, to avert defeat and enable Brazil to retain the trophy. The 'back four' of Di Sordi (or Djalmar Santos), Bellini, Orlando and Nilton Santos had introduced a new concept of defensive play. Although Hungary four years previously had effectively played with a back line of four, it was the Brazilians who established the cross-play possession game among four defenders which, in the sixties and seventies, would become a distinguishing mark of the Dutch and of the European champions, Liverpool.

In midfield, Zito and Didi were a pair without equal: and this 4-2-4 formation set a pattern which would be copied round the world for the next six or seven years. England were among the imitators in 1962, but the vulnerable aspect of the formation was that the opposition had only to eliminate one of the midfield pair for the team to grind to a halt. Didi, a pearl of a player with an aristocratic bearing, was to move subsequently to Real Madrid, but he was overshadowed by Di Stefano and the venture would prove a flop. He was far from having it his own way against Wales, too. Bowen recalls:

'I suppose Didi was at his prime around this time, and it was the first time we'd seen 4-2-4. I spent the first half of the game looking after Pele, and then switched to Didi. Mel did a good job in looking after Mazzola and, quite frankly, we did far better than we'd hoped. The intention beforehand had been to hang on, try and shut out Garrincha and Pele, and rely on John to snatch us a goal. It was a great blow when he couldn't play, but, even so, we were on level terms for more than an hour, and should have had that early goal from Webster.'

It was a stormy day in Gothenburg, the weather keeping the crowd down to 15,000 in the lovely new stadium. After Webster's early miss, Kelsey had to make three fine saves, twice against Mazzola and then a thirty-yard thunderbolt from Garrincha. Kelsey was in his most commanding form and, for the rest of the first half, nobody would have guessed that Brazil were the World Cup favourites. Mel Charles had subdued Mazzola, Garrincha was shooting from longer and longer range, and it was anybody's game. At half-time, Murphy convinced his players they could go out and win. John Charles remembers: 'He was a great motivator, a great talker. There was probably a lot of similarity between him and Brian Clough with Nottingham Forest. He made people play—because until we got to Sweden, we weren't really much of a side.'

The only goal, in the sixty-second minute, was a tragedy for Wales. Pele received a short pass from Didi on the edge of the penalty area, and hit a shot which was more of a flick than a drive towards the goal. Kelsey recollects: 'I had it covered; it was nothing, but our right-back Stuart Williams didn't realize, made an attempt to stop it, the ball struck him on the knee and was deflected. It just dribbled over the line.' Wales fought back but the absence of John Charles was too much of a handicap; the forwards were never able to create sustained pressure on that calm defence, even though John still insists: 'On the day the better side lost.' Just once, in the last few minutes, Brazil nearly cracked when Bellini mistimed and sliced a cross from Cliff Jones over his own bar.

Murphy, wretchedly disappointed at the finish, said: 'I think we have shown the best defence of the four British teams out here. If John Charles had played we would have won. For the first time in the tournament, our wingers Medwin and Jones were really getting the ball over properly—for the head that wasn't there.' It was a sad but proud exit for the smallest country in the finals.

Wales: Kelsey; Williams S., Hopkins; Sullivan, Charles M., Bowen; Medwin, Hewitt, Webster, Allchurch, Jones
Brazil: Gilmar; Di Sordi, Bellini, Orlando, Santos N.; Zito, Didi; Garrincha, Mazzola, Pele, Zagalo

CHAPTER SEVEN

Scotland
v
Czechoslovakia
WORLD CUP
1961

A goal which was awarded by a Belgian referee from twenty yards away, the ball allegedly bouncing behind the line after hitting the crossbar, sinks a super Scotland team devastated by injury.

The Scottish team in 1961 reads like a Hall of Fame: Bill Brown, slim, hawk-like goalkeeper from Spurs; brilliant, barrel-chested Dave Mackay of Celtic, and soon of Spurs, at right-back; Eric Caldow, the captain of Rangers, who were busy blazing trails across Europe; a half-back line of Paddy Crerand, master of tactics and the measured pass, and Celtic colleague Billy McNeill, with incomparable Jim Baxter, the most luxurious, sometimes the laziest but certainly one of the most feared, Scots of any generation; and a formidable front five which, at full strength, read Scott (Rangers), White (Spurs), St John (Liverpool), Law (Manchester United), and Wilson (Rangers). But that night in Brussels, they were nowhere near full strength.

With such a team, Scotland and not Brazil could have been the rulers of world football. Yet, incredibly, all had been in sackcloth a few months before when the Scots were humiliated by their worst ever defeat, going down 9-3 to England at Wembley with a team including six of that top eleven and a goalkeeper named Frank Haffey. He was to inspire a joke in

Glasgow for years to come, when anybody asked the time the answer was, 'Nine past Haffey'. That result was part freak, part tribute to a superb England line-up which included Greaves, Haynes, and Charlton and which, in little over three years, hit a century of goals but flopped in the finals in Chile. The Scots, however, recovered their pride with four wins and a draw against England in the next six years, a sequence which further entrenched Alf Ramsey's feelings about the Scots.

All seemed comfortable again only weeks after the Wembley crash that year, when Scotland put four past the Republic of Ireland in their opening World Cup qualifying tie at Hampden, though I did venture to say in the *Daily Telegraph* that their problems 'are only superficially solved'. In this match, as in so many others in his illustrious career, an unsettled team did not give Law the service which might have enabled him to reveal the true breadth of his genius.

The Scotland manager was Ian McColl, an amiable but rather ineffective former international who, even more than the England manager, was at the mercy of the whim of his selectors. Law recalls: 'In those days, the manager did no more than work on a few set pieces, free kicks and throw-ins, and it was simply hoped that you would reproduce your club form in the position in which you were picked, irrespective of the players alongside you.' Paddy Crerand remembers: 'Those were the best players I had played with or even *seen*, other than going back to the prime of Matthews and Finney just after the war. And they were *all* in one team. McColl had almost no influence, but it was difficult for him because the team was full of great players, and it was expected they would decide for themselves how they were going to play.'

A month before the game in Brussels—at that stage the Czechs still needed to beat Eire twice to force the play-off— Scotland went to Belfast and scored six, without Law, against an Irish team in which Gregg, McIlroy, Blanchflower and Peacock were in decline. Baxter, Crerand and White were in full song, the team rippled with skills, so much so that Mackay, not then a man of experience, tended to use his rich vein of ability more for exhibition than effectiveness. Crerand said:

'We had more players who were "naturals" than England at that stage, great players who could make it easy for each other, but, looking back, this probably produced a sense of false optimism in both the team and the Scottish crowds. You could almost say, ironically, that the crowd in those days was the biggest thing against us, rather than for us. They didn't care about anything so long as we beat England. and this naturally encouraged us to take the same attitude, because you always want to please your own people!'

This feeling is echoed by Law. 'In a strange way, the World Cup then didn't really *mean* much to Scotland. The press didn't make all that much of it, and when we failed to qualify for a place in Chile, although I was bitterly disappointed, it didn't seem the tragedy for Scottish football that it did in later years—when we didn't even have the same potential.'

Crerand and Law are right, of course; indeed, for the next twenty years, the disproportionate importance invested in the clash with England would continue to undermine Scotland's overall approach to international football. Even in 1978, immediately prior to the finals in Argentina, the manager, Ally MacLeod, was more concerned with picking a team to beat England in the final game before departure than in the proper preparation of his side. I travelled to the home qualifying game against Czechoslovakia at Hampden that season on the local rattler from Glasgow Central and all the way the crowd, jam-packed on the train, said not a word about the Czechs but spent the journey chanting: 'If you hate the f—— English, clap your hands.'

A week before the 1961 game in Brussels, Scotland had a chance for a last warm-up in the Home Championship meeting with Wales, and won without difficulty with a couple of goals from Ian St John. Crerand and Baxter were in total command and White conducted the attack with the refinement and dignity of Sir John Barbirolli conducting the Hallé Orchestra. It was such a pity that, in his peak years before his tragic early death, the gentle, frail, artist from Falkirk was never truly appreciated by Scottish fans. As Alf Ramsey was to say of Martin Peters, so John White, too, 'was ten years ahead of his time'. I gained almost as much pleasure watching him as I did watching Baxter. But whereas the buccaneer Baxter had all the eye-catching flamboyance and a left foot which could bring huge swathes of colour to any game, White went about his business with all the precision of a researcher at the Cavendish Laboratories. You half-expected him to appear in a white coat. He seemed apart from the game at times, distant, yet he was always available to colleagues; his perception was remarkable and his influence could be deadly.

Only two of the sixteen places in the World Cup finals remained to be filled when Scotland travelled to Brussels, and both places depended on play-offs: France would meet Bulgaria the following night, and lose. The two victories by Czechoslovakia over Eire meant that while Scotland needed to win, the Czechs had only to draw on account of superior goal average. From all angles, Scotland's had suddenly become the most difficult task. Far more serious than their psychological disadvantage was the loss, at the weekend, of their Rangers wingers Scott and Wilson, and of Bill Brown of Spurs. Even at full strength, Scotland knew they would be extended against one of the most accomplished teams in Europe, and this sudden depletion was critical. Scott and Wilson were replaced by Brand of Rangers, an inside-forward, not a winger, and more often deputy for Law, and Robertson of Dundee, making his first appearance. In goal was the wholly inexperienced Connachan of Dunfermline. Quite within their rights, the Czechs refused Scotland permission to call up Leslie of West Ham unless Connachan was unfit. For reasons known only to themselves, the selectors had failed to name Leslie, superior to Connachan, in their official squad of twenty-two.

Although I have stressed the quality of the Scottish team, the Czechoslovakian team should not be underestimated: it was drawn primarily from three outstanding clubs, Dukla and Sparta of Prague, and Slovan of Bratislava. Schroif of Slovan was a superb goalkeeper, and Pluskal (Dukla) and Popluhar (Slovan) were world class defenders. In midfield Masopust (Dukla) and Kvasnak (Sparta) were the most experienced midfield pair in Europe at the time, while the left-wing combination of Jelinek and Kucera (both Dukla) was formidable. Law recalls: 'I remember Masopust most, he was the Johnny Giles of the Czech team, a brilliant little general but, as well as him, they had some outstanding, big, strong players. I was not surprised when they got to the Final in Chile. Where would we have got to if we had beaten them? Nowhere, as usual, I suppose!'

It was a gripping, fluctuating match, with Czechoslovakia, immaculate and measured in their passing, only mastering the Scots finally in extra-time. The absence of Scott and Wilson almost certainly cost Scotland the match for, at every critical period, they did not have the balance to sustain their attacks, and thus the defence was overburdened. Hard though Brand and Robertson tried, there was no penetration down the flanks.

There was a flawless performance of subtlety and artistry from the Czech captain, tiny, swarthy Masopust, who gave a taste of what Spurs would have to overcome in their forthcoming European Cup quarter-final. For not only did Dukla have four men in the team, but all five reserves were from there, too. Only now and then were Baxter and Crerand able to get to grips with Kvasnak, while Hamilton, the Dundee right-back, was frequently in dire trouble against the speed of Jelinek. For some inexplicable reason, Hamilton had been preferred to Mackay for the last two matches, while an injury to McNeill meant that the ponderous Ian Ure of Dundee was at centre-half.

For half an hour the game was rather scrappy, with Czechoslovakia in control in midfield but finishing poorly. White, drifting into open spaces, kept Scotland's flame flickering. When Hamilton, attempting to clear, headed towards his own goal, Caldow headed off the line and then cleared again off the line from Scherer. At the other end, Popluhar headed away a seemingly certain goal by Law and, six minutes before half-time, Scotland went in front. Ian St John, whose intelligence made him such a fine player as leader of the Liverpool attack—which forced its way to the forefront of football in England, cleverly beat two men only to be hit for six by Popluhar on the left of the penalty area. Baxter curled over the free kick and St John raced in on the opposite diagonal to head the ball past Schroif.

Czechoslovakia pressed hard either side of half-time. Jelinek twice centred low across an open goal with nobody there to take advantage, and Scherer blazed a free kick over the bar. But Scotland countered, Baxter and Law combining to present St John with a good chance to make it 2-0; strangely, he hesitated.

Immediately, the Czechs threw everything into a furious onslaught which led to their first goal. In the space of two minutes, Connachan saved once from Kucera and twice from Jelinek. They forced three corners in a row and right-back Hledik advanced to head in the third.

Within forty seconds, Scotland were ahead again. Brand took a free kick on the right, and again it was St John who steered the ball home. Now it seemed Scotland were there and, without too many dangers, they hung on, the heavy pitch by now churned into a muddy battlefield. But with eleven minutes remaining, the Czechs equalized again with a disputed goal. Scherer crashed the ball against the crossbar, the ball bouncing down and out. The Belgian referee, who was in a poor position to judge, awarded a goal, but Crerand claims: 'I was very close to Scherer when he shot, I saw the ball all the way and I'm quite certain it did not bounce behind the line. Immediately it bounced I thought to myself "no goal" and I was dismayed by the decision.'

Versyp, the Belgian referee, said afterwards: 'I had no doubt it was a goal.' No doubt, face-on to the line from twenty yards away! Even so, in the last seconds of full-time, Law all but snatched victory with a fierce cross-shot which skimmed the angle of the posts and left Schroif groping. Then, in the first minute of extra time, White hit the crossbar. But now the Czechs really turned on the style, and Scotland disappeared in the mud, finished by two more goals in four minutes within moments of White's near miss. Right-winger Pospichal, cutting in at speed, beat Connachan with a shot he might have held, and then Kvasnak rifled the ball home from twenty-five yards. Law, who had travelled overland from Turin, where, for one happy, crazy year, he was playing with Joe Baker for Torino, recalls: 'It was a lonely journey going back to Italy, wondering where my career was heading. After a few months in Italy, I was dying to get back to Britain. It was a good experience, the people were lovely, but the football was terrible.'

Law returned to English football the following year, signed by Matt Busby for £115,000 after an arduous chase across France, Italy and Switzerland which, at one stage, almost persuaded Busby to pull out of the negotiations. In his foreword to Law's autobiography, Busby wrote:

'Once we had got Denis to Old Trafford, I knew that we had got the most exciting player in the game. He was the quickest-thinking player I ever saw. Seconds quicker than anyone else. He had the most tremendous acceleration and could leap to enormous heights to head the ball . . . often with the power of a shot. He had courage . . . and his passing was impeccable. He was one of the most unselfish players. But when a chance was on for him, even only a half chance, in some cases no chance at all for anybody else but him, whether he had his back to goal, was sideways on, whether the ball was on the deck or at shoulder height, he would have it in the net with such power and acrobatic agility that colleagues and opponents alike could only stand and gasp.'

I can vouch for the truth of that: not one word is an exaggeration. Yet Law's career was not without controversy and occasional violence. I have seen him aim a kick at an opponent lying on the ground and, in an infamous F.A. Cup semi-final in 1965 with Leeds United, become engaged in a brawl which was disgraceful. Fortunately, he married a strong-minded lady from Aberdeen and this in time helped to bring him to his senses. But certainly he was one of the dozen most exciting players it has been my pleasure to watch and part of his secret is contained in his autobiography:

'Perhaps it's the influence of television, or maybe something else, but kids don't spend the hours playing street football the way we did, and I honestly think this has a great bearing on the lack of skill in the modern game. Most of the great players I have met developed their skills in much the same way I did. I could never get too much practice. At home we had a small kitchen with a sink, a boiler, a cooker, a gas-meter and a table where we used to eat. Above all this was a clothes rack on a pulley which was used for airing the laundry. On winter evenings after everyone had eaten and gone into the other room, I used to clear everything off the table and suspend a ball of wool from the rack. I would then spend three or four hours at a time practising heading and kicking with either foot. I loved every minute of it.'

Stanley Matthews and Don Bradman will tell you the same sort of story about how they acquired their skills. Even genius must be supplemented with hard work.

Scotland: Connachan; Hamilton, Caldow; Crerand, Ure, Baxter; Brand, White, St John, Law, Robertson

Czechoslovakia: Schroif; Hledik, Tichy; Pluskal, Popluhar, Masopust; Pospichal, Scherer, Kvasnak, Kucera, Jelinek

CHAPTER EIGHT

Benfica

v

Barcelona

EUROPEAN CUP FINAL

1961

*The most experienced goalkeeper in Europe,
Ramallets of Barcelona, makes two unaccountable
errors and his incomparable forwards hit the posts
five times in a famous defeat.*

It was, quite simply, the most awesome and accomplished
forward line that has ever failed to win the European Cup—
three Hungarians, a Spaniard and a Brazilian. A forward line
so dazzlingly skilful that one supposed beforehand that it had
only to go out on to the field to win. A forward line which
for twenty minutes in its final appearance together came as
near to perfection as is possible under the stress of competition,
only to fail. The unforgettable climax left one numb with
excitement and disbelief, moved with involuntary sympathy
that such breath-taking, flawless artistry should go unrewarded.

Who were these players? Kubala, on the right-wing in this
match, but normally an inside-forward, had been longest with
the club. Born in Hungary, he had won international caps for
three countries, Hungary, Czechoslovakia and Spain. I had
seen him play, eight years before, for the Rest of the World
at Wembley, a miraculous dribbler with a two-way body
swerve, who contributed so memorably to England's near
defeat in a 4-4 draw. There had been a bitter, protracted

wrangle between the Spanish and Hungarian Football Associations when he first tried to join Barcelona, but eventually he had become its cornerstone, the idol of a fanatical crowd, more powerful within the club than the manager. Now, at thirty-four, Kubala was signing off at the top; this was to be his last match before becoming a coach—in which capacity he would later control the Spanish team in the 1978 World Cup finals.

In the early sixties, although the old WM formation had for some time given way to 4-2-4, as used by Brazil, or 3-3-4, as used first by Hungary and then Spurs, it was still fashionable to talk of a forward line of five. Midfield players, centre-backs and strikers were terms still to come. Kubala was a deep-lying creative winger in a 4-2-4 formation (like Zagalo was for Brazil). At inside-right was Kocsis, one of the great Hungarian side, a man with marvellous reflexes and a ferocious shot, and possibly the most powerful header of the ball of all time. He could, and regularly did, score with his head from the back of the penalty area. The centre-forward was Evaristo, a tall, swarthy Brazilian, tremendously fast, erratic, but also a scorer of spectacular goals. He had been voted third in the European Footballer of the Year Poll behind Suarez—his inside-left. For perception, Suarez was in the class of the classic midfield players before the game became ultra-defensive—Boszik, Blanchflower, Didi. But, in addition, he could do astonishing things with the ball. His feet possessed the versatility of a bag of golf clubs, enabling him to drive, drift, and chip, with a variety of spin. All this he could do while remaining unemotional to the point of detachment. More than Kubala, he had an uncanny awareness of the opposition's weak spot, able to lay it bare for the kill with one sharp pass. The fifth member of this glittering attack was Czibor, another of the marvellous Hungarians, a little bullet of a winger with the kick of a horse in his left foot. But a football team has eleven men, not just five, and therein lies this story.

Barcelona were the heirs presumptive to the crown worn with such majesty for the first five years of this competition by Real Madrid, arch Castilian rivals. The previous season, though winning the League title, Barcelona had been humbled by Real in the European Cup semi-final, losing 3-1 both at home and away. Real went on to trounce Eintracht Frankfurt in the Final. A few days after the second defeat, 50,000 Catalan supporters had demonstrated in the tree-lined boulevards of Barcelona, furious that Kubala had been omitted from both matches. As a result, manager Helenio Herrera, a hero when Real had been beaten 3-1 to clinch the League so shortly before, was sacked. This might have seemed an act of self-crippling appeasement but for the fact that, at the time, Barcelona were so good as to be able to function, more or less, without a manager. This was evident from the appointment of the new manager, Brosics of Yugoslavia, who merely kept the team ticking over, with Kubala the power behind the throne.

On the way to the Final in the 1961 season, Barcelona had gained revenge on Real, winning 4-3 on aggregate in the second round, then getting the better of a third match play-off with Hamburg in the semi-final. Few doubted their ability to beat Benfica, a growing force in Portugal but with nothing like the same reputation. There were those who thought that the Eagles of Lisbon had been underestimated, but certainly the glamour was all Barcelona's. I arrived in Berne for the final via Vienna, where England had come to grief against Austria at the end of their summer tour, following a World Cup qualifying draw in Lisbon and then a rousing victory in a friendly in Rome. Certainly I had seen nothing in Lisbon which led me to question Barcelona's superiority.

But soon, in the lounge of Barcelona's hotel, I detected an air of anxiety, derived from the factor which in the next ten years would steadily squeeze the colour from the game— finance. 'We must win—or die', exclaimed Juan Gisch, their genial, seventeen-stone general manager, spreading out his arms in a heavy, care-worn shrug of emphatic exaggeration. Certainly he had his cares. In desperate competition with Real's magnificent Bernabeu Stadium, the fiercely proud Catalans had mortgaged themselves to the hilt on their *own* new stadium, on which they still owed a million pounds, ten times its value today. As a result, they had been obliged to agree to transfer Suarez to Internazionale of Milan, now man-aged by Herrera, for £160,000 after the final. For Suarez also it was farewell.

As Real had won the League this time to qualify for next season's Cup, it was essential that Barcelona win their first Final to qualify as holders. Whom had they to beat? Benfica, regardless of their comparative inexperience and lack of acknowledged stars, had one potential trump card in their manager, the veteran Hungarian, Bela Guttman. He had purposely never remained long with one club, believing that his influence, if it were to work, had to be instant. From Budapest he had gone to, among others, A.C. Milan, Sao Paulo of Brazil, and then to Benfica's rivals Porto, with whom he won the League. In 1959 he joined Benfica, taking the unusual step of signing a two-year contract on the cool and logical assumption that, if he won the League, he would wish to guide them in the European Cup the following season. And thus it was.

In a few weeks, he had transformed the team, building on a principle of attack which was a fluid variation of the WM formation and a 3-3-4. His key player was the scheming inside-left Coluna, a wonderfully supple and powerful negro from Mozambique, then a Portuguese colony; a shrewd tactician as well as a complete technician. In addition, Guttman had great strength down the middle: Pereira, a fearless goalkeeper to rank with the Russian Yashin; Germano, a consuming, formidable centre-half; and Aguas, a spring-heeled centre-forward with the fantastic goal-scoring record, in Portuguese football, of a goal a game in nearly 500 games. Not without confidence, Guttman's motto was, 'If you score three, we will score four; you get four and we'll make it five.' In eight matches on the way to the final, Benfica had scored twenty-four goals. They would not be afraid.

On the day of the match it was a beautiful, early-summer evening, the air clean and clear as a bell, the tranquil, almost rural, setting in the picturesque stadium contrasting with the thunder to come. At the start, all was serene and uneventful for a while, nothing disturbing Barcelona's authority as they strode, elegantly rather than dramatically, towards the victory we all believed was theirs. Their forwards moved the ball about with the neat unconcern of a man going through the morning's post. Suarez, weaving this way and that before selecting the precise destination of a pass, directed the operation as if Benfica were but stage props for his performance. Gradually, the tempo quickened as the line, moving now slow, now in sudden electrifying bursts, began to turn the screw, all of them wonderfully relaxed, controlled, imperious, while behind them the defence went about its duties untroubled.

Yet Benfica held their ground. While the previous year's final at Hampden Park, Glasgow, had been memorable for Real's crushing power, *this* was to prove a great game because the teams, given one twist of fortune, proved more closely matched. Benfica's pedigree would be confirmed in the years ahead, and if their forte were then to be attack, it was now defence, theirs being physically stronger and more resilient than Barcelona's and keeping them buoyant. As Kocsis, Evaristo and Czibor swept down upon them, Germano and his backs held firm. Germano's interceptions thrilled the crowd and, behind him, Pereira's reach seemed to stretch from post to post.

But a goal had to come. Out on the right wing, the two masterminds conspired in a move so smooth that left-back Angelo never knew what happened. Suarez clipped a ball past Benfica's left-half, Cruz, to Kubala, and ran wide behind Cruz for the return, which never came. Instead, Kubala slid inside, cross-field away from Angelo, doing a scissors with Suarez, who was now going like the wind down the outside. Kubala's reverse pass behind Angelo was perfect, and on went Suarez, now with a clear run. With scarcely a glance towards the goal-mouth, he leant into the ball and sent over an away-swinger which seemed to come back towards the leaping Kocsis. A sharp, straining, sure blow off the forehead and Barcelona were one up.

Yet barely ten minutes later, the game had been transformed, the whole of Barcelona's elegant façade shattered in the space of forty-five seconds. It was one man's nightmare, an unbelievable combination of errors conceding not one but two goals in a twinkling. In the most important match of his long and distinguished career it was a disaster which Ramallets, the goalkeeper, would never forget. It was the thirtieth minute. The tireless Coluna who, with Santana, had steadily been bringing rhythm and consistency to Benfica's attack, put his winger Cavem away with a short, low pass. From wide out on the left, Cavem rapped the ball knee-high square across the back of the penalty area, behind the Barcelona defence. For no clear reason, Ramallets came rushing out fifteen yards from his goal-line, without hope of intercepting the ball. On it flew to Aguas, who had nothing to do but slip it forward into the now deserted goal.

Worse was to follow. Almost straight from the kick-off, Barcelona lost possession and Benfica surged forward. Yet the situation should have been under control. Foncho, Barcelona's right-back, could have cleared but, in attempting to do so, only sliced the ball high in the air, well inside the penalty area. Out rushed Ramallets again, leaping to punch danger clear. But fate conspired against him. As he went up, he lost sight of the ball momentarily against the lingering sun, not quite spent and low at the other end: he clashed with a panicking Foncho and, off balance, struck the ball backwards towards his own net. It hit the post, ran along the line and spun back into play, but the Swiss referee Dienst had no hesitation in awarding a goal.

Ramallets hung his head in remorse while his crestfallen colleagues stood around the pitch in disbelief, then slowly turned to face the uphill struggle. Not long ago, discussing the incident with Kubala, he told me: 'It finished Ramallets' career. They were two very bad mistakes. On any other day, he would have saved both goals. It was very sad. We knew Benfica were good, but we did not have any doubt beforehand not only that we could but we *should* win.'

Inevitably, for a time, Barcelona wilted and, though Joao had to clear a header by Kocsis off the line, even after half-time it was all Benfica. Germano commanded his half of the field with the stamina of two men. And in the fifty-fifth minute a tremendous twenty-five yard volley by Coluna, from a weak clearance, streaked through a crowd of legs and left Ramallets stranded: 3-1. Now, surely, Barcelona were finished. Yet slowly, like a gathering avalanche, their retaliation grew as they found reserves of inspiration for a final onslaught which burst upon an unsuspecting defence and nearly destroyed it. Sensing the need, Kubala moved into the middle, assuming control from Suarez, coaxing his colleagues back into action. 'We switched to oblige Benfica to change their formation—and it nearly worked!' Kubala explained.

Suddenly there was no holding Barcelona. Pereira saved superbly from Kubala; Kocsis shot over the bar and, almost immediately afterwards, with an open goal, headed against a post. How Barcelona were to curse their luck. Five times in that last blistering spell they were to be denied a goal by a post or crossbar. Once, a shot by Kubala from outside the penalty area hit the left post, rebounded across an open goal, hit the right post—and came out! With fifteen minutes to go Czibor, now playing with such fire that he seemed airborne, hit a glorious shot from way out which soared over the defence, on beyond the reach of Pereira and into the far top corner of the net. Only one more goal was needed to save the game. Surely it would come from the swarm of attackers around the vulnerable Benfica goal.

Evaristo cracked the ball against the bar yet again, but the equalizing goal was not to be, even though Benfica were spread-eagled. In the last couple of minutes, Czibor lashed a shot which grazed the outside of the post. It was all over. Perhaps with another few minutes, Barcelona would have levelled the score, even won, for Benfica were on their knees. Yet they had ended Spain's domination of the cup and, the following year, they retained it, beating Real.

But they lost it the next year to Milan at Wembley, with Coluna injured. Thus ended Barcelona's ambition to become Europe's foremost club, a status which has eluded them ever since, even during their illustrious spell with Johan Cruyff. Having sacked Herrera, and then sold Suarez to him, Barcelona saw these two bring Internazionale the success that *they* so coveted. Twice Inter would win the Cup. Would Barcelona have won with Herrera at the helm? Perhaps. The man who subsequently became the high priest of method defence, almost crippling European soccer in the process, until Celtic blew Inter apart, would have put Barcelona on the field with less vulnerability at the back—though Ramallets' errors would have finished almost any team.

Benfica: Pereira; Joao, Angelo; Netto, Germano, Cruz; Augusto, Santana, Aguas, Coluna, Cavem
Barcelona: Ramallets; Foncho, Gracia; Verges, Garay, Gensana; Kubala, Kocsis, Evaristo, Suarez, Czibor

CHAPTER NINE

Tottenham Hotspur
v
Benfica
EUROPEAN CUP
1962

The magical Jimmy Greaves, in the pack of possibly the greatest ever British club team, has three goals disallowed in an unforgettable European semi-final with Benfica.

The measure of the greatness of teams is not so much the loyalty of their own supporters as the admiration they arouse throughout the rest of the country and even overseas. The Liverpool team, which twice won the European Cup at the end of the seventies, was respected if not feared all over Europe, as was the Leeds team at the end of the sixties. But when Spurs were in their prime from 1960 to 1963, they inspired an affection which has been aroused by no team other than the pre-Munich Manchester United. Grounds were bursting at the seams wherever Spurs played, and not merely because they scored a magnificent 115 goals when winning the 1961 League Championship, the year they also achieved the elusive Double.

As with almost all the English teams which have triumphed in Europe, Spurs were a blend of the four British nationalities. The side which won the Double had three Scots, Brown, Mackay, and White; a Welshman, Cliff Jones; six Englishmen, Baker, Henry, Norman, Dyson, Smith and Allen; and one incomparable Irishman, Blanchflower. Their great strength was that an almost unchanged team played throughout the entire nine months of the League. Of the reserves, Welshman Terry Medwin made fourteen appearances, and Tony Marchi six. When they beat Leicester City 2-1 at Wembley to complete the Double, the match was something of an anticlimax, but there was not a glimmer of doubt that here was the most complete team we had seen in Britain—a harmonious blend of strong, intelligent defence, rare perception in midfield, lethal finishing up front. All except right-back Peter Baker and the left-wingers Allen and Dyson were internationals.

The test of their ability would come in the European Cup and, on a memorable Saturday in December, 1961, the team received a vital addition. 'Is Greaves a genius or something?' the plumber asked when he happened to call at my house that morning. 'I suppose,' I replied, 'that he is, in a way.' The opinion was wonderfully substantiated that afternoon when the most-publicized player of his era returned to League football after an unhappy year in Milan and maintained his sequence of scoring on his first appearance with any team for whom he played—a hat-trick in fact. And his first goal encapsulated all the skills which made him the idol of crowds wherever he played. Mackay took a throw in, Medwin slipped the ball overhead and, as it came down, Greaves took off with his back to goal and, spinning through ninety degrees in mid-air, hooked a left-footed shot which even he has never bettered. Blackpool were beaten out of sight 5-2.

Spurs, in fact, did not retain their League title, throwing it away over Easter to rustic Ipswich and their, as yet, little-known manager, Alf Ramsey. They did retain the Cup, defeating Burnley in a beautifully fluent match at Wembley, one of the few classic exhibitions. But, undoubtedly, the climax of Tottenham's season came against Benfica in the European Cup semi-final in April. As for all other English teams confronted with the same situation—the outdated, social-religious absurdity of the Easter programme in conjunction with European and F.A. semi-finals—Spurs stumbled in pursuit of the Treble. But what thrills, what heartache, what memories they left us!

Benfica were the holders, having unexpectedly overcome star-studded Barcelona in the previous year's final. They were managed by one of the shrewdest, most experienced men in the game, Hungarian-born Bela Guttman, now sixty-two but wise with the accumulation of years. Spurs by this stage had switched Cliff Jones to the left with his Welsh colleague, Medwin, on the right, Greaves displacing Les Allen as twin spearhead with Bobby Smith. For the away legs of European ties, Bill Nicholson had made a concession to defensiveness, usually omitting Medwin from the normal 3-3-4 formation, playing Tony Marchi as an extra fourth defender, with Blanch-flower filling a more forward role somewhere between midfield and attack. It was this formation which was to cause some controversy in the first leg in Lisbon where Spurs went down 3-1.

They were two down after nineteen minutes, with two scrambled goals by centre-forward Aguas and right-winger Augusto. Smith scored with a header from Blanchflower's cross soon after half-time, then Augusto made it 3-1 from a corner by Simoes. Greaves recollects:

'I think the critical factor was the game out there, on two counts. Firstly, we went to play defensively, and not our normal game. I don't believe we were really equipped to play it. Had we gone at them, which they would not have expected, it might have been different. And then there was the Swiss referee, Muellet. I reckon to this day he refereed us out of the final. When we were only one down, I took on the full-back, beat him, and scored—and was given offside. Nine minutes from the end, I crossed the ball from the right-wing for Smithy to score, and Muellet pointed to the centre circle for 3-2. Then he saw the linesman was flagging and disallowed the goal without even consulting him. It can only have been offside, yet I was ahead of Smithy when I crossed the ball.'

Costa Pereira, Benfica's goalkeeper, complained that 'Smith and Greaves are not gentlemen; they play very rough.' That was perhaps so with the burly Smith, who won a reputation, for which the English cannot be proud, of batting Continental goalkeepers around like tennis balls. Greaves, on the other hand, hardly did an ungentlemanly thing in his life, other than dropping the occasional Cockney reproach in the ear of the referee following some alleged injustice. If football is said to be, at its pinnacle, a combination of war, chess, and ballet, then Greaves and Cliff Jones in that Tottenham team provided the ballet. There never was a more graceful running (as opposed to dribbling) winger than Jones who, near goal, could leap to heights unknown to Nureyev with utter fearlessness and self-disregard. Greaves scored his many goals almost always with the ease with which you or I post a letter—a casual glance, an outstretched foot, and the ball was there. His greatness lay in the regularity, the certainty with which he took the simple chances. To many footballers the ball is a leaping, squirming, elusive devil. To Jimmy, it was simply a friend needing a pat on the back. He *was* a genius.

Guttman also thought Tottenham were overphysical in Lisbon and reckoned Benfica's two-goal lead 'might not be good enough'. There were arguments within the Spurs squad, as they flew home, about whether Nicholson should have switched Blanchflower back to his normal position once it was seen that Spurs were not functioning properly with Marchi in defence, and it was resolved not to use the same formation again. A bitterly disappointed Nicholson observed: 'Our players failed to reach their own normal level of skill. Passes were inaccurate, and a lot of heading, particularly in defence, was a help to Benfica. We gave away the first two vital goals because three players in a row made mistakes which can only be described as stupid.' Mackay, who always reckoned he could climb Everest any day of the week provided there was time for a few beers on the way up, promised: 'We shall do them at Tottenham.'

The day before the return leg at White Hart Lane, the skies opened and it was inevitable that the pitch would be heavy. Previewing the match for the *Daily Telegraph*, I thought this would be in Tottenham's favour, limiting Benfica's more lightweight forwards and also Eusebio, who liked to run with the ball, whereas Smith was used to running through mud as well as walls and goalkeepers. Benfica had been enormously strengthened, since beating Barcelona the year before, by the switching of Cavem from left-wing to partner Coluna in midfield, and the advent of Simoes and Eusebio in attack. But they were still a less effective team away from home, and 65,000 people ignored the rain to take up their positions for the most electrifying ninety minutes of European football I have seen on an English ground. At the end of a titanic drama which left the nerves trembling and the throat dry, Spurs bowed out, but seldom if ever was there such a match. Spurs had their chances to win, or at least to force a play-off, but luck was against them once more and, by the finish, none could really deny that Benfica, with their technique, agility, and anticipation, were a match for Spurs, their hearts and lungs as big. Events tumbled over each other so desperately, so swiftly, that the whole incredible ninety minutes left the mind spinning. In the final reckoning, the two defensive errors in Lisbon and the three disputed, disallowed goals, one at White Hart Lane, were the handicaps which finally consumed Spurs. But oh! the agony as, with strength sapping, they hurled themselves recklessly into attack again and again over the last half-hour.

It was a memorable match and, more than anything, it was Mackay's match. At times it seemed he would willingly have played Benfica single-handed. No player ever possessed more energy or resilience, more power to charge and charge again. Nobody will ever forget his solo efforts in the last quarter of an hour, bringing Pereira to his knees in goal and, with mere seconds to go, hitting the bar. Greaves, in his book with Reg Gutteridge, *Let's Be Honest*, said: 'If somebody asked me to name *the* greatest player in this great team it would have to be Dave. He had just about everything: power, skill, drive, stamina and, above all, infectious enthusiasm.'

As the sun dipped away behind the stands, giving way to night, the 65,000 were already there—half an hour before the start. And once Benfica were into their stride, they made North London realize, as they attacked without respite, just why they were champions. It was all one could do to keep up, on paper, with the pace of events; the roar of the crowd reached a crescendo which not even Hampden or Old Trafford had heard before. Augusto, on Benfica's right wing, was extending Henry; Eusebio's long, raking runs had Brown threatened in goal. And, with fifteen minutes gone, Benfica went into an aggregate 4-1 lead: Aguas out to Simoes on the left, then sprinting for the return as it skimmed across a muddy penalty area to glide in feet first past Henry and stab the ball home. Almost immediately Spurs, compelled by the dynamic roar, surged forward and Mackay lashed the ball against a post via a defender.

In the twenty-third minute, for the third time in the two matches, Spurs had a seemingly fine goal disallowed. Danish referee Aage Poulsen was the man in the middle. One of John White's perfect centres was volleyed forward by Smith to Greaves, who scored from close in, though tightly marked. Poulsen gave a goal, but the Benfica players dragged him over to his linesman, Hensen, who had momentarily flagged but then taken his flag down. It was no goal and Greaves recalls: 'I ran through *between* two players after Smithy had played the ball, so how could I have been offside? If you ask me, that decision deserved an enquiry, and I'm not usually one to complain.'

Neither outdone nor disheartened, Spurs scored to make it 4-2 seven minutes from half-time. White, at the second attempt, chipped into the middle, Smith chested down and let fly an unstoppable shot. On the stroke of half-time Aguas hit the bar. Such was the impact of this great Portuguese side that, while at the start they had been mildly booed, when they reappeared after the interval they were applauded on to the field. Within four minutes came the most dramatic turn possible—a penalty for Spurs. White was fouled by Cruz and, in an awesome hush, Blanchflower prepared to take the vital kick. Calmly he shuffled up to the ball and sent Pereira the wrong way: 4-3. Pereira claimed: 'I'd never been sent the wrong way before.'

It looked like another penalty when massive centre-half Germano seemed to handle Medwin's header, but Poulsen waved play on. To a frenzied crescendo from the crowd, Spurs hurled themselves forward in a desperate bid to force extra-time. Germano's arm which kept out Medwin's header had been on the blind-side of the overworked Poulsen and it was the final straw in the string of decisions which had gone against Spurs. A heroic encounter closed as Mackay, going through the mud like a snow plough, blasted the ball against the crossbar.

Benfica went on to defeat Real Madrid in the final and retain their title, leaving Spurs to reflect on what might have been. Guttman, who had resigned officially before the start of the match—'what more is there for me to do with Benfica?' —was fulsome in his praise of Spurs. He could afford to be. He said: 'It was the hardest game of my life. I thought Spurs would equalize in the last ten minutes. They can win the European Cup soon. The crowd did not affect our players because they are experienced.'

Sir Stanley Rous paid tribute to Benfica: 'Everyone of their players is a ball artist; they can play the ball from any angle. They are masters of the game.'

Blanchflower, Tottenham's ageing field marshal, whose own contribution to a tactical battle had been colossal, told me:

'Some people said we played it the wrong way at home, that we played at too fast a pace, but Pereira in goal did so well and Coluna was marvellous in midfield. Over two games we were slightly the better team, perhaps one goal better, but they were the more experienced. I think Guttman was sharper than we thought. He had experience all over Europe and South America. Certainly it ought to have been 3-2 in Lisbon, not 3-1 but, when Guttman came to London, he used the press before the match to criticize the tough tactics of Bobby Smith and Dave Mackay and put pressure on the referee. That's probably what persuaded Poulsen to disallow our early goal at home. I wouldn't say the referee did it deliberately, but it was all part of the psychological battle. I'd talked to Guttman after the first leg and told him I thought we'd win. "No, we'll do it", he'd said. But he was more worried about us than about Real Madrid. He had had admiration for us; he knew what was good and what was bad.'

Coluna, that marvellous half-back who came from Mozambique like Eusebio, probably had it right when he said: 'The Tottenham midfield line of Blanchflower, White and Mackay is the best in the world. Mackay is an extraordinary player.'

The most extraordinary comment came from League secretary Alan Hardaker, who claimed: 'It is the best advertisement for League football for a long time.' Which is about as illogical as claiming that roses are an advertisement for fertilizer. Cliff Jones put his finger on it: 'You can't give a team like Benfica three goals start.'

Tottenham Hotspur: Brown; Baker, Henry; Blanchflower, Norman, Mackay; Medwin, White, Smith, Greaves, Jones

Benfica: Pereira; Joao, Angelo; Cavem, Germano, Cruz; Augusto, Eusebio, Aguas, Coluna, Simoes

CHAPTER TEN

Tottenham Hotspur

v

Atletico Madrid

EUROPEAN CUP-WINNERS CUP FINAL

1963

A fluke goal by Terry Dyson, unsung member of Tottenham's team of all-stars, seals Britain's first European title—without Dave Mackay and with Danny Blanchflower a tactical passenger.

The *Daily Express* headline screamed: 'A sixty-three-inch hero named Dyson rips through Spanish aces to win Britain's first major European soccer title.' That said it all. Little Terry Dyson, for so long overshadowed by Tottenham's glittering array of internationals, played literally the game of his life this night in Rotterdam, to rejuvenate a team which many feared was over the hill. Not only that, Spurs had been obliged to play the Final without the inspiration of Dave Mackay, laid low with torn stomach muscles. In a mood of foreboding before the game, Cliff Jones had admitted: 'With Dave in the team we feel we can beat anyone. He makes things happen. He makes us go. If he doesn't play tomorrow, then the odds will change.' For so long Mackay had been the talisman, the lion-heart leading them into battle. It was galling that he should now miss Tottenham's finest hour, just as his compatriot Dennis Law was to do with Manchester United five years later.

Although Spurs had again scored over 100 goals (111) in finishing second to Everton in the League, and had convincingly disposed of the opposition on the way to the European Final, their misgivings on arrival in Holland centred around not only Mackay but Danny Blanchflower, who that spring had had a cartilage removed at the age of thirty-seven. Normally, such an operation required a two- or three-month absence, but Danny, always different, was back after only four weeks playing at outside-right in the third team. He missed the first leg of the semi-final against O.F.K. in Belgrade, played in the second leg at home, and made the first of two goals. 'I was out there reading the game rather than playing it,' he recalls. But the week before the Final, Spurs were thumped 5-1 by Manchester City and all optimism drained away. The critics considered that Blanchflower was now a liability.

The mood of the team was not assisted by the manager, Bill Nicholson. This dour, sandy-haired Yorkshireman was Tottenham's most loyal servant. He had joined the club as a ground-staff boy from Scarborough, had been an endlessly dependable wing-half during the heady days in the fifties when Arthur Rowe, with his famous 'push-and-run' tactics based on the Hungarians, and had guided Spurs to the League title. Only Billy Wright's presence in the England side denied Nicholson a fistful of caps, limiting him to a single appearance. 'Nick' had early turned towards coaching. I first met him when he was coach to the Cambridge University side—while still playing in the First Division. I was a totally undisciplined winger, the product of old-fashioned public school football, in which the best players dribbled all day and all night until they lost the ball. At half-time in my first game for the University, Bill came across to me in the dressing room with a puzzled frown and exclaimed: 'Well, I don't know what we're going to do with you!' With his patient assistance, I spent the next year re-learning the game, and establishing a friendship which has lasted ever since. Beneath that rather severe, often pessimistic, perfectionist attitude beat a kind heart. His detractors rarely understood him, but it is a fact that he did not lift people emotionally and, in later years, he tended if anything to depress his Tottenham teams by being too critical. Yet his ultimate departure, the abject failure of the Tottenham board properly to recognize his sterling service over a lifetime, was the shabbiest episode in the history of a club which has often been so magnificent on the field and so mean off it.

By 1963, Blanchflower had become assistant manager, taking over some of the coaching from Nicholson. In Rotterdam, as the moment approached when a decision would have to be made as to whether he should play, Blanchflower was clearly in a compromised position. Nicholson argued, after a final six-a-side practice which did something to improve morale: 'It's not a simple choice.' Blanchflower, never one to mince words, answered: 'It is. It's either me on one leg, or John Smith on two.' Smith was a highly skilful but always overweight young player, for whom the promise of an exciting future faded early. After injections to remove soreness from his knee, it was decided that Blanchflower should play. He reasoned: 'At thirty-seven, you know *why* things happen. With younger players like Jimmy Greaves and John White, brilliant though they were, experiences were still happening *to* them.'

When the team assembled for their final tactical talk, Nicholson was at his most solemn. It was at this moment that Blanchflower was to play one of his smartest aces in all his time at Tottenham. One by one Nicholson went through the Atletico players. By the time he finished, they loomed as a team of supermen. This man was a giant, that man was a magician, another a wizard. When he paused finally, Blanchflower stood up and told the players to forget the lot. Greaves recollects:

'That was the greatest game Danny ever won—off the field. Nick's bottle had gone, because Dave Mackay was our best player, and he was out. Nick was full of doom and he made all their players seem ten feet tall. Danny totally counteracted this. He said that if their centre-half were big and ugly then ours, Maurice Norman, was even bigger and uglier. He made us laugh away all our doubts, and this was when we still weren't sure whether or not he would be playing.'

Blanchflower, who soon afterwards retired to journalism, came back briefly fifteen years later with mixed success as manager of Northern Ireland and Chelsea. He remembers:

'I knew it was the moment to lift them. It was an awkward time for Nicholson. Nowadays it's called motivation, but all I was doing, as Peter Doherty did for the Irish team, was to introduce some humour, to ease the players' natural anxieties, to bolster their self-belief. If Atletico had one or two expensive players, why, Jimmy Greaves had cost more than their whole team put together! They were worried, too, about bonuses, about the fact that the Madrid players were said to be on an incentive of £1,200-a-man to win. I told them to forget the bloody bonuses and to leave that to me, and of course by the time we went out to play everyone would have played for nothing. That's the only way it can be.'

And so the mood changed once more from gloom to optimism. Tony Marchi replaced Mackay, and the attack was the same as that which had become established during that season: Jones back on the right wing where he had been in the Double year, Dyson on the left. And, within a quarter of an hour, Spurs were in front. Smith sent Jones racing clear towards the right corner flag, over came a perfect centre and there was Greaves to put the ball away first time. The rhythm was back, the moves were flowing like clockwork and, over on the left, little Dyson was tearing the Spaniards to shreds. On the half-hour, with immaculate John White plaguing the Spaniards into error, Spurs went two up. Dyson hooked the ball back from the by-line when it had almost run out of play, and there was White in the middle to meet it with a crisp drive. But a minute into the second half found Spurs in trouble as left-back Ron Henry punched out a shot with Bill Brown beaten and Atletico's left-winger Collar scored from the penalty. For the next twenty minutes, Spurs wobbled dangerously.

Henry had to head off the line from Mendoza, who was denied a second time by a brave save by Brown. Chuzo and Ramiro both went close, Atletico forced a string of corners and the game was on a knife-edge. Now came the moment which was decisive: a fluke goal by little Dyson. He beat a tackle by right-back Rivilla and swung over a speculative cross which was half shot, half centre. Atletico's goalkeeper Madinabeyta went up for the ball unchallenged, groped, and somehow helped the ball into his own net. Dyson, with pardonable pride, awarded the goal rather more strategy than it contained when he claimed afterwards: 'Bobby Smith was screaming for the ball, and I was going to pass to him until I saw the goalkeeper move. Then I shot into the top corner of the net!' The Spurs players merely smiled in gratitude.

Now it was Atletico who were on the ropes. There might have been a penalty when Dyson was brought down by Rivilla and, ten minutes from the end, it was Dyson who floated over the centre for Greaves to hit a fourth. Dyson sealed his personal triumph with a shot from twenty-five yards for the fifth three minutes from time and, as Spurs tumbled joyfully back into the dressing room, Bobby Smith told Dyson: 'Terry, you'd better retire now; you'll never play any better.'

True to character, even in a moment of triumph, Nicholson was busy trying to keep everyone's feet on the ground, when they were already comfortably airborne on champagne, by reminding them: 'It was a fluke goal that put things right for us,' but he did unbend enough to say: 'I'm tremendously proud for the players, and to be manager of the first British team to win a European trophy.'

Leo Horn, Holland's world famous referee, said: 'This was the finest exhibition of British football I've ever seen. You can send the Spurs team anywhere in the world with pride. Why doesn't your national team play like this!' To which the answer is, as I have said, that Spurs were multinational. It has long been argued that Britain should field a single unified team in the World Cup, just as it does in the Olympic Games. But this overlooks the fact that the associations of England, Scotland, Northern Ireland and Wales were in existence long before the formation of F.I.F.A. or the creation of the World Cup, and historically there is no reason why they should surrender their individuality. Much as Eastern Europeans and the Afro-Asian bloc might like to alter it, football is an arena for sport and not politics. The pressures the other way are severe, but long may it remain so. It will not survive otherwise.

For Spurs, that night in Rotterdam was the culmination of fifteen illustrious years. From here, their path would be largely downhill, by their standards, though they did win the F.A. Cup again four years later and subsequently a couple of League Cups. Tragedy was close at hand. Within a year, John White had died, struck by lightning while playing golf. Dave Mackay and Maurice Norman suffered broken legs; Bill Brown, Bobby Smith and Cliff Jones had passed their zenith.

And Blanchflower was finished. It had been a glorious era while it lasted.

Tottenham Hotspur: Brown; Baker, Henry; Blanchflower, Norman, Marchi; Jones, White, Smith, Greaves, Dyson

Atletico Madrid: Madinabeyta; Rivilla, Rodriguez; Ramiro, Griffa, Glaria; Jones, Adelardo, Chuzo, Mendoza, Collar

CHAPTER ELEVEN

England

v

West Germany

WORLD CUP FINAL

1966

A free kick given the wrong way and an undetected 'hands' allow West Germany to force extra-time in the World Cup Final: a goal, hitting the crossbar and bouncing in front of the goal-line, is wrongly given by a Russian linesman and England win the World Cup.

From early in Alf Ramsey's period as England manager, I had believed in his ability to lead England to victory in the World Cup. Even through times when many doubted him and heaped scorn on him. Before the final tournament in England began, I had written, in the *Sunday Telegraph*, that if England were to win, it would be with the resolution, physical fitness and cohesion of West Germany in 1954, rather than with the flair of Brazil in the two succeeding competitions. And so it proved, with the added coincidence that it was the Germans themselves, as usual bristling with all these same characteristics, who were the unlucky and courageous victims of England's methodical rather than brilliant football.

Yet having been their advocates through thick and thin up to the moment of triumph, I was bound to concede that they were the most efficient team rather than the most skilful—Hungary held that distinction. And in succeeding years, even though I believe the excellence of Ramsey's tactical organization might well have retained the Cup in 1970, it became obvious that his management was flawed with caution, and with too ready an acceptance at times of over-physical players, both of which factors, in the long term, were detrimental to the national development of the game. That should not detract from the brilliance of the man in his early days, his iron will, his unflinching resolution to win the Cup as he had promised to do from the outset. They had fetched him, three and a half years before, from quiet Ipswich, the second or even third choice of the F.A. following Walter Winterbottom's resignation. Taciturn, shy, reserved, Ramsey had calmly led with his chin and promised victory. There were those who laughed, and there were some who were still laughing when the tournament began.

There remains also the controversy which will be there for all time: whether England *did* win the World Cup, whether Geoff Hurst's second goal to put England 3-2 ahead in extra time was in fact a goal. But there was also dispute, certainly, surrounding Germany's equalizing goal moments before the end of full-time, so that probably justice was done. It was fortunate indeed that Hurst's third goal erased much of the argument and concluded the match on an emphatic note. Yet while the English like to believe that Hurst's shot, which struck the bar, bounced behind the line, there is scientific evidence, as opposed to photographic or television evidence, which quite clearly demonstrates that it bounced in front of the line. Let me explain.

The problem with all photographs and film of this celebrated incident is that they flatten a three-dimensional situation into two dimensions. The photofinish camera, sited on the line in the Olympics, never lies: but no camera shot of the Hurst goal can prove that the ball was touching the ground where, in some pictures, it appears to be behind the line. The ball could be, in fact, *off* the ground with the angle of the picture allowing the goal-line to be seen *beneath* rather than in front of the ball. But a German photograph holds the proof. With the ball quite clearly about two feet off the ground, its shadow is seen *on* the goal-line. The sun at this moment, late in the afternoon, was directly in line with the west-east axis of the stadium, and the shadows of the goal-posts are seen at right-angles to the goal-line. *Therefore*, since the shadow of the ball in the eastern goal-mouth would move forward, *into* the playing area, to meet the ball at the moment it was touching the turf, the ball *must* have landed at least a foot in front. No goal. The fact that the Russian linesman Bakhramov was badly out of position, ten to fifteen yards down the touchline, yet insisted to the Swiss referee Dienst that it was a goal, has always been cause for the gravest suspicions. Bakhramov did not raise his flag for several seconds.

Hurst himself was not really able to give an opinion, because he hooked the ball on the turn with his right foot, his left shoulder towards the goal, fell, and did not see the ball beat goalkeeper Tilkowski. The strongest evidence for a goal, though only visual, is Roger Hunt's. He was following up, only six or seven yards from the goal. After the ball bounced, he could have attempted to head it, had he not thought it bounced behind the line; and his instant reaction was to swing round in a dramatic appeal to the referee. Hunt, who now works with a transport company, recollects:

'Normally in that situation, I would have gone in and, looking back, I still don't know why I didn't. I don't think, in fact, I'd have got the ball. It bounced down and high up to my left, and Weber, their centre-back, headed it away for what would have been a corner. I've thought many times since, why did I not go in? The linesman definitely couldn't have seen: when I looked across, moments later, he was still moving back towards the corner flag, he was still so far away and still hadn't got his flag up.'

Although Hunt appealed instinctively, in the manner of most professionals, it now seems that he himself was far from sure.

Helmut Schoen, the German manager, then and ever since has taken a typically sportsmanlike stance. When I talked to him recently at his home in Wiesbaden where he is retired, he said: 'I was in the middle of the field, I simply couldn't say. From the evidence of TV I would consider it was not a goal. But in that game, the English team was better by one goal. It was a very great final, and it was a pity that the decisive goal was so controversial.'

Going on to consider the merits of his opposition on the day, Schoen remarked:

'The outstanding thing about that England team was that they had great personalities. We look around the world now and we don't find them anywhere, in Brazil, in England, in Italy or in Germany. The England team was, above all, a very good mixture of battlers like Jack Charlton, Nobby Stiles and George Cohen, and the skilful players like Bobby Charlton, Bobby Moore and Martin Peters. Alan Ball was not a personality then, but he had great worth for the team in that match. I knew when that third goal was awarded that it would be very difficult to equalize again: England were at home and were playing very well. I was proud of my team; they played very correctly after that goal.'

Schoen is a man of impressive dignity, pleasantly free of prejudice or resentfulness, concerned throughout his career with the image of the game: more concerned than the English, should I say? When I talked to him he would not bring himself to criticize Stiles, merely observing that he was 'a good worker—players of other teams didn't like to play against him'. This was particularly true of the French, I recall, whose skilful player, Simon, was lying on the grass after a challenge by Stiles in the first round when England scored a goal. Subsequently, the F.A. attempted to put pressure on Ramsey to exclude the demonic Stiles from the team, but he made it clear that if they wanted him as manager, they would have to accept Stiles as part of the package.

Ramsey was the absolute pragmatist, the essence of professionalism. If Styles could neutralize key men in the opposition, as he neutralized Eusebio in the semi-final against Portugal, then there was a place for Stiles. If there were no wingers in England at that time capable of giving a ninety-minute performance, contributing as much to defence as attack, then there was no room for wingers. It is not true to say that Ramsey disliked wingers. If England had possessed a George Best, Ramsey would have used him. From 1963 to 1965 he had persevered with Peter Thompson of Liverpool and Terry Paine, and had used John Connelly and Paine in the first round in the finals. It was the tactical breadth of Martin Peters and Ball which secured them their places as the finals progressed. Ruthlessly, Ramsey subjugated all considerations to the overall interest of the team, as must any successful manager: a prin-

Gaetjens, who scored the only goal in the United States' historic victory over England in the 1950 World Cup, is carried off shoulder-high by Brazilian fans in Belo Horizonte

The legendary Puskas equalizes for Hungary in the last minute against West Germany in the 1954 World Cup Final, but is ruled off-side by the English referee

Mortensen lunges forward to bring the score to 3–2 at the start of Blackpool's never-to-be-forgotten recovery against Bolton in the 1953 F.A. Cup Final

In incomparable Matthews style, the ball is crossed for Perry to score the injury-time winner in the F.A. Cup Final in 1953

Above: The collision between Aston Villa winger McParland and Manchester United goalkeeper Wood which determined the 1957 F.A. Cup Final (Byrne and Edwards in background)

Left: Harry Gregg, who survived the Munich crash, in action for Northern Ireland in the 1958 World Cup a few months later

Benfica centre-forward, Aguas, lashes the ball past Spurs' centre-half, Norman,
but Brown saves in the European Cup Semi-final second leg in 1962 (Henry and
Baker look on)

Hat-trick hero Dyson is hugged by Baker as Smith, Blanchflower and Norman
carry off the Cup-Winners Cup for Tottenham Hotspur in 1963

Eusebio rips past
Sadler in the 1968
European Cup Final
at Wembley, but he
failed to beat Stepney

Best (on the right) slides the ball home at the end of a brilliant run for the first of
Manchester United's three goals in extra-time in the 1968 European Cup Final

Weber equalizes for West Germany in the 1966 World Cup Final, with Wilson and Banks beaten. Seeler, Cohen (on ground), Moore, Schnellinger and Jack Charlton watch

Hurst shoots past Schulz to hit the cross-bar for a disputed third goal for England in the 1966 World Cup Final (Beckenbauer centre background)

Weber, Hunt and goalkeeper Tilkowski watch the ball come down off the cross-bar, and Hunt appeals for a goal for England. *Left:* The shadow of the ball just behind the goal-line proves the ball must have bounced in front of it since, when the ball was on the ground, the shadow *must* have moved forward

Chalmers (9) turns to receive acclaim from colleagues for his winning goal in the European Cup Final in 1967. Other Celtic players, left to right: Lennox, Johnstone, Murdoch, McNeill, Auld, Gemmell

The ball, coming off the back of Seeler's head, sails over Bonetti for a goal for West Germany in the 1970 World Cup quarter-finals, with Mullery watching

Müller hooks the 1970 World Cup quarter-final winner for West Germany from only three yards

Ian Porterfield hits Sunderland's historic winner against Leeds in the F.A. Cup Final in 1973, with Bremner and Reaney helpless on the line

England's Channon drives the ball against a post watched by Chivers in the ill-starred World Cup match against Poland in 1973

Poland rejoice – their hero Tomaszewski (left) – while Peters and Clarke (right) hang their heads. The 1–1 draw puts England out of the 1973 World Cup

McDermott hammers home Liverpool's first goal in the 1977 European Cup Final.
Vogts arrives too late for Borussia München-Gladbach

Jansen fells Holzenbein to give West Germany their equalizing penalty against
Holland in Munich in the 1974 World Cup Final

McIlroy shoots Manchester United's equalizer past the Arsenal goalkeeper, Jennings, in the 1979 F.A. Cup Final

Sunderland scoops a last minute winner past Albiston for Arsenal, with Bailey watching after failing to reach Rix's cross

ciple which ultimately became self-defeating. What can never be denied Ramsey is the fact that he created for England the kind of team spirit which previously had only been found in club teams. He was the first professional manager with exclusive rights of selection, a long overdue innovation and, although his inability to express himself was eventually to cause him grave problems in public relations, he was a caring, sensitive man, deeply loyal to his players and his country. I remember him correcting me on one occasion soon after he took over, as we drove across Blackfriars Bridge on our way back to Liverpool Street Station from a training session at Crystal Palace: 'It's not *my* team you know, it's England's.'

Bobby Moore began his first volume of biography shortly before the 1970 finals: 'There is a message sewn with invisible stitching inside every England cap . . . "Just remember you are here to play for me, for England, and to do as I say." Ramsey's words to every new England player.' The authority of a coach must be absolute, even though he must be susceptible to opinions from his senior players; his leadership and the team's unity are synonymous, and a manager must carry the ultimate responsibility, must stand or fall by his own decisions. All great leaders are of necessity lonely men.

The anecdotes concerning Ramsey are legion. He had a passionate, competitive dislike for the Scots, and when a Scots journalist once greeted him on landing at Glasgow Airport with 'Welcome to Scotland', Ramsey replied with icy disdain: 'You must be f—— joking.' Moore recounts the occasion of Alf going up to Allan Clarke during the flight to Mexico in 1969.

'Enjoying yourself Allan? he asked.

'Yes Alf, great, thanks,' replied the uncertain new boy.

'You don't enjoy yourself with me. Remember that,' snapped Alf. And to a Polish interpreter, on a wretched bus journey from Cracow Airport to Katowice at the end of an eight-hour journey on tour before the 1966 finals, who cautiously enquired what Mr Ramsey intended to do later that evening: 'To get to Katowice . . . I hope,' with a look which would have shattered a crossbar.

Ramsey's most unenviable and most objective decision came on the day of the Final, when he decided to keep an unchanged team against Germany, thereby excluding perhaps the greatest of all talents available to him, Jimmy Greaves. It was a decision which few would have wanted to shoulder. Had England lost, the criticism would have been colossal. Greaves had been injured in the first round game with France, a gashed shin required stitches, and had missed the quarter-final—in which his replacement, Hurst, had headed the only goal from a cross by Peters, to clinch a game remembered primarily for the cynical malevolence of the Argentinians and the sending off of their captain, Rattin. Greaves was still unfit for the semi-final with Portugal but was available for the Final. It is an entrenched maxim not to change a winning team and Greaves, who scored forty-four goals, second only to Bobby Charlton's forty-nine, in his fifty-seven internationals, remembers:

'I felt in my bones that Alf would stick with the semi-final team. Alan Bass, our doctor, couldn't do anything about my cut in a hurry, and I couldn't have played against Portugal. It was a devastating experience, the slow realization that I was going to miss what for everyone else would be the pinnacle of their whole career, a moment that would never occur again. Alf didn't say a lot to me, just that it would be the same side, and I said "Fair enough", and there was never any vendetta. I recognized that he was under tremendous pressure and that, if he lost, he'd have been wrong whatever he did.'

There is that famous photograph of the England benches at the final whistle with all the England trainers and reserves leaping exultantly into the air, all except Ramsey, still resolutely seated and, in the background, a sad, pensive, unsmiling Greaves. Hurst had just scored the only hat-trick of a World Cup Final. Greaves did not begrudge him his hour of glory, but knew that his own genius had missed the biggest curtain call of its life.

A fact which tends to be forgotten after all this time is that Bobby Moore, England's blond Adonis of a captain, had approached the World Cup uncertain of his place. In friendly matches against West Germany and Yugoslavia in the spring and against Finland on tour immediately beforehand, he had been replaced by Norman Hunter. Ramsey had been acting shrewdly, conscious of a complacency in Moore's play, anxious to invigorate him with a dose of uncertainty. In football as in life there is no driving force greater than ambition. Once Moore had recognized the signals, he emerged to become an inspiring captain, and was voted the outstanding player of the tournament. Franz Beckenbauer, just twenty, was still a leader of the future.

Many complained during and after the finals that England were helped by playing all their matches at Wembley, a decision taken by F.I.F.A. for financial expediency; yet on their form of that time, England certainly could and would have won anywhere in the country. The overwhelming nationalistic fervour which was generated at Wembley would have been every bit as intense at Goodison or Old Trafford, though it was a pity that the North, providing six of the team, should not have had at least one opportunity to clasp the potential national heroes to their bosom. Yet it was overlooked that, in some ways, the pressures on England at Wembley were more intense than anywhere else and that much of their best football in the seasons before and after was played abroad. They were far from being exclusively a 'home' team. The two results which had most convinced me that England were potential winners were the 1965 2-0 win over Spain in Madrid, when Ramsey first introduced a 4-3-3 formation, and the one-goal victory over Poland in Katowice, immediately before the World Cup.

England asserted themselves in the Final from the start, with Bobby Charlton exerting a telling influence in midfield though closely shadowed by Beckenbauer, whose responsibilities were subjugated, as they would be four years later, to a largely negative role. Yet with the game only thirteen minutes old and the crowd riding on a 'high' of expectation, England found themselves a goal down for the first time in the competition. It may stretch credulity to say so now, but it was in fact the result of the first *unforced* error made by England in their six matches so far. Sigi Held, Germany's blond, urgent right-winger, had momentarily switched to the left and floated over a high cross. Ray Wilson, who was probably the most accomplished left-back, other than Roger Byrne, ever to have played for England, stood in isolation, eyes riveted on the dropping ball. He made to head it down to Moore, but his judgement betrayed him and he directed it instead straight to the feet of

Haller, standing in an inside-right position some fourteen yards out from Gordon Banks. With time to spare, Haller whipped a low, skidding shot into the far left-hand corner beyond Banks.

The strapping Germans and their banner-waving supporters noisily bounced with joy but, within six minutes, England were level. Midway inside the German half on the left, Wolfgang Overath, that fine midfield player with a velvet left foot, tripped Moore and, even before referee Dienst had finished waving his finger at Overath for the second time in a few minutes, Moore had spotted a gaping hole in the German rearguard. He placed the ball and took the kick almost in one move: a dipping floater which carried thirty-five yards over to the right and was met by Hurst, timing his run superbly to slip through the defence, with another graceful, expertly timed header like that which had beaten Argentina.

The pattern swung once more in the ten minutes before half-time. The three German strikers, Held, Uwe Seeler, and Emmerich, nosing in and out of England's defence like carnivorous fish, began to create havoc which was only calmed after extreme anxiety. In between Hunt, from a glorious pass by Bobby Charlton, hammered a thundering shot, a difficult one running away to his left, straight at Tilkowski. But Beckenbauer was occasionally able to neglect Charlton and venture forward. Overath was commanding, and nearly beat Banks from twenty-five yards. Three minutes before half-time, Hunt squandered the kind of opportunity which invited unfavourable comparisons with Greaves. At the other end, England were lucky when a fast, dipping shot by Seeler was tipped over the bar by Banks, arched in mid-air like a stalling buzzard.

Little happened for nearly twenty-five minutes after half-time, but then England's rhythm began to gather momentum. Alan Ball, the baby of the team who, over the two hours, grew to become the man of the match, began to stretch the Germans. He and Bobby Charlton and Peters almost freed Hurst and Hunt again and again. With only eleven minutes to go, Ball pressurized Schnellinger into conceding a corner and swung the ball across; it was headed out but hit back first time by Hurst. It struck a defender, fell free and Peters, whose menace was from the start strangely undetected by the Germans, swooped to lash the ball home on the half-volley. England, sensing victory, now played it slow, slow, but Hunt wasted a priceless chance on the edge of the area, when it was three red England shirts to one white German, by misjudging his pass. The price of that squandered opening was exacted quickly.

With just over a minute left, a high ball was knocked down the right flank of England's defence. Held made no real attempt to jump, creating only a stooping obstruction to Jack Charlton as the big centre-half took off. Dienst gave a free kick against Charlton when, if anything, it should have been the other way. Emmerich blasted the free kick into the goal-mouth and, with a protest that Schnellinger had handled scarcely off England's lips, Weber had forced the ball past Banks. England sank to the ground as they waited for the start of extra-time during the brief interval, but were sternly admonished by Ramsey: 'You have won the match once, now go out and win it again. Besides, they are more tired than you.'

None responded more than the dynamic little Ball, who gave a foretaste of the dedication which was to characterize a long career. In extra-time, he ran Schnellinger into the ground and was an inspiration to the rest of the team. It was Ball's pass which now led to the decisive third goal. Twelve minutes into extra-time, Stiles fed the ball up the right, Ball made space for himself and turned a pass square into the path of Hurst. With both teams beginning to feel physically distressed, Bakhramov's decision in England's favour was bound to be psychologically defeating for Germany. Again England sought economy with gentle passes, keeping precious possession, yet right at the finish Germany might have snatched another shock equalizer. But Seeler lunged at a cross by Held—and missed. Now Moore dribbled clear of the defence once more, spotted Hurst on the half-way line, and lofted a long pass which set his West Ham colleague clear. With three spectators prematurely already on the pitch, Hurst forged forward and lashed a left-foot shot into the roof of the net. It would have been hard to produce a more fitting final flourish.

Only a month before the finals began, Hurst would have been given small chance of playing, and now he said: 'I had a bad game on England's tour and, when Hunt and Greaves played in the opening game against Uruguay, I reckoned that was it. I have played in two Cup Finals for West Ham at Wembley but I have never known anything quite like this.' In the moment when he had the world at his feet Ramsey was as phlegmatic as when he had been ploughing his lonely furrow in the preparatory years. He had not forgotten the criticism and the doubters. I myself had helped script an ITV profile of him screened the day of the draw for the finals in January, the day after a scruffy draw with Poland at Goodison. When I walked into the studio that morning for the final run-down on the programme, the producer was tearing his hair out.

'Ramsey must go,' he bellowed at me. *World Cup—England to Win* was the title of the programme. I held my ground. In the event, someone lost their nerve and placed a question mark on the end when the titles came up on the screen.

Ramsey was back in his shell within twelve hours of his greatest feat. With the world waiting for information and opinions from the man at the pinnacle of world football, he was almost monosyllabic in his statements. Some British journalists tried to see him the next day, men who had been loyal to his ideas for three years. 'I can't talk to you today . . . it's my day off!' But he did at least venture to say: 'I do not think we can ever match the individual technique of the Latin-American or Latin-European. We play a different kind of football. We were the *fastest* and the *strongest* side in the World Cup. I was a little worried before the tournament started that we were behind the rest of the world. I think this result shows we have caught up.' Events would prove that, instead of developing and expanding his new-found power and influence, Ramsey remained fundamentally cautious. Within seven years, his power had waned.

England: Banks; Cohen, Charlton J., Moore, Wilson; Stiles, Charlton R., Peters; Ball, Hunt, Hurst
West Germany: Tilkowski; Hottges, Weber, Schnellinger, Schulz; Haller, Beckenbauer, Overath; Seeler, Held, Emmerich

CHAPTER TWELVE

Celtic

v

Internazionale

EUROPEAN CUP FINAL

1967

The loss of the genius of Suarez in midfield, and Helenio Herrera's belief that one goal was enough to win any match, sees Celtic inflict the demise of Internazionale.

My most enduring memory of Celtic's inspired triumph in the European Cup in Lisbon—the first in this competition by a British team—is not of Tommy Gemmell's blistering shot for the critical equalizing goal, nor of the thousands of delirious Glasgow supporters cascading on to the pitch at the finish, but of a small Portuguese policeman whose emotions finally overwhelmed his sense of duty. As Gemmell, whose perform- ance still ranks among the most notable of any full-back in a major match, turned to receive the acclaim of colleagues and crowd, the policeman ran forty yards to the trainers' bench on the half-way line as fast as his legs could carry him, one hand holding his hat on, the other steadying his holster, and grabbed the hand of Celtic's manager, Jock Stein, in a spontaneous gesture of mutual joy. This one man conveyed the feeling in that instant of almost every football enthusiast in Europe; for whether you were watching on television or were there in Lisbon's lovely tree-lined stadium out towards Estoril, at that moment you knew that Internazionale's expedient and diseased four-year domination of European soccer was at an end, that obsessional defence had capitulated to insistent attack, that eleven Scotsmen and a fine manager had breathed vitality and positive thinking back into the game.

No less ecstatic than the Glaswegians, who enlivened the boulevards through to the dawn, were the Portuguese. The pageboy back at the hotel greeted me with a broad smile and one word 'Herrera . . . ' whilst simultaneously drawing his finger slowly across his throat. The destructive, negative, mathematical tactics of Inter's manager, Helenio Herrera, had made him widely despised. 'Celtic won the field, the Cup and the public' proclaimed the headlines in one Lisbon paper. Yet if Celtic had ended an era of Latin monopoly of the Cup—Real Madrid, Benfica, Milan, Inter—they had also begun an argument which only they themselves could end.

For their victory had only confirmed what we already knew, that they were a lion-hearted, supremely fit, fast and disciplined side, but it had not proved what every Scotsman would have liked to believe: the team were still without evidence of true greatness. Just as most people believed that the 1966 World Cup Final was between the two most efficient rather than the two most skilful teams, so this was not a vintage year in the European Cup, Celtic apart. They themselves admitted that they probably won the title when they beat Voivodina of Novi Sad, the Yugoslav champions, in the quarter-final. Inter, masters of everything that was negative, were not the team which had two seasons before beaten Liverpool, or who had beaten Celtic the previous year. I think we can rely on Bill Shankly for an objective view on Celtic's triumph when he said: 'Liverpool would have beaten Inter easily on this form.' Even Stein himself, perhaps, knew it in his heart.

I had followed Celtic most of the way in this momentous season, travelling with them for the victories over Nantes and Voivodina before I was denied a visa to Prague for the semi-final with Dukla. Like any Englishman in the Scots camp, I was regarded as something of a friendly interloper, and sometimes my detached viewpoint had been categorized under the old maxim, 'If you're not with us, you're agin us.' Stein's first cautious words to me after the match were: 'Don't say we won because Inter played badly.'

Jean Escanazi, one of France's most respected journalists, was of the opinion: 'Inter just stood and waited for defeat', while Spain's former World Cup manager, Pedro Escartin, observed: 'You cannot hope to win the European Cup with only two forwards.' A Swiss national morning paper ran the headline: 'The dead men of Inter beaten—painful to regard.'

Celtic had established a new dimension in collective effort. It was marvellous the way in which, as one player faltered, another would rise to meet the situation: Jimmy Johnstone, Bobby Murdoch, then Bertie Auld, all at different stages. Yet my belief then and now was that Celtic lacked two individual players who could possibly have made them unbeatable, especially a truly great striker. How long, physically, could they sustain their momentum? Although they continued to have unrivalled success in Scotland, to the almost total eclipse of Rangers, they were eliminated in the first round of the European Cup the following year by Dynamo Kiev and, when they reached the Final again in 1970, were defeated by Feyenoord. A team's place in history must to a large extent be judged by its performances over a period, by the style of those performances and by the quality of the opposition it beats. It was unfortunate for Celtic that credit for their victory against Inter was diluted by the poverty of the Italians' resistance. It is interesting that in the 1967 Glasgow Charity Shield at Hampden Park, Celtic's Lisbon team were held 3-3 by Spurs, who by then were not the power they had been, even though they had just won the F.A. Cup Final against Chelsea. While the Celtic all-action machine almost crushed Spurs like so many coffee beans in the first half, it was touches of pure skill from Greaves, Terry Venables, Alan Gilzean and Dave Mackay which earned Spurs equality.

Not the least remarkable aspect of Celtic's achievement, however, was that it came in only Stein's second season as manager. Previously unheralded, he came upon the British scene like a whirlwind, even upstaging his revered compatriot, Sir Matt Busby. Sir Robert Kelly, chairman of Celtic, wrote in a history of the club shortly before he died:

'Jock has exceptional enthusiasm. He is generally recognized as a players' manager. He knows the value of players receiving the best treatment possible, but woe betide the player who lets the club down. He is a firm believer in discipline as he has shown on several occasions. He has his own methods of coaxing and cajoling, even of bullying. I have never known a manager so close to his players as Jock, or one who can so read them like a book. His ambitions for the club and himself have led to a vast amount of publicity, most of it favourable. His ability to put his points of view over in the club's newspaper has been of the utmost value in establishing liaison with our supporters and in helping to raise the standard of behaviour. He can be an intense and even an angry man, especially if he thinks his club is not getting a fair deal.'

Almost from the word go Stein had the Glasgow public, and the Scottish press, in the palm of his hand. He would even push Rangers off the back page of the popular papers on the morning they were due to play a European match, by releasing some news story about Celtic which would grab the headlines. He didn't miss a trick. And I remember well when centre-half Billy McNeill scored the winning goal, with only forty-seven seconds to spare in the second leg of the quarter-final against Voivodina, a Scottish journalist rising solemnly to his feet at the finish, moments later, and announcing: 'Jock cut the margin fine tonight.' At this time an eclipse of the moon would have been attributed to Stein: though it must be said that, with all the adulation and success, he remained pleasantly approachable to one and all.

That win against the Yugoslavs was indeed critical. At that stage, in March, Celtic were without the leading Scottish goal-scorer, McBride, and Wallace, his replacement, was ineligible for the two games. Losing by the only goal in Novi Sad due to an error by Gemmell, Celtic were hard pressed in the return. Voivodina might well have increased their lead in the first half and there was only half an hour to go when Chalmers levelled the score after an error by goalkeeper Pantelic, until then as strong as the door of a safe. McNeill's header from Gallagher's corner in the last minute nicked an important victory. Dukla were overcome in the semi-final, Celtic hanging on for a goalless draw in Prague after a 3-1 home win.

Before the final Stein wrote, rather guardedly, in the club newspaper *Celtic View*:

'It is important for Celtic to think that they can win every match they play. But it is equally important for them to keep in mind that there is always the possibility of losing. It is a must that they remember that though we all hope to win the European Cup, and believe we can, there's more than a slight chance that we won't. If it should happen that we lose to Inter, we want to be remembered on the Continent and indeed all over the world for the football we have played. Never has good behaviour on the playing field been so important. Winning or losing tomorrow night in Lisbon, I want our great club's name to be even more respected than it is at present.'

On the eve of the game in Lisbon he told me: 'We must show variety. That's my reading of the match. I think we have as much variety as Inter, and we have more stamina. Extra-time is not worrying us, nor the prospect of a replay in two days' time.'

It was, as almost always, a beautiful evening in the elegant, horseshoe-shaped national stadium, open on one side to give a view of the Lisbon hills, strong with the aroma of pine and cypress. Inter, who had beaten Torpedo of Moscow, Vasas of Budapest, Real Madrid and the Bulgarian Army team C.S.K.A., were everybody's reluctant favourites. This was their third final in four years and they had been built by the Spaniard Herrera on the wretched principle that one goal is enough to win any match. It is surprising how much men are conditioned more by their bad experiences than by their good ones. It happened with Alf Ramsey. Herrera had been manager of the brilliant Barcelona side which in 1960 had lost home and away in the semi-final to rivals Real, resulting in Herrera's sacking as 50,000 people demonstrated in the streets! From that moment he had pulled down the tactical blinds.

Now, when a tackle on Cappellini by Celtic's right-back Craig, after only seven minutes, brought a penalty for Inter, it seemed that everyone's worst fears were about to be realized. As Mazzola stroked home the penalty, we all braced ourselves mentally for another display of non-football. We had reckoned without Celtic, who proceeded to pulverize the Italians relentlessly with wave after wave of attacks as the shadows lengthened on that glorious sunny evening. Stein has always made the claim that 'the best place to defend is in the other team's penalty area'. By this reckoning Celtic were defending for the rest of the match! Territorially, it must have been the most one-sided European Final ever played, as Inter retreated without any semblance of a plan to counter-attack and increase their lead. Had it not been for a quite exceptional performance by Sarti in goal, the game would have been over long before the end. As it was, it remained on a knife-edge all the way to the finish.

The one mitigating factor for Inter was that they were without the injured Suarez, one of the most accomplished of all midfield 'play-makers'. He had been brought by Herrera from Barcelona, and it was upon the accuracy of Suarez's distribution that Inter relied for their sharp counter-attacks. Now there was no Suarez and, as they fell back after the penalty, they played into Celtic's hands, totally conceding the initiative.

With a five-man rearguard of Burgnich, Bedin, Facchetti, Guarneri and Picchi, Inter were well equipped to weather any amount of pressure, but they experienced an onslaught which left even them breathless. Bertie Auld and Gemmell both hit the crossbar, all four forwards and Murdoch forced Sarti into desperate saves. Yet it was an hour before Celtic managed to equalize. The goal stemmed from Auld and Murdoch, who were the fulcrum of the team in midfield. For many critics, Murdoch was the most dynamic player to emerge in Britain since Duncan Edwards, a barrel of a man with unlimited reserves of power and courage. Auld was a total contrast: small, wiry, cunning. Murdoch blazed in through the front door, Auld stole round the back. Now they combined on the right to send full-back Jim Craig through on yet another over-lapping run. At the same time, Gemmell was streaming down the left, yelling for a pass. With the defence waiting for a high cross, Craig pulled the ball square across the back of the penalty area; and there was Gemmell going at full speed, taking the ball first time without checking his stride and hitting a goal from twenty-five yards or more. Inter must have known that it heralded the end. What should they do now: play for time and a replay, or open out in an attempt to win the game? In the circumstances, with Celtic maintaining their frenzied attack, Inter were able to do neither.

With six minutes or less to go, Gemmell and Craig were on the rampage again. This time it was Gemmell who swept down the left with the ball, squaring it into the middle. Murdoch drove hard at goal. Sarti had the ball covered but, at the last minute, Stevie Chalmers darted across the line, got a deflection . . . and Celtic were champions, the first from Britain. In Lisbon and in Glasgow, Scottish supporters hurled themselves into an orgy of celebration. More than 12,000 Scots had made the trip from home by every possible means of transport. In the early hours of the morning, the Lisbon police were collecting the insensible, liquor-loaded tartan army off the streets by the bus-full, carting them to the airport, and piling them on to charter planes until each was full. Sometime the following morning, a red-eyed Jock knocked weakly on his own front door.

'It's me, we won, I'm hame.'

Said his wife: 'I can see that—but where's the car?' It was in Lisbon.

The thrill of Celtic's victory, and its style, rippled round Europe. They had had forty-two attempts at goal to Inter's five, nineteen to three inside the penalty area. Stein claimed proudly: 'It was a triumph for offensive football, and it will start a new trend.' But when I questioned him on this years later, after he had become manager of Scotland at the third time of asking, he had to admit: 'I don't think it really had any effect in the end. The freshness of the thing gave everyone hope at the time, after the sterility of the World Cup in 1966 but, in the end, the need to be successful, the need not to fail, turned against it. We had no alternative then, with the players at our disposal—it was the only way we knew how to play.'

As Brian James, the outstanding writer of the time on any national daily paper, reported in the *Daily Mail*: 'Celtic never faltered, not when their better shots struck the posts, or flew wide, not when their sharpest moves dwindled to nothing in the mesh of Inter defenders, not when time galloped away, with every minute bringing fresh cause for cursing fate.'

Celtic: Simpson; Craig, McNeill, Clark, Gemmell; Murdoch, Auld; Johnstone, Wallace, Chalmers, Lennox
Inter: Sarti; Burgnich, Facchetti, Bedin, Guarneri; Picci, Domenghini; Bicicli, Mazzola, Cappellini, Corso

CHAPTER THIRTEEN

Manchester United

v

Benfica

EUROPEAN CUP FINAL

1968

Eusebio, perhaps the fiercest striker of the ball who ever played, tries to bust the net instead of scoring a simple goal—and Matt Busby achieves his ambition.

Bill Foulkes, a survivor of the Munich crash, a stalwart who played in over seventy European Cup ties, is quite emphatic. Foulkes, who has spent time in management in America and in English non-League football, said when we discussed Manchester United's memorable night at Wembley recently: 'It was one of the worst United teams I'd played in at any time, when you consider the teams we've had, and the players we've had. But it was a justifiable reward for Matt Busby, for what he'd done for United and for football.' Matt Busby had taken over as manager after the war and had guided the club to the League title in 1952, 1956, 1957, 1965, and 1967. A remarkable seven times they had been runners-up. Twice they had won the F.A. Cup, twice they had been runners-up. Three times previously they had reached the semi-finals of the European Cup, and this season they had made it to the Final thanks to a freak goal by Foulkes in the semi-final second leg in Madrid. It was certainly the last chance for Busby and folk-hero Bobby Charlton, if not for United. It was obvious to all that it would take United time to build a new team under a new manager. For Busby, this was it.

Denis Law was missing, forced out of action with a cartilage operation and, as Pat Crerand says:

'We should have won in 1966, but George Best was injured for the return leg of the semi-final against Partizan of Belgrade, and we threw it away. It was not a good Manchester United side in 1968. But in spite of this we were pretty confident, because we had slaughtered Benfica twice in 1965. In the event, I thought George played badly, for him, in the final at Wembley—he was a bit greedy although he scored a vital second goal at the start of extra-time.'

United had come perilously close to elimination again in the semi-final. Winning the first leg at home against Real, they were 3-1 down at half-time in Madrid. As Stepney recalls: 'Amancio had murdered us and it seemed we were in for a real pasting, not just defeat. At half-time Matt, as always, told us to keep trying to play football and then, just as we were going out of the dressing room, called out, "Don't forget, there's only one goal in it." '

Foulkes, who had endured the disappointment of those three previous semi-finals, vividly remembers that night in Madrid. 'We hadn't really seen George or Bobby, we weren't in the game, but then, in the second half, a ball hit David Sadler on the knee and went in to make it 3-2 and level on aggregate. Real began to panic, but so did we. What should we do: should we attack and go for the winner or hold on to what we'd got? Then we got a throw-in on the right, taken by Paddy Crerand. Nobody seemed to want the ball, so I made a run at the last minute, which pulled the cover off Best.' Stepney remembers that everyone was screaming at Foulkes to get back, but he kept going! Foulkes continues: 'Zocco and all their defenders went to cover the near post as George cut in on the right. I'd kept running and bellowed at him, but I didn't expect him to give it to me. Then he pulled back a perfect pass to me just inside the area. I thought "If I drive it, I'll miss it", so I side-footed it and it went in the far corner. It really silenced that 130,000 crowd!'

It would be Foulkes' job at Wembley to help take care of the towering, six-foot six-inch Portuguese striker Torres, a job he did well. In fact, fear of the opposition was to play a more important part in the match, until extra time, than the skills which were the cause of that fear. The football was a complete anti-climax, with more than thirty fouls in the first half, an exhibition of all the worst trends in the game which in Britain and abroad were reaching a climax. Celtic had had a disgraceful encounter with Racing of Buenos Aires in the descredited World Club Championship the previous autumn; United would have another with Estudiantes of Buenos Aires as a result of their win at Wembley. Everywhere the game was getting out of control, not least in this match refereed by Italian Concetto Lo Bello. In the violence charts, Britain were well to the fore, a fact noted with alarm by Jim Manning, that eminent columnist of the *Daily Mail*, the day following United's victory. Was Britain's prominence in world football at this time, he rightly asked, the product of an increasing concentration on physical intimidation?

Not that the Portuguese were blameless. It was they who had kicked Pele and Brazil out of the World Cup two years previously. Now there were fearful fouls by Cruz and Humberto in the frenzied first half, an appalling tackle by Eusebio on Crerand. Yet Eusebio himself was enduring the close attentions of Nobby Stiles, about whom the arguments will never be resolved, for the fifth time in four seasons. The subjective view of United players and of Stiles' England colleagues was that the toothless Nobby was a character, a battler and a great competitor. When United were on their knees after being forced into extra-time in this game, it was Stiles who rallied them and, as Crerand says: 'Nobby could have persuaded the dead to get up and play.' But abroad, and among United's rivals throughout Britain, Stiles was seen as a demon. I accept the argument that many of his tackles were simply badly timed rather than malicious, but that did not make them any the less provocative . . . or illegal. In Argentina and Mexico, he was caricatured with the devil's pointed tail.

So what of the game itself? Foulkes says:

'As a game of football, it was a non-starter. But for drama, it would take some beating. The loss of Denis was a bad blow, and we just had to hope that George would turn it on as he had against Benfica in Lisbon two years before. In the event, Benfica were so busy keeping George quiet that they

left the other flank wide open for John Aston and he took
full advantage of it. It was only in extra-time that George
came into the game.'

But for all the domination of Benfica's right-back Adolfo by
young Aston—son of United's left-back in the 1948 F.A. Cup
Final, and who had been a member of the defeated England
team in Belo Horizonte—there was still no score at half-time.
They had had their chances: Sadler, primarily, had missed
them. Eusebio had hit the bar, but otherwise had succumbed
to the attentions of his personal, ferocious traffic warden.

Early in the second half, United went in front at last. Sadler
and left-back Dunne combined down the left wing, Sadler
swung the ball over and Charlton, breaking into a space, scored
with a rare header. He claimed afterwards, 'It was my first
headed goal for about ten years. Maybe if I hadn't been going
bald it wouldn't have gone in! I didn't notice the goalkeeper
coming off his line and, in fact, I thought the ball had gone
wide.' This gave United the platform to begin to play with
some confidence. A series of glittering runs by Aston had
Benfica on the ropes, but again Sadler missed, shooting over
the bar with goalkeeper Henrique out of position. Then, with
only ten minutes to go, Benfica equalized. Torres headed across
the face of the goal and Graca, having stolen forward from
midfield unmarked, steered the ball wide of Stepney. Stiles
says: 'It was like the World Cup all over again when Germany
pulled level just before the end. We were shattered. If there
had been more than another ten minutes to full-time we would
have lost.' They should have lost, too, but Eusebio, that renowned striker with a catapult in both feet, now missed one
of the most important goals of his whole career only four
minutes from the end, a goal which surely would have buried
Busby's long cherished ambition. Eusebio was clear of United's
defence and 100,000 people had their hearts in their mouths as
he bore down on Stepney.

It is best to let Stepney recall what happened next. Recently,
he has been keeping goal with much of his old reliability for
Altrincham and it still surprises him when he looks back on
that vital, isolated incident.

'Eusebio hadn't caused us too many problems. He'd hit

the bar early in the first half, a shot with a lot of top spin which I thought was going over but then dipped at the last minute. There'd been a free kick which got through our wall but I was able to get down to it at the last minute. I'd played against him in America in the summer on tour, when Benfica won, and he'd scored a penalty. He was always a player who wanted to score great goals rather than simple goals, and I think it was this fact which went against him now. If you remember, it was still the old Wembley pitch, before the drainage was broken up by show jumping, and the turf was still thick and heavy. When Eusebio was put through, I thought the ball was coming faster than it was, and I was off my line a bit early, but the ball slowed. Instinctively I thought, "If I keep going, he'll chip me", so I checked for a couple of paces. Eusebio then gave the ball another nudge, slightly too far ahead of him, so I moved forward again. I should have been dead! If he had hit the ball accurately, low down to the left or right, I wouldn't have had a chance, but he belted the ball straight at me and I was able to hold it. If he'd scored, it was all over.'

Watching from the same angle directly behind Eusebio's run was Paddy Crerand, who tells the same story:

'Frankly, I blame Eusebio more than I give credit to Alex. My head was bursting with the thought that in the next few seconds our dream of the European Cup would be "blown" again. But Eusebio loved to make the net bulge, and that was probably what he wanted to do then. I can remember Wembley going dead silent, it seemed to me, for a split second. Eusebio had acres of room. George Best or Jimmy Greaves would have side-footed the ball, but Eusebio drove it at Alex, thank God.'

Busby went out on to the pitch before the start of extra-time and told his players: 'You're throwing the game away with careless passing; you must start to hold the ball and play again.' Gloriously, Best took him at his word. With extra-time only two minutes old, Stepney cleared upfield and Kidd headed forward. Cruz seemed to have the ball under control, but Best took it off him. With the defence trailing at his heels, Best ran on, the whole stadium already on its feet in a concerted roar; on he went, and Henrique advanced. Best sold him a dummy to the right, rounded him to the left and tucked the ball into the inviting, empty net.

A minute later, the issue was beyond doubt. Charlton curled over a centre and teenager Brian Kidd—a bag of nerves in the hours leading up to the final—forced Henrique to turn a header on to the crossbar. As the ball rebounded, Kidd, having kept his balance, was there to head it home. Then Charlton made it three in eight minutes from a cross by Kidd, and Busby's greatest hour was accomplished.

It was belated reward for the courage with which he had pulled himself and the club together after Munich; reward for a vision of the game in which, in the main, he had tried to steer towards what was noble; a reward of sorts for the families of the Munich dead who had been invited to the match. The players, the older ones in tears, tried to get Busby to go and receive the Cup, but he declined. Pride and satisfaction is not measurable in polished silver. This victory, and his subsequent knighthood, were the justifiable climax to a life dedicated to the game.

For Best, sadly for such a player, it was his last appearance on the international stage at the climax of a major event. The following season, United were beaten in the semi-finals by Milan and, by 1970, the career of this charismatic figure was deep in trouble. I do not think there will be many critics, even those who have been around longer than I, who will argue that Best was the greatest British player of his or any generation. He had literally everything: amazing ball control and swerve, blistering pace, marvellous tactical awareness when he did not overdo his phenomenal dribbling, the ability to score incredible goals with both feet, tremendous stamina and power in the tackle for one so comparatively small, even ability in the air (though not on a par with Law's). For a few brief seasons, he raced like a meteor across the night sky, only to burn himself out prematurely. Had he been English instead of Irish, he would have been a world-wide sensation.

It must be doubtful whether any player could have coped with the pressures imposed upon him by his fame, adulation and wealth when barely out of his teens. His emergence coincided with the explosion of pop culture in the sixties and, undoubtedly, Busby's handling of him should have been less avuncular, more patrician. But Busby, almost at the end of his own span, was growing tired, and was as dazzled by Best's prodigious talent as was United's youngest fan. He granted him a licence which proved fatal. Lacking a family life in Manchester, lacking true friends as opposed to sycophantic hangers on, lacking a fulfilling relationship with women in sharp contrast to the sex-symbol status of his self-appointed publicists, he was simultaneously devoured and nudged towards self-destruction by an unheeding public. His personal collapse was our loss, but we should recognize our share of the blame.

Manchester United:	Stepney; Brennan, Foulkes, Stiles, Dunne; Crerand, Charlton, Sadler; Best, Kidd, Aston
Benfica:	Henrique; Adolfo, Humberto, Jacinto, Cruz; Graca, Coluna; Augusto, Torres, Eusebio, Simoes

CHAPTER FOURTEEN

England

v

West Germany

WORLD CUP

1970

The sudden illness of Gordon Banks on the night before a World Cup quarter-final, and the personal problems and subsequent nightmare errors of his deputy, Peter Bonetti, result in an astonishing reversal.

The 1970 World Cup opened with world-wide speculation over whether Bobby Moore's arrest in Bogota, the Colombian capital, while on tour shortly beforehand, would affect his and England's performance. The England captain had been detained at the airport when the team were en route from Quito, Ecuador, to Mexico City, accused of having stolen a bracelet from a jeweller's boutique in the foyer of the team's hotel during England's visit to play Colombia the previous week. As the team flew onwards to Mexico, Moore was detained under house arrest at the home of Alfonso Senior, chairman of the Millionarios Club. Such a scandal involving the captain of the World Champions was front page news throughout the world. The facts of the matter, never properly revealed, were that none of the five sets of fingerprints on the showcase was Moore's, and the police had been aware of this from the start.

I was there in Bogota during the court proceedings, and the

most unruffled man throughout was Moore. Considering there was no knowing for how long he might be detained under Colombian law—he was never charged—his equanimity was itself proof of his innocence. His performance under colossal stress in Bogota was almost as impressive as his lofty, imperious displays in Mexico, notably against Brazil. After five days, Bobby was released and I flew with him back to Mexico City and a president's reception. He remained unimpaired by the experience, even though controversy continued to surround the England team.

There was the question of Nobby Stiles, depicted in the Mexican press as some kind of diminutive vampire. There was the offence given to the Mexican people—wholly imagined by a nation which fluctuates from extremes of charming hospitality to almost child-like hostility—by the importing of a private team bus by England. There was the antagonism generated by Ramsey's total inability to compromise with his own blunt, honest and, admittedly, slightly perverse personality when dealing with the Mexican press. Since he could not even cope satisfactorily with the British press, what chance with the Mexicans? Not for him the overflowing insincere compliments as from some visiting screen goddess about 'your beautiful country' and 'your beautiful people'. In the public relations department, Ramsey bore the hallmark of the British bulldog in Mexico, and was resolutely and exclusively concerned with the welfare of his players and little else. The result was that England were about as popular as sharks on a surfing beach.

Their popularity did not improve after a quite breathtaking encounter with Brazil, as fascinating in its play and counter-play as a confrontation across the chessboard between Bobby Fischer and Boris Spassky. Played on a scorching midday in Guadalajara, it was an encounter of ninety of the most fascinating minutes and, although Brazil won by the only goal from their dazzling right-winger Jairzinho, the champions had enhanced their reputation even in defeat. Gordon Banks had made the most memorable save of his life from Pele; Alan Ball and Jeff Astle had wasted chances to draw or even win the game; and the local hostility to England mounted with the realization that there was every chance they could still go on to a second meeting with Brazil in the Final . . . and win.

England had opened with a 2-1 win against a Rumanian

team intent on kicking lumps out of them, and qualified for the quarter-final, following the Brazil game, with a lacklustre win over Czechoslovakia which produced a mixture of pessimism and criticism when viewed on television back at home. Having seen this game, and also having been to see West Germany in an unconvincing though comfortable victory over Peru, I had not the slightest doubt that England would win their quarter-final in Leon. In all my twenty-eight years of watching England, I've never been so sure, and I said as much in the *Sunday Telegraph* on the morning of the match. It was to be ironic that the concluding sentence of my argument in that preview was that Banks, at that time, was unquestionably the best goalkeeper in the world.

Germany, in reaching the quarter-finals, had been behind against Morocco, of all people; they had struggled initially against Bulgaria, and again against Peru. Such was the now almost perfected competence of England's 4-4-2 formation that I had written before the tournament began: 'It is not so much a question of whether England will retain their title in the heat and altitude, which they can, as whether there is any opposition which is capable of beating them, which is uncertain.' Germany at this stage, on paper, were not.

The justifiable criticisms of England up to then had been their lack of penetration, the fact that they had scored only three goals in three games, and that Geoff Hurst and Francis Lee up front were receiving little if any support from midfield. This could be traced to the fact that Martin Peters, the eighth highest post-war England goal-scorer, had been restricted to a more defensive role in the early matches. Almost every important goal which England had scored in the previous four years had at some stage involved Peters but, apart from a header over the bar against Brazil, we had seen little of him within striking range. Ramsey had deliberately built a team for the Mexican conditions which would take as little out of itself as possible by not losing the ball and not catching too many men going forward. England would play largely 'behind' the ball, leaving Hurst and Lee to pull the opposition out of position.

The one cause for concern the day before the game, although we didn't know it then, was the illness which had overtaken Banks. Throughout their stay during the first round in Guadalajara, England had been on a rigidly-controlled diet that was almost boring, and had consumed pills daily, until they almost rattled, to counter the possibility of Mexican tummy—Montezuma's Revenge as it is known, and which I had experienced the year before when England were on tour. It is as sudden as it is devastating, and now it overtook Banks at a critical hour. As he recalls in his autobiography, it felt as if 'an army of soldiers were marching in my head as the room kept spinning around!' It was said at the time that Banks had eaten some ice cream, contrary to all instructions, but he makes no mention of this in his book. Only that he felt like death as the team made its five-hour trip to Leon, where he had to ask Alex Stepney to carry his bags for him. He attended the team meetings on the morning of the match but, at ten o'clock, it was clear that he was far too unwell to take part. Peter Bonetti had a mere two hours' notice that he was to be plunged into the most important game of his life, kicking off at midday. The start had been scheduled to accommodate European television by satellite and, in the little desert town of Leon, the dry heat was soaring into the high nineties by the time the game began.

There was no obvious reason to suspect Bonetti's competence at this stage. He was widely respected for his performance with Chelsea who, a month or so before, had rubbed salt into Leeds' wounds, beating them in an F.A. Cup Final replay to deny them the only surviving leg of a League-European Cup-F.A. Cup Treble, which had been on the cards at one stage.

The news that Banks was out must, however, have been some sort of encouragement to the Germans. Helmut Schoen had admitted that he arrived in Mexico with no more than 'an idea of a team'. He had moved Beckenbauer into midfield to combine with Overath, leaving Schnellinger and Fichtel as centre-backs. Seeler had also been given a midfield role to accommodate Muller; and he was playing with two wingers, Libuda and Lohr, in a front line of three. This meant that, with Muller's disinclination to come to life until the ball entered the penalty area—where he became a magician— Germany had no central thrust from the middle of the field unless Seeler pushed forward. Their penetration was down the flanks, and England were confident they could cope with that.

Each side had five of the team which had played in the last Final—Moore, Ball, Bobby Charlton, Peters and Hurst for

England; Hottges, Schnellinger, Beckenbauer, Seeler and Overath for Germany. About Banks' absence, Schoen later told me: 'For England it was a great pity; he was an outstanding goalkeeper and, in such a competition, it was a great loss. If he had been there, I cannot say he would not have allowed our three goals, but he had a fine understanding with the other defenders which must always be an important factor. Bonetti was a good goalkeeper but he was not a Banks.'

It was soon apparent that Peters was, for this match, being liberated by Ramsey, because he took part in the first three attacks and was not far off with a header. After seven minutes, Maier, a spidery goalkeeper who always looked as if he would have been happier playing basketball, dropped a centre by England's right-back, Newton, and this nervousness communicated itself to the rest of the German defence, who for a while repeatedly cleared with an anxiety which suggested they were bailing a leaking boat. England's rhythm was building up nicely, Ball burning with urgency. When he was tripped by Muller, who was booked, it was another sign of anxiety. Muller was being forced deep into midfield because Labone and Moore were bristling with authority in the centre of defence.

Another cause for concern for Schoen on the bench was that Libuda, who had been the supply line for all but two of Muller's goals in the first round, was getting nowhere against Terry Cooper, the tenacious little Leeds left-back. Eliminate Libuda, and you were halfway to victory. This Cooper did, forsaking the direct tackle on which the nimble Libuda thrived and holding off instead, so that Libuda found himself like a conjuror without a hat, unable to perform his one outstanding trick. Cooper stalled, back-pedalled, feigned to tackle, and had soon reduced Libuda to passing the ball square or even back to his full-back, Hottges.

With half an hour gone, Bonetti had not really been tested, comfortably punching the ball away after twenty-five minutes when Libuda did get a rare centre across. Beckenbauer, busy as he had been at Wembley in shadowing Charlton, was unable to augment Germany's attack, and he remained somehow aloof from the game as if he were too good to become involved in the toil and sweat of lesser men. It was left to Seeler to try to hold the side together in midfield but, with Moore again in commanding form, reading every German attack as if with radar, the Germans were totally neutralized.

Just after the half-hour, England took the lead with a fine goal: a classic counter-attack which moved from the penalty area to the opponents' goal area in five passes. Cooper dispossessed Libuda yet again and slipped the ball inside to Alan Mullery, England's defensive midfield player who was the 'bolt' in front of the back four and who had so successfully helped shut out Pele in the game with Brazil. Now Mullery, hearing a call from his right-back Newton, swung the ball forty yards out to the flank into Newton's path, and set off on a diagonal, supporting run himself. By the time Newton was level with the German penalty area Mullery was steaming through, and met Newton's cross on the edge of the six-yard area with the sweetest of volleys. It was Mullery's first goal for England in over thirty appearances and, at the time, he couldn't believe that the Germans had permitted him to make such a penetrating run without impeding him illegally. The goal was no more than England deserved at this stage, but a further demonstration of Schoen's concern came at the start of the second half when he replaced his right-back Hottges with the dour Schultz, another survivor from the 1966 Final. Schultz took over as sweeper with Schnellinger going to full-back.

There was applause from both teams and from the crowd when it was announced just before the restart that this was Bobby Charlton's record 106th appearance for England. Within four minutes, England scored again with another superbly executed counter-attack. Moore gained possession, Ball and Hurst kept the move going and, again, an overlap by Newton on the right caught the Germans off guard. Taking Hurst's reverse pass in his stride, Newton finally crossed the ball to the far post where Peters drove it home. In that moment, the game was effectively finished. Germany were going through the motions only, like a boxer who knows that his opponent is too far ahead on points to make exposure to further pain worth the effort. Schoen now made his second substitution, replacing Libuda with Grabowski, who was given instructions to wander with the intention of stretching a defence which might be tiring.

In the next quarter of an hour, the two main chances were England's, Hurst being flattened as he dived for a header with a fine chance of scoring, and Ball, clear on the penalty spot, losing control with only Maier to beat. England had the grudging respect of the hostile Mexicans at last. They were witnessing a performance even better than England had given against Brazil. Germany were playing out time: England realized it and began to slow-ball with man-to-man passing. Ramsey, sensing the danger, and wanting to maintain England's forward momentum and to preserve Charlton for the semi-final, instructed Colin Bell to warm up on the touchline. Bell was about to replace Charlton when the second critical blow of the day fell on England.

Beckenbauer, who for an hour had tried a succession of rather aimless, harmless shots from long range, advanced on another of his casual dribbles. Mullery forced him out to the right and, from an angle which Bonetti had well-covered, Beckenbauer shot from some twenty-five yards with only moderate power. 'He shot because there was nothing better to do', somebody in the press box said afterwards. Yet Bonetti went down late, allowed the ball to pass underneath him and cross almost the middle of the goal line into the inside of the far side-netting. The magnitude of the error was starkly apparent to Ramsey and his substitutes on the bench immediately in line behind the shot. But even at this stage there was no need for it to have been disastrous. England still had one foot in the semi-final.

Bell now replaced Charlton as intended and, with only twelve minutes to go, England were within a whisker of going 3-1 in front. Ball put Bell clear on the right, and his early cross was met by Hurst, breaking clear of Schultz and the glancing header beat Maier. I was directly in line with the ball in the press box and it was going a foot inside the post when it bounced and broke wide. Lee, convinced it would hit the post, waited for the rebound which never came.

With only ten minutes to go, Ramsey made his second substitution, replacing Peters with Norman Hunter with the intention of giving the defence that extra bite to check a German attack which was taking wings. But Hunter had only been on the pitch a few moments when Germany equalized with a fluke goal. Moore and Labone failed to clear properly, and Schnellinger lofted the ball back into the penalty area. Seeler and Mullery went up together; Seeler made contact for a back-header but had little idea of its direction. He was not

to know that Bonetti had come off his line towards Schnellinger's cross which he could not hope to reach, was caught
helplessly in no-man's-land and could only watch in agony as
the ball curled in a slow parabola over his head and into the
net.

Now the substitution of Peters was a genuine handicap,
because England had forfeited a vital link in their striking
armoury. Yet, for the first half of extra-time, they continued
to carry the game forward. Hurst, Ball, Labone and Lee all
went close. The winner came five minutes into the second
half of extra-time. Grabowski, who had been causing England
increasing problems, crossed the ball high over the goal-
mouth to the far post where Newton, under pressure from
Lohr, headed back across his own goal. Labone had followed
Grabowski's cross towards the right and failed to notice
Muller steal back towards the left, where he was waiting
unmarked as Newton's misdirected header fell. Yet even now
Bonetti might have cut out the ball before it reached Muller,
because it was well inside the goal-area and, as Muller hooked
it home, he was no more than four yards from the line where
Bonetti stood as if transfixed. In vain England tried to save
the match, Mullery and Ball shot wide, Maier saved from
Newton, but the 'impossible' had happened.

Bonetti had made two, possibly three, glaring and uncharacteristic misjudgements. I remain convinced to this day that
these errors, and not Ramsey's substitutions, were the root
cause of England's failure. It is a view shared by England's
captain, Moore, though in his biography he chooses his words
with care. It was known by some people in Mexico, and not
only those within the England camp, that Bonetti was to some
extent concerned about the welfare of his wife Frances, who
was making her first prolonged trip abroad without the
constant companionship of her husband, to follow the games in
Mexico. The wives of Moore, Hurst and Peters were also
there but it was known that Bonetti had shown anxiety about
his wife. This factor could well have contributed to his uncertain state of mind when thrust into a vital match at short
notice. As Moore wrote:

'Now I'm not a specialist goalkeeper but I do know a good
shot from an ordinary shot, and that wasn't anything like

one of Beckenbauer's better shots. The ball went under Peter into the middle of the net. If Peter's going to be honest with himself, he must be disappointed. I know how bad the rest of us felt. Psychologically, it was a desperate goal to concede . . . it was the sort of goal which cut into your confidence from the back.'

And on the second goal: 'Uwe did a feat, straining to get his head to the ball. He admitted he had no intention of scoring. He was just trying to keep the ball in play. Yet it flopped over Bonetti into the net. Peter's concentration might have been adrift.'

Ramsey, who had been positioned with horrifying clarity in line with the first goal, showed no hint of recrimination afterwards. As he said goodbye to Bonetti on the lawn of England's motel in Leon when Bonetti departed to rejoin his wife, and while other England players lay about in the sun in a state of stunned disbelief, Ramsey said: 'Thank you, Peter, for all that you've done for us; have a good journey.' Never have I witnessed a better demonstration of Ramsey's loyalty to his men, his refusal to criticize them publicly.

Ramsey's comment to the press had been:

'We should never have lost. When we led 2-0 it was all over. Germany were dead. But they were brought back into the game by an unfortunate goal, then got another and their tails were up. I don't think I've ever seen an England team give away goals like this—or indeed give away three goals at all for a long time. There were errors and panic in defence and we were made to pay for it.'

He did not need to specify whose errors. The intensely competitive, patriotic Ball could scarcely contain his tears of anguish for several hours. 'For the first seventy minutes, I was playing for the best England team of all time. This was the best performance of any side I have been in.' And Mullery: 'Since we came out to Mexico, we have taken everything thrown at us and still we were going to win the Cup. We had overcome the lot, the climate, the altitude, the crowds. I didn't think anything could happen to us. We were armour-plated. Just don't ask me how I feel.'

Schoen, discussing it with me ten years later, admitted:

'When England's second goal went in, I said to myself, "It's over." But our team has always had a tremendous fighting spirit. Some of the England players showed they were tired. It was not a good shot by Beckenbauer but a *surprising* shot. My opinion at the time was that Ramsey's substitutions were a sign that he was unsure, and so often when a team is leading 2-0, the 2-1 goal can be decisive for the whole game.'

Ramsey's 'armour-plated' 4-4-2 formation only came to be seen as an error in subsequent years because of its negative influence on the development of players and teams in England as a whole. As a system for winning that tournament, at that time, in those conditions, against those opponents, I still believe it could not be faulted. What Ramsey had not done, in the long-term interest of England football, was to use his position of unrivalled power to create advantageous trends within the game. As Dave Sexton, who has always attempted to be in touch with international styles and trends and was there in Mexico, observed afterwards: 'We have not played our usual running off-the-ball game in recent years. We have been behind the ball nearly all the time.'

In fact, Italy and Uruguay both reached the semi-final with only two strikers and far more negative tactics than England. The so-called 'entertaining' semi-final in which Italy beat Germany 4-3 only became a carnival with five goals in extra-time as fatigue, heat, and altitude took their toll on both sides. And, as usual, the comparisons drawn with Brazil, who trounced Italy in the Final with classic displays from Jair-zinho, Gerson, Tostao and Pele, were a red-herring. England could not copy Brazil because they did not possess such players. Ramsey was subsequently pilloried for saying at a post-mortem press conference back in London: 'We have nothing to learn from Brazil.' That was not tactical myopia but further evidence of his stilted inability to express himself. What he meant in fact was: 'There is nothing which Brazil possesses or does which we can practically or usefully attempt to emulate.' Where Ramsey now began to betray his own professional brilliance was in persisting with a principle of safety first in the coming years.

England: Bonetti; Newton, Labone, Moore, Cooper;
                    Ball, Charlton, Mullery, Peters; Hurst, Lee
West Germany: Maier; Hottges, Schnellinger, Fichtel, Vogts;
                    Seeler,   Beckenbauer,   Overath;   Libuda,
                    Muller, Lohr

CHAPTER FIFTEEN

Leeds

v

Sunderland

F.A. CUP FINAL

1973

The inexplicable eclipse of Eddie Gray, the tactical misjudgement of Johnny Giles, the incredible miss of Peter Lorimer or, equally, the 'impossible' save of Jim Montgomery, all conspire against Leeds, the team which could not lose.

From 1971 to 1973, the European Cup was dominated by Ajax. At the time they won it for the third year running, their Rumanian manager, Stefan Kovacs, told me that he regarded Leeds as, without doubt, the second best team in Europe, a view which would have been shared by almost everybody other than the Yorkshiremen . . . who thought that they were the best. Their record, as opposed to their reputation, under Don Revie had been one of quite exceptional success. They were top of the First Division in 1969 and 1974 and were runners-up five times between 1965 and 1972. They were F.A. Cup winners in 1972 and runners-up three times; League Cup winners in 1968; U.E.F.A. Cup winners in 1968 and 1971, runners-up in 1967; European Cup-Winners runners-up in 1973. Yet, at the same time, they were one of the most despised teams in English history, not merely because rivals are always jealous of success, but because their most consistent characteristics were seen to be tinged with a cultivated meanness of spirit and sharp practice.

The Sunday before their meeting with Sunderland at Wembley, I had written in the *Sunday Telegraph* under the heading 'Sunderland Can Win in Midfield':

'If Leeds lose the F.A. Cup Final next Saturday to Second Division Sunderland in what would be the most unlikely of all stories, there will be few other than Yorkshiremen who will shed a tear and many will openly rejoice. Why? The regrettable fact is that, along the stony road to success, Leeds have allowed too many imperfections unnecessarily to mar their repertoire . . . there has been no need for Leeds to use the gamesmanship and uncompromising "professionalism" which has forfeited their claim to greatness. They are far too good to have to resort to what at best is unsportsmanlike, at worst invokes the use of far stronger words . . . my opinion of Hunter is by no means an isolated one . . . he is a good enough player not to need to do the things he does. The public might be more sympathetic towards Leeds if, just occasionally, Revie would admit that his team were guilty of phvsical excess and gamesmanship.

'Yet when Hunter gets his third suspension of the season, Revie claims he is "just a natural ballwinner", another euphemism of the modern game . . . Hunter is by no means the only transgressor. Sprake developed the foot-up goalkeeper's jump to an exaggerated degree. Giles, a superb player, is a notorious, if subtle, tackler. Lorimer's histrionic, instantly-evaporating injuries falsely bring the wrath of referees on opponents and do more damage than even his fearsome shooting. Clarke, the best close-range finisher since Jimmy Greaves, spoils himself by his niggling. Bremner, besides some still provocative tackling, far too persistently questions the referee. The only three players to whom one can give unqualified approval are Cooper, Gray and Madeley.

'Let me say that nothing would give me more pleasure than that Leeds should beat Sunderland on Wembley's fiftieth anniversary by six goals with a masterly display which could be placed among the historic exhibitions of football. People suppose that one is vindictive towards certain clubs or players. Nothing could be further from the truth. All that matters is the quality of the game, which alone will determine its capacity for survival. Leeds are capable of winning by a record margin but will they? . . . I am increasingly suspicious that Sunderland have an outside chance if they can get hold of the match in midfield as they did against Arsenal in the semi-final. Bremner is not having a good spell and Giles, at thirty-four, will be feeling the strain of a long season. Sunderland's midfield trio of Horswill, Kerr and Porterfield are capable of giving Bremner and Giles less breathing space than they are accustomed to and, if Sunderland once get some encouragement, the pace of Tueart and Hughes could trouble even Leeds' defence.'

I have quoted from that article extensively because I think it is important to demonstrate what my feelings were before the match was played. I was by no means alone. When Leeds complained about the article, through their solicitors, the *Sunday Telegraph* had five First Division managers, within a week, who were prepared to testify that it was true. Bill McGarry had observed after Wolves' semi-final with Leeds: 'I was staggered at the way Bremner went the whole ninety minutes disputing every decision given against his team.' And Bob Stokoe, the manager who had inspired a fairy tale revival of Sunderland's fortunes, said before the Final: 'I want Mr Burns, the referee, to make the decisions on Saturday, and not Mr Bremner.'

Within weeks of Stokoe's arrival at Sunderland earlier in that season, with the club slumped near the bottom of the Second Division, attendances of 12,000 had jumped to three times that. They beat Notts County in a replay, then Manchester City with 53,000 people locked inside Roker Park. Fancied Arsenal were tipped over in the semi-final and Sunderland found themselves at Wembley with a team containing only three changes from the time when Stokoe's predecessor Allan Brown was sacked: the addition of Guthrie in defence, Halom in attack (£50,000 from Charlton) and the switching of Watson from centre-forward to centre-half.

To know the emotion aroused by football in the north-east, you need to know the geography: to see and understand the still visible signs of decades of hardship, of life lived close to the bone; of community and comradeship in the almost village-like atmosphere which exists in the huge, shipbuilding towns on Tyneside and Wearside. Go a mile or two from Newcastle or Sunderland and you are in open country. Walk down the High Street and, if you are a local celebrity, as Stokoe had become even before the Final, everyone will want to shake your hand. There is a warmth and identity which surpasses that found in other cities. The Sunderland ground itself, its presence proclaimed by the tall, staring floodlight pylons, is an oasis in the sea of grey slate roofs and identical, back-to-back terraces.

Before Stokoe's arrival, the game in Sunderland had died. He himself had been a Newcastle player through their glorious years in the early fifties, when they won the Cup three times, a reserve in 1951 and 1952, playing in the winning side against Manchester City, and Don Revie, in 1955. Subsequently, he was manager of Bury, Charlton, Rochdale, and Carlisle, taking the latter to the semi-final of the League Cup. When I went to talk to him at Roker Park before the 1973 Final he had said:

'I didn't bring back the magic—it's always been here. I came back to find it. I consider myself to be a players' man, to try to know what makes each one of them tick, to distinguish their different senses of humour, to understand who needs to be driven, who to be coaxed. At the moment, they are not ready for the First Division—they are way off. I wouldn't like anyone to think they are a great side. Whether they'll be ready next year remains to be seen. At present, we're doing two things: scoring exciting goals, and not giving much away. But we need depth and experience, and we just haven't got it. When I came here, thirty-one of the thirty-four players on the staff were local. Football *needs* clubs like Sunderland at the top. When you think of teams like Norwich, Ipswich, Southampton in the First Division, and Sunderland out of it, it's daft.'

Yet there was nothing daft about the composition of the team that went to Wembley, even though Wembley itself was an undreamt-of adventure. Whereas some of the Sunderland players had never been there before, even to watch a game, the Leeds team were virtually regulars, either with the club or with England. Most of them had been there in the team which drew with Chelsea before losing the replay in 1970, and then when Arsenal were beaten two years later. Clarke, Madeley and Hunter were currently in the England squad, and Lorimer, Bremner, Giles and Yorath were long-standing pillars of Scotland, Eire and Wales. But Jim Montgomery, in Sunderland's goal, had been international class for thirteen years, Watson was about to become England centre-half, Tueart could catch pigeons, and Hughes and Halom were seriously underestimated. However, as Revie said beforehand:

> 'We know all about the tension of Cup Final morning when minutes seem like hours. We know the awe-inspiring experience of driving up Wembley Way. We know what it is like to stand in the tunnel twenty minutes before kick-off, when legs turn to jelly and throats turn dry. We know what it's like to walk out into that thundering sound. We know that strange feeling just after kick-off when men become a little bit slow in their thinking and legs begin to feel heavier than ever before. For Sunderland this is an experience still to come.'

The main threat to Sunderland was likely to come from Eddie Gray down Leeds' left flank, where his opposing fullback, the slightly unbalanced, top-heavy Malone was potentially vulnerable. But Malone was to be cleverly supported by dynamic little Bobby Kerr, Sunderland's skipper; and when Sunderland had survived the first twenty minutes with only occasional anxiety, the impossible had already become a distinct possibility. From the very first deafening roar, when Sunderland had turned to wave to their supporters before the presentation to the Duke of Kent at the start, the Wearside team drew the strength of a twelfth man from the surging tide of noise from the west terraces. 'Haway the Lads' the tens of thousands cried, as stirring and emotional as hunting horns. Right from the start, Sunderland achieved what they set out to do; to cramp Leeds' midfield style, to hustle them and prevent them from building a platform of authority from which to launch the destruction so widely forecast.

It never happened. Never for a moment were they overawed. Slowly Gray faded from the scene until, at last, he was substituted by Yorath with a quarter of an hour to go. Without the expected penetration from Gray, it was up to Bremner and Giles to crack the Sunderland nut. They could not. Horswill was superb, forcing Giles deep into his own half of the field from where, cool though he remained, he was unable to exert a telling influence. Even allowing for the fact that Clarke should have won the match for Leeds, with a number of half chances before Sunderland scored the only goal, Sunderland's defence was magnificent, with Watson demonstrating beyond dispute that he was ready for England.

There was a spate of fouling by both sides at the start which, for a time, made it look as if the game were deteriorating into a dog-fight. Leeds were making unaccountable errors, Hughes went close for Sunderland with a twenty-five yard drive over the bar. A minute later, Clarke was guilty of his first miss as Reaney set up the opening. The ball broke free as Clarke was smothered when delaying his shot, Hunter hooked the ball back into the middle and Lorimer deflected it into the side netting. Sunderland had had their first two escapes.

Soon afterwards, Watson snuffed out Clarke as Cherry forged through on the left to create an opening and, with Leeds losing their composure, there was a flurry of fouls: Madeley on Guthrie, Clarke on Hughes (for which he was booked), then Guthrie on Lorimer. Mr Burns failed to spot this last one and, immediately, there was a flash of steel as Hunter came in and demolished Tueart as reprisal. On the half hour, Gray had a half-chance at the back of the penalty area, putting the ball wide; a minute later, Sunderland were in front.

Porterfield, who had been playing with conspicuous elegance and awareness, swung a thirty-yard pass out to Kerr on the right. Seeing that Harvey, in the Leeds goal, was off his line, Kerr floated a high ball and Harvey had to back-pedal hard to turn it over the bar. Hughes sent over Sunderland's first corner from the left and the Leeds defenders, imagining the ball was intended for Watson, were caught off guard when it flew on beyond them to Halom, who knocked it back across the face of the goal. Porterfield, with the aplomb of a Pele, caught the ball on his left thigh, swivelled and, taking advantage of the space granted him by the attention focused on Watson, cracked the ball into the roof of the net with his right, and reputedly weaker, foot. 'I normally only use that one for standing on,' he said afterwards.

Leeds were obviously shaken: incredibly, Sunderland were on top, with chants of 'easy' from the ecstatic west end. Those should have been silenced a minute before half-time when a superb through-ball by Madeley gave Clarke his best chance yet, but again he delayed and again Watson smothered him. Leeds' confidence cannot have been improved when, as they walked out from the tunnel for the second half, the Sunderland team ran past them at a smart trot—a singular piece of psychological one-upmanship.

Soon after the restart, Bremner cannoned a shot off Montgomery's chest, and now he was desperately pushing forward with that unquenchable Scots fighting spirit in the attempt to revitalize his side. But Tueart, Porterfield and Guthrie rattled in a succession of shots to prove that Sunderland were long past being intimidated. With half an hour to go Sunderland were remarkably fortunate not to concede a penalty when Watson brought down Bremner as he was put through by Lorimer. How Mr Burns failed to give a penalty, nobody knew, least of all Leeds. Maybe Bremner was paying the price of years of influencing referees, and Mr Burns subconsciously leaned the other way at the vital moment. If that were so, there was a grain of justice in a seemingly unjust decision, Mr Burns waving play on so vigorously that he almost took flight.

There were twenty-six minutes to go when there came the moment for which this Final will be remembered more than any other. Lorimer centred from the right and Cherry, coming in hard on an overlap on the far post, headed for goal. Montgomery parried the ball, twisting cat-like in mid-air and plunging to his right. The ball ran free to Lorimer, who had followed in behind his centre, and from a few yards he had only to tap the ball inside his right hand (Montgomery's left hand) post. Instead, he chose to drive it: and he was, after all, the most powerful kicker of the ball in Britain. Astonishingly, Montgomery, lying on the ground after his save from Cherry one second, the next second had flung himself the other way to deflect Lorimer's shot with his right wrist up on to the crossbar and away. Now, as Leeds made a last vain bid to save the game, it was Horswill and Halom who came closest to scoring. Sunderland had won the Cup because Leeds had passed it straight to them, and because Montgomery had made one of the most notable saves in F.A. Cup history. The trophy went into the Second Division for the first time since West Bromwich won it in 1931.

Bobby Kerr, whose liquid celebrations were as wholehearted as had been his performance on the pitch, said: 'Our victory had one outstanding moment, and not when I collected the trophy. It was when I hugged our manager, Bob Stokoe. For this man has transformed the lives and standing of everyone at the club. Only five months ago we were deeply involved in relegation.' Stokoe, who at the finish had sprinted halfway across the pitch for that mutual embrace, claimed: 'Leeds did not know us. They had watched us in the wrong sort of matches. You can go and watch League matches, but you don't really get the picture. Our players have exploded in the Cup.'

Montgomery, who was the hero of the hour, said of his save: 'I was stranded on the ground and I just flung myself in the general direction of Lorimer's shot. The ball hit my arm and flew on to the underside of the bar and I didn't know much about it.' It is a measure of the improbability of that save that Jones, the Leeds centre-forward, had already half-turned to congratulate Lorimer.

Trevor Cherry, Leeds' left-back, who was one of those always to take an objective view of things, told me later:

'We'd played a lot of hard teams to get there. I was surprised how many players froze on the day. It was the most experienced team in the League: they'd been there the year before, but it just shows that no one can go to Wembley and be sure they'll play well. It was the right result on the day, on the way the play ran. We only came good in the last twenty minutes. Revie had said at half time, "You've got to get forward more." But, on the day, Sunderland had average players who played like they have never played before. Bremner and Giles didn't get to grips with their midfield, and there's just no explanation. I never expected a defence such as ours to give away a goal like that, even though it was my first season with the club after joining them from Huddersfield. We just didn't concede that sort of goal.'

Billy Bremner, defiant to the last, insisted afterwards: 'This team will last another four or five years before it breaks up. We wanted to play well and win at Wembley, but what happened will all be forgotten once we have won the Cup-Winners Cup!' That, too, was to prove a further wretched experience for Don Revie and his team ten days later, when they went to Salonika for the final against Milan. Such was the blatant bias of the Greek referee, Michas, that the match should have been re-played. When the winners are booed out of sight by neutrals and the losers are cheered to the echo, there is something deeply wrong. Sadly, U.E.F.A., as always, were too weak or too uncaring to take action. Even the Greek Federation, accustomed as it is to intrigue and corruption in club football, cared enough to suspend Michas for two years for 'incompetence'.

His bias towards Milan was the worst I've ever seen in football and just one in a long run of refereeing scandals involving Italian clubs which has darkened the image of European football. *The Sunday Times*, in vain, has campaigned for years for a proper investigation of the facts, which show that over a period of years the same handful of referees were appointed to control the matches of the leading Italian clubs. Liverpool were shamefully treated by the Spanish referee De Mendebil in their semi-final with Inter in 1965, and there was the celebrated case of the attempted fixing of Derby's semi-final with Juventus in 1973. *The Sunday Times* proved that an intermediary, named in the Juventus scandal reported by the Portuguese referee, Lobo, had previously been on the official payroll of Italian clubs. But in such dire matters, U.E.F.A. remains as neutral as Pilate.

Leeds: Harvey; Reaney, Madeley, Hunter, Cherry; Bremner, Giles, Gray; Lorimer, Jones, Clarke
Sunderland: Montgomery; Malone, Watson, Pitt, Guthrie; Kerr, Horswill, Porterfield; Hughes, Halom, Tueart

CHAPTER SIXTEEN

England 5

v

Poland ○

WORLD CUP

1973

Norman Hunter, controversial hard man, replaces fading Bobby Moore—and makes the uncharacteristic, unforced error which costs a World Cup place . . . with Polish goalkeeper Tomaszewski giving a 'freak' display.

It is not too far-fetched to say that, by degrees, Sir Alf Ramsey dug his own grave with his continuing negative policies, his use of the hard men, and his perverse attitude to public relations. It should be remembered that while Ramsey achieved the most notable result in England's soccer history to this day, the victory in 1966, he also suffered some historic reverses: as a player, the defeats by the U.S.A. and Hungary; as a manager, the rout by Brazil in 1964, the collapse in Leon, and the home defeat by West Germany in the 1972 European quarter-finals. I am certain that these setbacks coloured his judgement, and intensified his caution.

Following the Mexican trauma, England's next major confrontation was the game with Germany in 1972 after some nondescript qualifying rounds against Malta, Greece and Switzerland. For a while, Ramsey had been flirting with the intimidators who characterized the dominance by British clubs of European football in the early seventies—Hughes and Smith for Liverpool, Hunter of Leeds, Storey of Arsenal. There was

considerable criticism and, under all-round pressure from the
F.A., from English managers, from the press and TV—Ramsey
swung spectacularly the other way with his selection against
Germany that autumn. His middle and front three were all
attacking players: Ball, Bell and Peters, Hurst, Chivers and
Lee. It was the *one* night when he needed a defensive midfield
player. Gunter Netzer ruled the pitch and Germany won 3-1,
though on the scoring chances of the night, England were a
shade unlucky. Ramsey was bitterly resentful of what he
regarded in retrospect as his own weak-mindedness.

When England went to West Berlin for the return leg in the
spring, with everything to gain and nothing to lose, Ramsey
reverted to a perverse, wilfully negative formation including
Hunter and Storey, for a boring, goal-less draw. Needing to
attack, Ramsey chose defenders; rather than creators he preferred destroyers. Geoff Hurst, who was out of the team by
now, was persuaded to say:

> 'I think we've got to take a look at things, as a football
> nation, and get our priorities right at all levels. If you look at
> England's system you have to admit it's got results. I've seen
> both sides of the picture, playing attractive football at West
> Ham and not getting results, playing less attractively with
> England and achieving things. From a professional's point
> of view, I would always say that results are more important.
> This tie was lost, obviously, at Wembley. Ramsey didn't
> think, none of us did, that Germany would come and attack
> us at Wembley.'

Helmut Schoen, manager of the German team which would
take the title with a style which won admirers throughout
Europe, observed cryptically: 'I thought the England team's
tackling was brutal and aimed at the bones.'

So now it was on to the World Cup in which England were
drawn with Poland and Wales. In another wretchedly physical
match in January, 1973, England were held 1-1 at Wembley
by Wales. Money was taken from the public under false
pretences. The public was quick to smell that what it had been
offered was rotten, fake and degenerate; and they rightly
booed. Dave Bowen, the Wales manager, claimed that his team
had played well, yet all they had achieved was their share of the

derision of a 62,000 crowd. The players tore lumps out of each other. Noel Coward said contemptuously of the contemporary theatre around this time, that if one wishes to see people in the nude one goes to the Turkish baths, not the theatre. If we wanted to see the antics of Roberts, Yorath, Hunter and Storey in that match, we ought to have gone to the bear pit.

In the previous autumn, England had scuffled a 1-0 win against Wales in Cardiff and there seemed to be few people in the game, at the F.A. or anywhere else, who cared to heed the words of Danny Blanchflower. 'It is thought that the game is first and last about winning. This is nonsense. The game is about glory, about doing things with style.' Ramsey had allowed England's style to sink to its lowest point ever in the name of functionalism and expediency. Ramsey's ambivalent attitude to his job, to his responsibilities to the game, was neatly summed up when he said before the game against Wales in Cardiff:

'While nothing would give me greater pleasure than to see a classic battle between England and Wales, graced by a display of smooth skill, neither team can afford to sacrifice a successful result to the interests of pure football. I was most impressed by the attitude of the countries taking part in the Olympic Games. They had not travelled to Germany to entertain; they had come to win medals and that is a philosophy no manager can ignore when his team is engaged in competitive football.'

One of those teams had been Poland and, already, Ramsey's thinking was veering to the negative. At the annual meeting of the F.A. in May, 1973, Bill Dunlop of the Sussex F.A. suggested that players with bad records or recent suspensions should be prohibited from playing for England, that their international selection, carrying as it does the implication of official approval, made it difficult—if not impossible—to achieve effective discipline in the lower reaches of the game, where life is modelled on that at the top. The F.A., privately agreeing to a man, did nothing to support him publicly. Such was the slide into indiscipline that I suggested in the *Sunday Telegraph* that Ramsey's teams should wear armbands carrying a government health warning.

Certainly Ramsey had problems of availability in selection. Allan Clarke withdrew, for example, from almost more matches than he played in. Players such as Summerbee, Marsh, MacDonald, Curry, and Chivers were tantalizingly gifted, frustratingly inconsistent. And, most critically, Bobby Moore was nearing the end of his career. When England travelled to Katowice in the summer of 1973, for their first tie with Poland, they had descended a long way from their memorable win there, seven years previously, immediately before the 1966 finals. Now they were shrouded in fear and uncertainty. And it was this fear which persuaded Ramsey to drop Mike Channon after a successful run of five consecutive games and to re-introduce Storey, the destroyer in a defensive 4-4-2 formation.

In the event, England went down 2-0, Bobby Moore being at fault with both the goals. I had suggested several weeks before the game that Ramsey should consider dropping Moore, because the evidence of his decline from his own peerless level was well-established. The problem for Moore was accentuated by playing alongside a ball-playing centre-half, Roy McFarland, instead of a conventional stopper like Jack Charlton or Labone. The result in Katowice gravely exposed all England's shortcomings. Ramsey, carrying perversity to extremes, claimed he was 'impressed' by England's performance. By what score had they to lose before he was dismayed? The king, one had to proclaim, was wearing no clothes. Even after half-time, when England were two down, Ramsey refused to introduce attacking substitutes, the tactical use of which he never fully grasped. These opinions, then and now, are not vindictive. It is far more agreeable to be reporting the fortunes of a team which is successful and admired. For three years England's team had been neither.

Mike Channon, recalling his surprise exclusion, says: 'I was certainly disappointed. I'd already played ten games, I'd been scoring. I think Alf went for experience, went for the draw, opting for caution. But things went wrong in the first few minutes. After that I played regularly until Alf got sacked. He was loyal to the players and had their support.'

Ramsey had some willing accomplices in the propagation of his theory of expediency. Jimmy Hill, who was then being paid over £20,000 by BBC TV for his alleged expertise, claimed on radio, the day before the match in Katowice, that Ramsey would be justified in recalling both Storey and Hunter, saying: 'It does not matter *how* England win as long as they do.' It was alarming that someone with a seemingly authentic professional background should be supporting Ramsey's sterile philosophy in such a powerful medium.

Even Ramsey's admirers among the public were beginning to cross the floor in droves. I travelled to Poland in a chartered plane taking supporters, young and old, united in their loyalty, and paying £50—a lot at the time—to prove it. On the flight home they were unanimous in their condemnation not of individual performance but of lack of adventure by the manager. As Joe Mercer commented on England's formation of five men across the middle of the field with only Chivers up front: 'You do not run forty yards and then give a three-yard pass as England were doing.'

Ramsey's public relations, too, were an increasing irritant. Regettably, he had not always behaved like a knight. His aloofness and his inhospitable attitude to foreigners, as at the formal press conference at Katowice, were grudgingly tolerated eccentricities while he was successful. Now that he was not, they were merely an additional burden for England to carry. In 1963 Ramsey was given a mandate to produce an England team possessing spirit and organization. He did so beyond all expectation, but not only had he squandered his own achievement but he had helped to send English soccer down a blind alley in which functionalism would eventually bring the development of the game grinding to a halt. The F.A. had not the wit to know the difference. It was too busy manning the turnstiles and running to the bank.

From the gloom of Katowice, England went to Moscow where they won a friendly 2-1, then to Turin where their limitations were again exposed in a two-goal defeat. All was euphoria, briefly, that autumn when, with Norman Hunter replacing Moore as sweeper, Austria suffered a seven-goal hammering at Wembley in a warm-up for the return with Poland (the goals coming from Channon and Clarke, with two each, Chivers, Currie and Bell). The week before the moment of truth at Wembley, Ramsey went to see Poland in a warm-up in Rotterdam. Holland showed the way to beat them, repeatedly exploiting the Poles' weakness down the flanks. But England were a team without a winger, or anybody resembling one, with only Peters and Channon occasionally making wide runs. It was also apparent in Rotterdam that the Polish goal-keeper, Jan Tomaszewski, was vulnerable to high crosses from the wing. Yet he was to prove the hero of the night at Wembley.

The warning for Ramsey lay in the pace of Poland's right-winger, Lato, who was constantly dangerous. Ramsey, after giving a lengthy interview to Dutch television in pouring rain, had little to say to the British press but he did admit: 'That was the first time I have seen Lato since the Olympics and he is a vastly improved player. He was extremely dangerous.' The threat of Lato made it certain that Hunter would keep his place instead of Moore. The other player who seemed bound to give England trouble was Kazimierz Deyna, a midfield player with an awareness and a fine touch. In a long interview before the match Deyna told me:

> 'This is a new Poland that comes to Wembley. Always in the past, before we played England in Katowice, what we had been lacking was the *hard* game, but now we know we have to answer opponents with the same action. If they attack we must counter-attack. If they kick, we shall kick. It will be an eye for an eye. I have read much about the Ramsey plan to shackle me with a bodyguard, but I have had many body-guards in the past and I do not care who it is today. I do not believe the game will be brutal the way it was against Wales last month. What we need is a draw, and we will do every-thing we can to get it. But there is no talk of defence from the beginning. To play the whole match defensively would be stupid, tactically. Very few teams have won at Wembley. But we do not need to win!'

After much speculation, Ramsey fielded the same side which had beaten Austria, with Currie, Bell and Peters in mid-field, Channon, Chivers and Clarke up front. He was going to rely heavily on the ability of Chivers to batter the Poles into submission in the air, yet he had not got the player who could get round behind the defence to pull the ball back on to Chivers' head. There were grave fears, after the injury inflicted on Poland's outstanding attacker Lubanski, in the first leg, that Poland would be out for revenge. In the event, the match was surprisingly lacking in physical intimidation from either side.

Ramsey had scorned picking an assassin in midfield: indeed, it was difficult to understand why, with such a team now entrusted with the most important match for three years, Ramsey had gone through the negative and defensive process of the previous sixteen matches. It was a change in policy which was to prove to have come too late.

Everybody knew how the game was likely to be played, with Poland pulling nine or ten men back behind the ball. Ramsey said on the day of the match: 'It's not a question of motivating the players, so much as keeping then composed and patient.' With Peter Osgood out of action with an injured ankle, Ramsey's attacking alternatives on the substitutes bench were Kevin Keegan, who at that stage had played only twice previously, and Kevin Hector, the little Derby striker who could wriggle through keyholes. But on this controversial night, when everything which England hurled at the Poles, in an almost unbroken attack from start to finish, was fended off, Ramsey delayed introducing a variation, taxing the Poles with a different set of problems by sending out Hector to replace Chivers, until only two minutes from time. It was an extraordinary tactical blunder. How the Poles survived nobody knows to this day. It was a massacre in all but the scoreline, and strong men like Hughes and Hunter wept in frustration at the finish.

England's opening onslaught lasted for twenty minutes, but somehow Poland weathered it, with unbelievable luck and some improbable saves by Tomaszewski. So bizarre were some of the ways in which he blocked England shots with every part of his anatomy that Brian Clough, one of ITV's panel of experts, called him 'a clown'. But clown or not, Tomaszewski was the man who so often during the ninety minutes stood between England and a place in the finals in Germany. Channon recollects:

'I think about it even now, about the amount of control we had throughout the game. Sometimes in a match you have the control but are still vulnerable on the counter-attack, yet it wasn't like that. We weren't vulnerable. We totally dominated them, but our shots hit the post, hit bodies standing in the way and, on the night, their goalkeeper was brilliant. The way the luck ran was unbelievable. I remember one incident early in the first half: I was on the left close to the six-yard box when Chivers knocked a ball square to me quite hard. I'd got a defender close in on me but he couldn't see the ball. I stuck out a foot and the ball caught me on the heel. I was only three yards out by then and the ball hit the post. The goalkeeper was nowhere near it. It could have gone anywhere—but it hit the post!'

The longer the game went on, the more inconceivable it was that England should fail to win, but the 90,000 crowd was stunned when Poland scored first after fifty-seven minutes. Four times before that, Poland had cleared off their own line, Peters, Chivers and Bell had missed open goals and now, disastrously, England were one down. Ironically, the goal stemmed from an error from Hunter on the halfway line on the right. He failed to control the ball properly with his right foot and Lato broke free, sweeping the ball cross-field to an unmarked Domarski, whose long-range shot was misjudged by Shilton. Shilton had been England's regular goalkeeper for the past ten matches, after a car crash and the loss of sight in his right eye had ended the career of Gordon Banks the year before.

Poor Hunter. Whatever his physical excesses of the past, it was an unjustifiable burden which he now had to carry, the tag of being the man who cost England their place in the World Cup finals. That is the side of the game which the ordinary man, the F.A. official, the TV commentator, or the journalist never experiences: the glare of mute public accusation. Even Hunter's young son was to say to him: 'Daddy, is it true you lost us the World Cup?' A sad Hunter admitted his share of the blame afterwards:

'Blame me, it's partly my fault. I tried to be clever and flicked the ball round a player with my right foot. Suddenly it was lost. As the ball hit the back of the net I thought "Blimey, I caused that." I could have put the ball anywhere, away for a throw in. That's my job. I'm a defender. But I forgot years of experience, tried to use my right foot, and the nation paid the penalty.'

The magnitude of the importance which a game of football has wrongly assumed in our lives is reflected in Hunter's un-

witting use of the word 'nation'—a substitute for the loss of
Empire?

The other half of the blame for the goal was Shilton's. Today
he remembers:

'I had almost nothing else to do at all. It was all at the other
end. I blame myself for it, though it was a more difficult
ball than people realized at the time. Domarski's shot went
through Emlyn Hughes' legs as he lunged for an intercep-
tion, and for a split second I lost sight of the ball. Nowadays,
I think, I'd have saved it. Then, I was trying to get my body
behind the ball for the *perfect* save, but the ball bounced
just before it reached me, which is always hard. My game
has developed since then: if it had happened now I'd have
been prepared to stop it with anything. It was coming so
quickly I didn't know what to use, body or arms. I'm not so
upright these days, I'm a bit crouched, but that was over six
years ago.'

England equalized with a penalty by Clarke after Peters had
been fouled on the edge of the penalty area and, suddenly, all
the pressure was on Poland again, though England forfeited
some of the right to sympathy with an outrageous 'professional'
foul by McFarland. In a rare breakaway, Lato might well have
scored with nine minutes to go had he not been pulled off the
ball by his neck, a foul for which McFarland should have been
sent off. But the catalogue of England near-misses, of the
twenty-six corners they forced, would haunt people for
months.

As the minutes ticked by, Ramsey sat stonily on the bench,
unable to believe his eyes, making no move towards the substitution which might have tipped the balance. Moore, sitting
on the bench beside his general, was desperately urging him
to make the change. In his biography with Jeff Powell, he
recounts:

'With fifteen minutes left, there was a break for treatment
to an injured player and I said to Alf, "It's getting desperate;
don't you think it would be a good idea to get a left-sided
player on?" Alf merely said he'd pushed Norman Hunter
forward. Again I said, "Stick a left-sided forward on, Alf;

we might get 'em down that side." Again Ramsey said he'd push Norman forward, and didn't think he could do any more. How long was there to go? Someone said five minutes and Alf said it was too late. I said, "It's never too late, get Kevin Hector on for two minutes and see what he can do. Come on. Come on. Just get him out there." Ramsey nodded, transfixed, his world collapsing before his eyes. He sent on Hector for the shortest international career on record with just ninety seconds left. Once Alf agreed, I was tearing at Kevin's track-suit trousers. Someone else was trying to get his top off. You could feel the seconds ticking away. We almost threw him on the pitch. And in that ninety seconds, he nearly got Alf another knighthood. Alf ended up taking stick for forgetting the time and sending on a substitute so late. Yet Kevin knocked a ball only inches past the post, just before the final whistle. He might have put us in the finals with his only touch of the ball. I think Kevin might have saved us if Alf had acted sooner. It was obvious we needed a left-sided player to go through them. Emlyn was doing his best from left-back but, as usual, he was cutting the ball back on to his right foot and losing the angles.'

Channon is less sure. He says: 'Should we have changed earlier? When you're playing, it's not always easy to see. The commitment out there was fantastic. We'll never know what Hector might have done earlier but, looking back, I don't think I would have changed anything.' At the finish, Ramsey, England's fallen knight, shuffled off the pitch, head down, hands in pockets, towards an uncertain future.

I am totally with Moore on this issue. It was a blunder. For eighty-eight minutes, Ramsey had persisted with football played too much in the air. Since the middle of the first half the match had cried out for the ability of a man like Hector who might have beaten the Poles on the ground. Twenty years after the Hungarians taught us the same lesson on the same pitch, we had to learn it again: there is no substitute for skill. Helmut Schoen told me after the game: 'When a defence packs the penalty area as Poland did, you need wingers. England's tall, powerful forwards were not supple or flexible enough to tight situations.' This was echoed by Ron Greenwood, who said: 'What worried me was the lack of intelligence in the

England play. I feel players should be more observant at world level.'

Ramsey had reaped the whirlwind of the unchecked thuggery of the last ten years which had stifled the development of players of the class of Jimmy Greaves, Johnny Byrne and Joe Baker. For Ramsey to substitute Chivers with Hector was a contradiction in strategy, like pouring petrol into a car with a flat tyre. Ramsey said afterwards: 'It was a shattering blow. This was the most disappointing night of my life. The lads were great but we just did not have the luck. If I could play the match again I would do the same. If we failed it was in the end product in front of goal.' A few weeks later, England took it on the nose again from Italy, beaten 1-0 in a friendly at Wembley. On the morning before departure for England's next match against Portugal, in the spring, the decision was taken secretly at Lancaster Gate that Ramsey would have to go.

England:6Shilton; Madeley, McFarland, Hunter, Hughes; Bell, Curry, Peters; Channon, Chivers (Hector), Clarke

Poland: Tomaszewski; Gorgon, Szymanowski, Bulzacki, Musial; Kasperczak, Deyna, Cmikiewisz; Lato, Domarski, Gadocha

CHAPTER SEVENTEEN

West Germany○

v

Holland○

WORLD CUP FINAL

1974

Bobby Rensenbrink misses a sitter—and Holland pay the price of scoring 'too soon'. In Rudi Krol's opinion, 'It was better for Germany than for us that we scored after ninety seconds.'

Holland in 1974 were the most exciting team there'd been since the Hungarians twenty years before. When they were playing at a peak, they lifted the game with a level of inventiveness and collective intelligence which not even the Brazilians of 1958 or 1970 had equalled. Brazil had supreme players, but I do not believe their intelligence matched that of Johan Cruyff and his colleagues under the leadership of their manager Rinus Michels. That Dutch team were exceptional, and not just with their feet. Almost all of them were multi-lingual and it was a fascinating experience to move among them as they held open court on their special press days at their headquarters in Hiltrup, just over the border from Holland. Cruyff, Neeskens, Krol, Rep, and Van Hanegem would discourse fluently with the world's press in five languages: Dutch, German, English, Spanish and Italian. They were the aristocrats of their profession: a product of three superb club sides, Ajax, Feyenoord, and PSV Eindhoven, who dominated Europe in the early seventies.

The Dutch approached the Final against West Germany in a mood of quiet, controlled anger, the result of scandal-mongering stories in the German press deliberately aimed at undermining the Dutch players. Michels, in the days before the Final, refused to speak a single word to any German correspondent, in retaliation for the scurrilous attack by *Bild Zeitung*, with its false accusations of an all-night orgy the previous Sunday. When I talked with Michels at Hiltrup, he said: 'This attack was aimed at the players' wives and families, in an effort to undermine our harmony through emotional disruption at home. There are no limits in this kind of cold war.' But he went on to admit:

'Six weeks ago, I would not have believed such success as we have had to be possible. Normally it's out of the question with such short preparation. You cannot hope for a team which will express themselves with such unity as this team has. The most important factor has been the responsible attitude of the players. They accepted they had to do more than normal. Brazil had four months' preparation yet their eventual team appeared only in the last two matches.'

Cruyff echoed Michels' opinion. 'The players are united mentally. Michels was vital because, although the experience was there, he excluded outside interference and gave us one voice.' Michels' innovation had been to dispense with a sweeper, using Arie Haan in a deep midfield position instead, *in front* of the previously uncapped defender Wim Rijsbergen—behind whom goalkeeper Jongbloed was effectively the sweeper out on the edge of his penalty-area. Michels, controversially, had also preferred the dribbling skills of Bobby Rensenbrink on the left wing, instead of the more direct running of the ageing Piet Keizer. It was a team which took hair-raising risks, confident in its own ability to survive errors if they were made; a team which put the clock back twenty, thirty, forty years to a time when the game was, in Blanchflower's words, not just about results but about glory, to an era in which Matt Busby, as a wing-half for Manchester City, gave his supporters heart attacks with his dribbling on the edge of his own penalty-area.

Holland's formation with Cruyff presented opponents with a unique problem—a team playing without a central striker, leaving the space in the middle vacant for any one of half-a-dozen players to break into. Cruyff would take up a position in midfield, to one side or the other, behind his wingers, Rep and Rensenbrink, and then attack that flank of the opposition's defence as a pair, probably with a supporting run from Neeskens or Jansen. The way the Dutch grouped and supported each other, the player in possession always had three or four alternative passes at any one moment.

Holland had come steadily to the boil throughout the finals, really exploding for the first time when they thrashed Argentina 4-0 in the second round. They had given notice of their quality when they had scientifically and systematically outplayed an ugly, expedient, defensive Uruguayan side in their first match. Then, against Argentina in the vast new stadium at Gelsenkirchen, they set the World Cup alight. There were two spectacular storms in the Ruhr Valley that night: and the first of them was Holland's. Long before an artillery of forked lightning split the inky night sky, illuminating the forest of chimneys and the pithead wheels of this huge industrial sprawl, Holland gave a truly great performance, restoring to the World Cup some of its magnetism and tradition.

As the rain came down as straight as stair rods, Holland tore the helpless Argentinians to shreds in the most formidable exposition the competition had yet seen, convincing everyone that nothing could stop them from becoming champions. Cruyff and Krol scored twice in a breath-taking opening spell, then Rep and Cruyff hit two more in the last quarter of an hour. As the thunder shook the towering cantilevered roof of the stadium, Holland's display sent shivers of apprehension through Germany's supporters throughout the country. The Dutch attacked with ten men, interchanging at bewildering speed. There were times when they actually manoeuvred Argentina's goalkeeper Carnevali off his line with tactical cunning, only to have the final shot cleared off the line. If the magic of Cruyff was the pinnacle of this performance, the value of the others was not far behind: the incredible perception of Neeskens, Jansen, and Van Hanegem in midfield, the anticipation of Rep and Rensenbrink, the supporting roles of full-backs Krol and Suurbier. Argentina never knew what hit them. In the middle half hour Holland coasted, merely raising their eyebrows in bemusement and refusing to retaliate when

Argentina, fearing the rout that was already upon them, began to bend the laws and go 'over the top'. In London, the book-makers drew breath sharply and cut Holland's odds to make them favourites for the first time at 6-4, ahead of Germany at 7-2.

It was a coincidence that both the final matches in the two second round groups should effectively be 'semi-finals', the results determining which of the four teams would dispute the Final. On a waterlogged pitch at Frankfurt, West Germany defeated a fading Poland while, in Dortmund, Holland thrashed Brazil. Not only did Brazil surrender their proud, prized crown as champions, but also their illustrious reputation in one of the fiercest World Cup ties since the Chile-Italy encounter in 1960. Holland surged into the Final with two classic, peerless, second-half goals which epitomized all they stood for: style, refinement, speed. Their regal authority, precarious for the first forty-five minutes, was ultimately overwhelming. How sad that Brazil could not accept with grace the kind of lesson which they in the past had so crushingly inflicted on others. 'Brazil were disgraceful,' commented Sir Alf Ramsey at the finish.

Predictions about the quality of Brazil's defensive play had proved misleading. George Raynor, for instance, manager of the 1958 finalists, Sweden, who had been beaten by Brazil after leading, now had said: 'Brazil's back four of Ze Maria, Pereria, Mario Marinho and Francisco Marinho, is defensively the best in the competition. Holland will find it very difficult to score.' Pele, though retired and personally depressed by his country's loss of favour, claimed: 'Our back line reads the game faster than any other. If we beat Holland, we shall win the Final.' Mario Zagalo, outside-left in Brazil's victories of 1958 and 1962 and now their manager, had predicted: 'Argentina committed suicide against Holland. The Dutch will not find our penalty area the same playground. It will be a hostile place.'

In the event, Holland surged into the Final leaving Brazil broken and discredited. When Luis Pereria was sent off for a brutal, waist-high tackle on Neeskens, a few minutes from the end, he was paying the price for his colleagues' stream of far worse tackles which had gone before. Brazil attempted to steal their way into the Final by spoiling, defensive tactics by all ten outfield players. It was they who first pulled the knives. Yet Holland, among their many qualities, possessed immense physical toughness, a capacity to look after themselves whatever the weapons. Nobody was likely to intimidate them and, within ten minutes, they were matching the Brazilians tackle for tackle, trip for trip. From the start, the Brazilians regarded Neeskens as more of a threat than Cruyff. Not long before half-time, Neeskens was laid out cold by either Mario Marinho's elbow or fist while the ball was at the other end of the field, an act of violence undetected by referee or linesman but picked up on television. With Neeskens on the ground, Jairzinho missed an open goal at the other end. Had Brazil scored then, the second half would have been a bloody battle. Instead, in the first quarter of an hour after half-time, Holland scored two brilliant goals, Cruyff making the first and scoring the second, and each was perfection.

In the fiftieth minute, Neeskens made ground on the right and slipped the ball wide to Cruyff, who was hovering on the touchline. Almost before the ball had reached Cruyff, Neeskens was off in the direction of the penalty area, taking Mario Marinho with him. Cruyff not only played a first-time return but bent the pass, curving it ahead of Marinho and back into Neeskens' path. Hitting the ball first time through an angle of at least 140 degrees as it came from behind him, Neeskens scooped his shot over the advancing goalkeeper Leo and just under the bar for one of the most memorable goals of all time. The second had no less distinction. Rudi Krol broke down the left, clear of right-back Ze Maria on an overlap, hit an early, square, waist-high cross, and there was Cruyff coasting in effortlessly to meet the ball on the volley, a goal taken with calm finality. Afterwards, Michels said: 'We thought things might be easier once we were two up, but the war went on.'

And so the Final. Holland were unique in possessing simultaneously the greatest individual in the tournament, Johan Cruyff, and the most integrated team. In the *Daily Express* I forecast:

'If Rinus Michels' exciting Dutchmen score first, and in the opening twenty minutes, then I think their eventual margin may be more than two goals. In every respect except

one, that of being the home team, Holland are ahead of
West Germany. Their goal aggregate is 14-1, Germany's
13-3. Holland have never looked like losing, while Germany
laboured against Chile, lost to East Germany, were lucky
against Yugoslavia and were twice behind against Sweden.'

Holland had three recognized match-winning goal-scorers,
Cruyff, Neeskens, and Rep, to Germany's one, Muller. Each
side had three attacking back line players, Suurbier, Haan and
Krol of Holland, Vogts, Beckenbauer and Breitner of Germany. Of the two stoppers, Rijsbergen and Schwarzenbeck,
the one more likely to be exposed was Schwarzenbeck. All the
speculation in the days before the match was whether Helmut
Schoen would give the job of shadowing Cruyff to Vogts or
Bonhof. To give it to Vogts would leave a huge gap on
Germany's right flank, inviting exploitation by Rensenbrink, or
his deputy following an injury against Brazil. To give it to
Bonholf would occupy Germany's midfield strongman totally
and Cruyff, I fancied, was more than capable of swallowing
Bonhof whole and spitting out the studs.

Dettmar Cramer, a F.I.F.A. coach and member of the
World Cup technical committee, said to me before the final:
'Watching Cruyff in this tournament has shown us how Di
Stefanc was twenty years ahead of his time for Real Madrid—
playing in every area of the field, scoring goals, technically
outstanding yet brave when necessary, the leader of the team
physically and mentally.'

The size of the task facing Germany was stupendous, and
Schoen was forced to admit: 'Of the three Finals I've managed,
Wembley in 1966, Brussels in 1972, and now here in Munich,
this is the hardest because the public expects the most from
us.' The confidence of the Dutch was well-founded but, above
all, they were intent on inflicting on the Germans a crushing
defeat to settle some old scores, not all of them arising from
the football field. It is not an overstatement to say that Michels'
brilliant team had their hearts set on humiliating the German
side in front of their own people. It was that secret wish which
was perhaps to prove their undoing.

Germany's team had only fallen into shape in the opening
second round match against Yugoslavia following a traumatic
defeat by East Germany in the first round. Gunter Netzer had

gone from the dazzling team which won the 1972 European championship. There was no doubting their customary virility and competitiveness, but they lacked balance and, it seemed, some of the essential qualities of a team. Following the defeat by East Germany, Schoen had had a long, late-night discussion with his senior professionals, Beckenbauer and Gerd Muller, turning over changes which he had in mind for the game with Yugoslavia—the introduction of Bonhof and Holzenbein, the one a muscular midfield player, the other a roving, hard-running flank player. It was Beckenbauer's 'leaking' of these suggestions at a press conference before the match against Yugoslavia which gave rise to the notion that he and not Schoen was running the team. Schoen told me with an owlish look some years later: 'That was not very correct of Franz!'

The two players dropped were Cullman and Grabowski but, by the time Germany beat Poland 1-0 to reach the Final, Grabowski was back at the expense of Flohe, with the same kind of formation up front which Schoen had employed against England four years before: two wingers, Grabowski and Holzenbein, on either side of Muller. It was Berti Vogts who was given the onerous responsibility of shutting out Cruyff.

When, in little more than a minute, Holland took the lead in the Final with a penalty by Neeskens, they seemed poised more than ever for the victory which everyone in the game, Germans apart, believed would be theirs. In that first minute, Cruyff gave Vogts the slip, and he did so again at least three times in situations which should have enabled Holland to win. Why did they not?

Rudi Krol, still playing with marvellous authority for Ajax in 1980, said to me at the time:

'You can score too quickly, things go through your mind, you start thinking about the result instead of the match. It is probably true to say that it was better for Germany that we scored so quickly than it was for us. It made them realize exactly what they had to do. The pity for us was that we did not score the couple of goals before half-time that we should have. Maybe we played it too easy. I admit that some of our players probably thought "We're World Champions", and in the end we woke up too late.'

Holland threw away the Final in 1974, and with it an un-
challengeable place in history because, for twenty minutes, they
forgot what professionals should never forget: that being the
best team is not enough. You have to prove it. West Germany
beat the favourites to take the title for the second time in
twenty years because as in Switzerland against Hungary, they
had the character, the mental tenacity, to refuse to allow
Holland to make fools of them. There is no denying that
Germany's gritty but less than polished achievement was an
example of that spice of uncertainty which makes football such
a fascinating game. As Schoen says: 'After that first goal, our
team was really fighting.'

It was a mesmeric, unforgettable opening, with Holland
kicking off and playing an unbroken sequence of fifteen silky
passes, backwards and forwards, square across the pitch,
Neeskens' eventual penalty putting the ball in the net without
the Germans having touched it. As Germany had fallen back,
Holland advanced; Krol, Suurbier, Haan and Van Hanegem
lazily rolled the ball across the face of the German penalty
area. Suddenly, on the left, Cruyff exploded into action, rip-
ping clear of Vogts, only to be brought down by a desperate
lunge from Hoeness barely two feet into the penalty area. Jack
Taylor, the Wolverhampton referee, stunned the 75,000 crowd
in the Olympic stadium by instantly pointing to the spot.
Neeskens scored, and Holland were poised for an historic
victory.

But instead of going for the kill immediately with a second
goal in the next ten or fifteen minutes which would have
demoralized Germany beyond recovery, the Dutch foolishly
stood back and started to toy with their opponents, supposing
they had them on a string. It was now, when they were on top
and saw half-a-dozen chances go begging, rather than in the
second half, that Holland really lost the match. If there was
one team unlikely to lie down in the first quarter of an hour
it was the vigorous Germans, playing in front of their own
crowd. Ignoring Holland's assumption of effortless superiority
—stroking the ball about as if taking time off on the beach—
the Germans closed ranks, gathering themselves for the
counter-offensive. With the determined running of Grabowski
and Holzenbein on the flanks, the tenacity of Muller in the
middle, the contrasting flair and energy of Overath, Hoeness,

and Bonhof in midfield, Germany began to probe for cracks in the Dutch edifice. And began to find them.

Grabowski and Hoeness, working through on the left, made an opening from which Holzenbein shot wide. Suddenly, Holland's back line, instead of being able to knock the ball off as they pleased, were under pressure. In the twenty-fourth minute, Muller, straining for the break which would put Germany back in the game, fouled Rijsbergen on the edge of the penalty area. Up came the swarthy Van Hanegem, the most volatile of the Dutch team, and stupidly shoved Muller in the chest, for which he was promptly booked. It was an indication that Holland were losing their composure, a quality which vanished totally two minutes later. Again Germany attacked down the left, fast, against the unsupported Suurbier, Breitner making the spare man. Holzenbein cut loose into the penalty area. Someone had to challenge; it was Jansen, and Holzenbein went flying over his outstretched leg. Breitner scored from the penalty.

What Holland had tried to treat as a formality had suddenly become a throbbing, vibrant match. In the next ten minutes, the Dutch were almost bowled over as the Germans, responding to the roar of the crowd, to the adrenalin now racing through their own game, swarmed all over them. Within a minute, Jongbloed, for the first time in the competition it seemed, had to make an important save—from the steely Vogts. Moments later, Overath, conducting the German revival with all his former assurance, put Hoeness clear; Grabowski and Overath himself kept the move going, Overath centred and the Dutch defence was in real trouble. From a free kick by Beckenbauer a few yards outside the penalty area, Jongbloed turned the ball over the bar.

Yet now came the moment when the Dutch could have settled the game, one of those stark incidents which will be remembered as long as the opening penalty, as long as the result itself. With eight minutes remaining to half-time, with Germany pressing and the crowd baying, Cruyff suddenly ghosted clear of Vogts with Rep alongside in support on his left, and with nobody between him and the goal but an anxious Beckenbauer. On and on went Cruyff, with that loping run, straight at Beckenbauer, 'fixing' the German captain by taking the ball straight at him. Rep intelligently held back, onside, until Cruyff finally rolled the ball into his path for the goal which could have been the knockout. But, with only Maier to beat, and the chance to go round him, Rep froze and struck his shot straight against Maier's body.

Six minutes later, Germany scored what was to prove the winner. Bonhof surged through on the right, went past Haan, and struck the ball hard into the penalty area. Muller failed to control it first time, but instantly showed why he was such a phenomenal marksman. Although the ball rebounded slightly behind him, he reacted quickest, turning in a flash with his low centre of gravity, hooking the ball wide of Jongbloed with that unerring instinct of where the gap is beyond the goalkeeper.

Apart from creating that one priceless chance for Rep, and forcing the initial penalty, Cruyff had been more subdued than in almost any game up to now, thanks to the relentless shadowing of Vogts. The Dutchman's opinion of the legality of some of Vogts' tackling, of his hustling from behind, was left in no doubt when he protested strongly to Jack Taylor as the teams left the field at half-time; for his efforts, he was rather histrionically booked. As a result of this, the crowd stupidly booed Cruyff intermittently in the second half with surprising small-mindedness. It was probably fear.

The second half belonged almost exclusively to Holland, but they were unable to exploit their advantage. After an early near-miss by Bonhof with a header which flew just wide, the Germans bore a charmed life; their midfield, which had a capacity for hard work rather than improvization, was now seen to characterize the whole side, Muller and Beckenbauer apart. Little was seen of Breitner's surging runs down the flank, for he was far too preoccupied with containing Rep. Rensenbrink, whose fitness had been in doubt before the start after an injury against Brazil, was replaced at half-time by René Van Der Kerkhof.

Holland made all the running but the luck all ran the other way. Breitner cleared off the line, the ungainly but agile Maier made a succession of competent saves and, when he was beaten, Bonhof cleared off the line from Van Der Kerkhof. With a quarter of an hour to go, Neeskens thundered a tremendous close range volley against Maier's body from Van Der Kerkhof's cross. Three times, Rep went close from good positions. Even though Cruyff was never permitted to display his normal range of skills, there could be no doubting that the better team lost. As Cruyff admitted afterwards: 'For thirty minutes in the first half, we played like schoolchildren. I am bitterly disappointed in our performance. Berti Vogt was very good but he was most certainly unfair, and this was what I was telling the referee.'

Krol, who was to captain the team four years later in Argentina, believes in retrospect that Rensenbrink should not have played in the first half. Shortly after his possible transfer to Arsenal in 1979 had fallen through, Krol told me:

'The decision was left to Bobby, and he told Michels he was fit, but he was not as fit as he said he was. We went out in the second half and took every imaginable risk, and it nearly worked. I think we were unlucky with our shooting, although some of it was bad. Obviously we would have been tremendously confident if Johnny Rep had scored that goal before half-time. Perhaps the pass from Cruyff was just a shade too hard. But, undoubtedly, we gave away the first half, we were too relaxed, we thought we were already World Champions but, in the second half, we played some of the best football in the tournament.'

Schoen reflects: 'We had time to talk at half-time and I warned the team that they must not be too defensive, that Holland would attack and this would give us a chance for a third goal. The victory was a tribute to the character of my team as much as anything.'

| Holland: | Jongbloed; Suurbier, Rijsbergen (de Jong), Krol; Haan; Jansen, Van Hanegem, Neeskens; Rep, Cruyff, Rensenbrink (Van Der Kerkhof) |
| West Germany: | Maier; Vogts, Schwarzenbeck, Beckenbauer, Breitner; Hoeness, Bonhof, Overath; Grabowski, Muller, Holzenbein |

CHAPTER EIGHTEEN

Southampton 1

v

Manchester United 0

F. A. CUP FINAL

1976

The whole country expected Manchester United's whizz-kids to win the F.A. Cup, but Southampton's old stagers, and a mishit shot by Bobby Stokes, determined otherwise.

So much of the luck of any cup competition extends to the luck of the draw, and never was this more true than in the pairing of the four teams for the semi-finals of the 1976 F.A. Cup. The Final for which every neutral was hoping, between Manchester United and Derby County, was forestalled when they were matched against each other in the semi-final at Hillsborough, Sheffield. They were, by general consensus of opinion, the two most engaging teams in the country at that time, each in the running for both Cup and League. Derby eventually finished fourth in the Championship, scoring seventy-five goals, but being failed by their defence, which conceded fifty-eight. And, in the semi-final, Derby gave a wretched performance, Leighton James and Kevin Hector failing to deliver up front, Archie Gemmill, Steve Powell, and Bruce Rioch being shut out in midfield by the tenacity of young Gerry Daly and Sammy McIlroy and United's wingers, Gordon Hill and Steve Coppell. At times, the gallant Roy McFarland seemed to be playing United on his own and he admitted to me afterwards: 'It would have been wrong if we had won on this performance.' So United moved into their fifth post-war final with a young team which brought back memories of that other young team two decades before . . .

The other semi-final was a comparatively low-key affair between teams from the lower divisions: Crystal Palace who, under the guidance of Malcolm Allison, were desperate to climb back out of the Third, and homely Southampton of the Second, who had stolen their way through almost without being noticed. Crystal Palace had staged a remarkable run, eliminating Leeds, Chelsea and Sunderland, all on away grounds. Southampton had survived a difficult passage against Aston Villa, Blackpool and West Bromwich and only narrowly scraped through a difficult sixth round tie away to Bradford City. Crystal Palace's euphoria evaporated as Southampton won competently by two goals at Stamford Bridge.

Much of Southampton's life had been spent outside the First Division and their only appearances in the F.A. Cup Final had been as runners-up in 1900 and 1902. They were widely regarded as even bigger outsiders for the Final than Sunderland had been three years before, though, of course, the pedigree of their Manchester United opponents could not compare with that of Leeds. Yet there was a sure, sound dignity about Southampton, which stemmed from the top: from a sensible board of directors, from a general manager, Ted Bates, who had devoted his life to the club and painstakingly built it up over recent years, and from their go-ahead young team manager, Lawrie McMenemy, who was rapidly making a name for himself with his shrewd handling of men and limited resources.

McMenemy, a towering Geordie ex-guardsman who had been on the books at Doncaster but who had never played League football, came to Southampton after taking Grimsby to promotion from the Fourth Division, an experience which had taught him much about the realities of football life and management. He was, and is, particularly conscious that the local football team is a living function of the community which supports it, without that support it ceases to exist; and he has never failed to impress upon his players this aspect of social responsibility, encouraging them to set a good example in the way they conduct themselves. This kind of awareness extended to tactics on the field. McMenemy might have had a limited pedigree, but he consistently showed himself able to organize his resources to the greatest possible effect. If there were one man who did not believe Southampton were lambs going to the slaughter, as they approached the Final, it was he. The lambs, he sensed rightly, were United.

It was the youth of Tommy Docherty's team which, together with their use of two wingers, had caught the imagination of the public. Wingers had been unfashionable, and Docherty had been cleverly exploiting the publicity generated by the feats of Hill, Coppell and their colleagues. Yet the basis on which almost everybody forecast a United victory, me included, was somewhat shallow. United were not all we cracked them up to be; Southampton were more than we supposed. Indeed, they proceeded to do precisely what I claimed they could not do in my preview in the *Express*:

'Second Division Southampton, full of goals and the wisdom of more years in the game, are just not equipped to win the only way that is open to them, the way Sunderland beat Leeds: by the only goal. Southampton's only strategy must be to attack—yet in that way, I believe, they are destined to lose, perhaps by the four-goal margin of their last final seventy-six years ago. In the form book there is no way that Southampton can score a single goal and hang on to it, as defence is their self-acknowledged weak suit.'

Which only goes to show how wrong you can be, and that the journalistic pundit cannot afford to be without humility.

Perhaps I should have been warned by Mike Channon, successor to Bobby Charlton as the brand-image of English soccer abroad, and the only man at that stage to have played in every international under Don Revie. Wembley was his scene and, without a trace of boasting, he had said:

'We'll handle the occasion better than United, I think. They've a lot of skill but they're young. We have more experience in players such as Peter Osgood, Jim McCalliog and Peter Rodriguez, who've all been at Wembley before. I'm more confident about this one than I was about the semi-final at Crystal Palace. Semi-finals are so edgy. Obviously we haven't the consistency to be a really successful side as yet in the League. If we've got a fault, that's it. But we've scored more goals than most in all divisions, and the country could be in for a shock.'

With hindsight, we can observe also a dangerous touch of arrogance in the way Docherty proclaimed beforehand: 'We haven't studied Southampton. We're not concerned with the way they play so much as with the way we play. What Sunderland did to Leeds is the perfect warning for us, but we won't talk about Southampton. A few English clubs have pumped life-blood back into the game by giving it more freedom. That's what we aim to do at Wembley.'

Like so many of Docherty's postures, the claim did not stand up to close examination. At the time, the United players were prepared to ride along with the manager on his free-wheeling bandwagon, which certainly had excited the crowd. But Lou Macari, who had been signed by Docherty from Celtic, now reveals that Docherty was merely doing his usual bit as fairground barker. Although Macari stands to be accused of sour grapes, following Docherty's controversial dismissal two seasons later, he has always been reliable for his sanguine views on both United and Scotland. He says:

'Docherty claimed we weren't concerned with Southampton but really, in my opinion, he didn't know much about anything in the game. He'd been kidding people this way for so long, but so much of what he said was wrong. All the talk about wingers was an ideal gimmick for him. In fact he was lucky; the results had gone for us but, at the end of the season, we had nothing to show for our entertainment. Okay, so we used two wingers, but Gordon Hill on the left was erratic, scoring a good goal every now and then. I always felt we were a team who could possibly flop on the day, and we did. When Docherty claimed he didn't know much about Southampton, the fact was he didn't know much about *any* team. We were labelled "the team of the future" when we were promoted that year, rather like Crystal Palace were in 1979. But the fact was that we'd developed an attacking style in the Second Division where the standard was terrible outside the first half dozen, and we simply tried to keep it going in the First Division.'

In his whirlwind passage through the managerial seats of Chelsea, Rotherham, Aston Villa, Queen's Park Rangers, Oporto, Hull, Scotland and Manchester United, Docherty had yet to pick up a major title. Certainly he had shown a capacity to motivate young players for a limited time, until the point, as with Terry Venables at Chelsea and again with Q.P.R., at which they start to think for themselves. If his Glaswegian humour was said to be razor-sharp, it was certainly capable of wounding; and it regularly did. In the day-to-day intimate relations of club football, his personality was seldom likely to create mutual trust and stability, with his profusion of transfers, in and out; and there was good reason to claim that he was 'full of sound and fury, signifying nothing'.

McMenemy talked less and thought more before the Final. He had a four-point victory plan: one, to use Nick Holmes and Gilchrist in midfield to assist full-backs Peach and Rodriguez in shutting out United's wingers, Coppell and Hill; two, for Jim McCalliog repeatedly to hit damaging, long, through balls to Channon and Stokes, to cause United anxiety in the middle of their defence and prevent them from pushing too many men forward; three, for Southampton to play early, first-time passes, contrary to their normal style, because of United's renowned tenacity in tackling back; four, never to waste four men defending against two at the back, but to defend in numbers whenever United had possession, even into their opponents' half, in the knowledge that United's short-passing system could be shut down.

Channon recalls: 'We rated ourselves very highly. People tend to forget that the previous season, United had been in the Second Division with us; we had two tight games with them and knew we could match them. I felt beforehand that we had the old heads, that they didn't have half the experience we did.'

In the first quarter of an hour, United missed two fine chances. First Coppell went off at speed on the right wing and hit a good cross-shot which Turner in Southampton's goal failed to catch cleanly. He succeeded only in pushing the ball out a few yards in front of him, where Pearson and Macari both reacted slowly on the six-yard line. Then Hill, who was dangerous only for the first half, made a perfect opening for Daly but, from eight yards, he shot weakly. On another occasion, when Hill was clean through, the ball bounced awkwardly: he attempted a lob as Turner came off his line but the keeper caught the ball brilliantly at close range and this proved to be a save which inspired Southampton.

They began to open out, and the intention of closing down United's inter-passing began to work. Now United were repeatedly caught offside and, with Southampton's left-back Peach attacking down the left, there were the first qualms for United and their supporters. Southampton's counter-attacking through Channon and Osgood began to click; McCalliog was finding time and space. Stepney in United's goal had to make his first real save, rushing out to smother a shot from Channon.

With the start of the second half, it was obvious that United had lost their usual rhythm. Hill and Coppell had been checked and Channon remembers: 'After five minutes of the second half, I was looking at Lou Macari and I could tell he was anxious, that United's confidence had gone. I said to Ossie, "Keep going, I know we won't lose this one, just keep playing till we nick one." ' Shortly afterwards, Coppell made a chance for Pearson but, taking a difficult ball on the turn, Pearson flashed his shot wide. McIlroy headed against the crossbar, from a corner by Coppell nodded back by Macari but, increasingly, it looked as if extra-time would be necessary. Then, with only seven minutes to go, Southampton scored.

Bobby Stokes, whose otherwise largely inconspicuous career was about to have its one moment of indelible glory, had just shot wildly over the bar—one of many inaccurate shots in an inaccurate match. But now he raced on to a perfect through pass from McCalliog. Momentarily, he thought he was offside, and so did United's defence. But his pace carried him clear of Buchan and, as he faced Stepney from an angle on the left, he hit a cross shot which crept just inside the far right-hand post. Stepney, who had so little else to do, remembers: 'Bobby didn't strike it all that well, but it bounced just before it reached me. That often kills the goalkeeper. If he'd struck it right, cleanly, I think I'd probably have got it. The only other real save I had to make was in the first half when I'd come out to block Mike Channon.'

Southampton calmly played out the remaining seven minutes, and television subsequently showed that referee Clive Thomas and his linesman had allowed Stokes to go through from a close but onside position correctly. Stokes, who would

never experience anything like it again and who, within a
short time, was playing in the Fourth Division, said modestly:
'Okay, I got the goal, but give credit to the old men in the
side', a comment which made his manager observe: 'The
modesty and the homespun image of the club has worked its
way into the players' bones.' Not the least irony was that Stokes,
during the previous six weeks, had had a nightmare of a time,
rarely hitting the target. Channon recalls: 'All the betting
shops were giving odds on who might score the winner, and
I remember Hughie Fisher, our midfield player, saying, "I'd
like to back Bobby" simply because he was having such a lean
spell and had to score sooner or later.'

With this result, McMenemy had arrived as a manager.
From then on, his name would be linked with almost every
important managerial post which became available but, probably wisely, he resisted temptations and remained with
Southampton, guiding them back to the First Division and a
League Cup Final in 1979. He said after this famous victory
in 1976:

'It would be utterly wrong to suggest that this was simply
a defeat for flair by organization, that our victory will in
some way turn English soccer in the wrong direction, away
from United's exciting leadership. The whole point is that
we are also a flair team. But we had the more flexible attitude, did our homework, organized ourselves and proved the
value of it on the day. Osgood, McCalliog . . . these are flair
players. And Mike Channon sees only his intentions in the
last third of the field. I could argue he should be more
organized. If United had had somebody to hit the forty-
yard cross-field pass, they could have used Hill much more
in the first twenty minutes but, by then, we were completely
adjusted to our new tactics. We were the side with the bad
defensive record, but we showed we could adapt, and Jim
Steele and David Peach were outstanding. McCalliog's long
passes were a vital factor, even if five out of seven did not
find their mark. Those who didn't give us a chance didn't
know enough about us. We're a team playing First Division
football in the Second Division. That's been our problem,
because it doesn't necessarily get you out of the Second
Division.'

In the matter of propaganda, McMenemy conceded little to Docherty when he put his mind to it. The important difference was that McMenemy stayed nearer to the facts. Southampton didn't get out of the Second Division the next season. Only four teams, including promoted Wolves, Chelsea and Nottingham Forest, scored more than Southampton's seventy-two goals, but only three teams conceded more than their sixty-seven goals. United went back to Wembley and won the Cup in an unexpected victory over Liverpool with a winning goal which came off Jimmy Greenhoff's shoulder. As Macari says: 'You can disregard the F.A. Cup as a guide to good teams!'

Southampton: Turner; Rodriguez, Blyth, Steele, Peach; Gilchrist, McCalliog, Holmes; Channon, Osgood, Stokes

Manchester United: Stepney; Forsyth, Greenhoff, Buchan, Houston; Daly, Macari; Coppell, Pearson, McIlroy, Hill

CHAPTER NINETEEN

Italy 1

v

England 6

WORLD CUP

1976

*Don Revie, under mounting public pressure, selects a
World Cup team which even the players believe is
crazy. A deflected goal seals the result.*

How was it that after two years as England manager, with
the experience of all his years at Leeds, with his profound
knowledge of European football, Don Revie should have
selected for the match with Italy in Rome a team which the
players themselves regarded as disastrously unbalanced? Sport
being what it is, the players would not be openly critical at
the time; they had to go out and try to win the match; they
would not wish to be disloyal to colleagues or to the manager
who might remain in charge for years to come. But looking
back, nobody in the England squad at the time is in the
slightest doubt that Revie took leave of his senses.

Mike Channon, who was one of the three most experienced
members of the team, and England's only goal-scorer of any
consistency at that period, says:

'I was really surprised and, quite frankly, I didn't think it
was Revie's team. I thought it was a team thrust upon him
in bits and pieces by the press and TV. I got the feeling
he didn't really know what he wanted. Stan Bowles was

picked and he hadn't even been in the reckoning for two
and a half years—he hadn't even been in the squad. When I
first joined the England squad, I spent the first two or three
years sitting in the stand before I got into the team. He
picked Dave Clement at right-back; I think it was only
his second cap. I've seen some nervous lads in my time, but
he was an absolute bag of nerves before the start, knowing
he was up against the guy who was expected to be their
match winner, Bettega. At centre-back, with Dave Watson
out of action, Revie had the chance of one of two pairs,
McFarland and Todd, or Thompson and Hughes, but he
goes and picks McFarland and Hughes. You'd think he
would have played a pair who knew each other. The whole
thing was a bloody shambles, though I blame myself a bit;
I'd had over thirty caps by then. Brian Greenhoff played
in midfield and had all the ball for us, but it's no disrespect
to Brian to say that he was never going to win the game
for us. He was a defensive player, not a passer.'

Trevor Cherry, one of Revie's own former players from
Leeds, also found himself in midfield, with Greenhoff and
Trevor Brooking, and he admits:

'I don't think we were prepared right. You could play me
or Brian in midfield but not both of us—we were too
similar. Any team needs a settled formation to get success,
but we were anything but settled. Revie did a lot of things
that were surprising when you knew him from his Leeds
days, but I think his problem was that he never had a
platform, one really good spell with good results and, in
the end, the pressure got at him. You could tell that. We
beat Finland easily enough, but then we only just beat
Luxembourg and we knew things were a bit dodgy. A lot
was made of the dossier before the game in Rome, and my
job was to look after Antognoni, but we weren't balanced
properly. That was where we lost the qualifying chance, in
Rome. Italy were a good team but they weren't a great team.
They just had some good individuals.'

Kevin Keegan, who, even after Revie's defection to the
United Arab Emirates, retained some loyalty and could see

some of the virtues in this strange paradox of a man, says: 'We had a new back four, a new midfield, a new attack! The three of us up front, Channon, Bowles, and myself, would all be playing the same way, running off defenders, making space, going out wide. But who was going to knock 'em in?'

It is interesting that today there is such unanimous admission by the players that the team was a non-starter. One of the most depressing aspects of the two-goal defeat was that, on the charter flight back home, there was hardly a player who seemed to sense the gulf between the teams. The general view was that the team was unlucky not to *steal* a result. Such is the subjectivity of players, too, when they are under pressure. Even today, Cherry considers, 'We still might have done something if their first goal from the free kick hadn't gone in off Keegan; the Italians took a lot of confidence from that.' The use of the word 'steal' by several of the players at the time was indicative that the basic mentality of the team had been reduced, by Revie's fluctuation, to a self-confessed second-class level; that the means by which they hoped to beat top-class opposition was through stopping them from playing and then nicking a goal on the counter-attack.

Yet this was not the real, natural character of born optimists like Keegan and Channon. Some time later, Channon, no longer in the reckoning under the new regime of Ron Greenwood, admitted to me: 'That afternoon in Rome is the only time in my life I've been disappointed I was English.' How did Revie allow himself to be manoeuvred into this position in which he compounded so many mistakes? After England's final training session, on a lovely, warm October morning in the Olympic stadium, I strolled off the pitch with Revie following his announcement of the team, and ventured to say to him that I thought there were a disturbing number of changes, six from the previous game with Finland; and was he not worried by the obvious lack of integrated teamwork; a team of experienced players without collective experience? With that expression he reserved for questions he resented, as if one had just burned a hole in his new suit with a cigarette end, he replied: 'I think it's the right team to do a job on the day.' Then, and throughout his chequered three-year period as England manager, I do not think Revie realized the differences between the role of club manager and international manager, which have been well summarized by Miljan Miljanic, manager of Red Star, Real Madrid and now, once more, of the Yugoslav national side. He says:

'The club manager selects his tactics according to his players, the international manager his players according to his tactics. The club manager is less concerned than the international manager with the creative part of the game; his concern is to motivate players at regular, short intervals, even when they do not feel like playing. The international manager must use players whose character and skill does not require motivation or months of arduous collective practice. The club manager selects his players for their form on the day; the international manager has to have a long-term vision on little practice or evidence. The club manager is pragmatic; the international manager should be concerned with the broader concept.'

As Revie walked from the pitch at the finish, head and shoulders down, he was the victim as much of his own caution as of the shortage of world-class players generated by a decade of over-emphasis on the physical aspects of the game, a trend promoted as much by himself as by others such as Bill Shankly, Don Howe and Alf Ramsey. Revie had attempted to reach the comparative sanctuary of the second leg at Wembley the following autumn with a team which, in Rome, consisted largely of tacklers. There is not the slightest doubt in my mind that Italy in Rome were a vulnerable team. Their fear was as great as England's and, had Revie sent his side into the game with a more positive attitude and with some sort of consistency of selection, there is every chance that they would have taken one point if not two. Ron Greenwood showed what could be done, abandoning caution in the return leg; and even though England then had home advantage, and though Italy could afford to lose and still be able to qualify by scoring the necessary goals against Luxembourg, the frailty of the Italians' morale was evident from the way they panicked and began to foul at Wembley. One of the key men in that England performance was Wilkins yet, for the match in Rome, Wilkins, having played in the previous match against Finland, was not even in the squad! In the space of six consecutive matches at this time, Revie used six different left-backs, five different right-backs, and seven different centre-backs. Truly this was the ultimate in straw snatching. By comparison, Enzo Bearzot, the Italian manager, had used a team containing seven members of the Juventus side which had eliminated Manchester City and Manchester United from European competition that season.

Certainly there were some mitigating circumstances for Revie's extraordinary mismanagement of England in general and the Rome match in particular. There were long-term injuries to key players such as Bell, Gerry Francis, Madeley, McFarland, Beattie and Thompson, while several outstandingly skilful players such as Hudson, Currie and George proved unreliable. England were scandalously kicked out of the European Championship in Bratislava by the Czechs' exploitation of a weak referee. But these difficulties were accentuated by Revie's unending change of policy on the use of target strikers, wingers, and defensive marking systems (as is evident from the use of fifty-two players in twenty-nine matches). His obsession with the quality of the opposition, the reliance on dossiers, was confusing and inhibiting, and he failed to advance the international experience of such players as Trevor Francis, Wilkins and Steve Coppell early enough. He believed that international players could be manipulated and controlled hour by hour, the same as club players. Even with a club team this can prove repressive; with an international team, it is impossible. To manipulate the characters whom it is necessary to have in an international team contradicts the objective. A lion taught to jump through a hoop is no longer a lion.

It was no more than predictable in Rome that the first goal by Antognoni, after thirty-six minutes, which finally liberated Italy from their fear, came from one of the many free kicks conceded around the penalty area by Roy McFarland and his defenders. In this instance it was Cherry, attempting to halt the endlessly elusive, probing, precisely-coiffured little Causio, who always looks as if he has stepped straight out of a tailor's window. From about twenty-two yards, Causio gave a short ball to Antognoni. The England wall broke up too soon as they attempted to charge down the kick, and Antognoni's shot was deflected by Keegan past a helpless Ray Clemence.

Football is essentially a passing game, but other than the

elegant Brooking, a player who, on his day, has all the grace
and vision of a Beckenbauer, the players who could pass the ball
were sitting at home or on the bench. The front line of
Channon, Bowles and Keegan never really functioned except
when Bowles demonstrated, briefly during the second half,
what he might have achieved with better support from midfield. Twice in a few minutes, with half an hour to go, England
created openings to level the match. First Bowles drew three
men on the right and slipped the ball to Channon, who went
round Tardelli, was tripped but recovered his balance. Yet
referee Abraham Klein from Israel, the best in the business
and specially appointed for this game because of his neutrality
and firm control, halted the play for a free kick, with Channon
dangerously positioned only twelve yards from goal with the
ball at his feet. Then Greenhoff, meeting a cross by Channon
on the half-volley, shot wide.

As Keegan recalled in his biography, *Against The World*,
Greenhoff was the one player the Italians would be happy to let
have the ball. 'England's team that day was the worst technical
error of Revie's life.' Keegan also highlighted the fact that
England had taken a turn down the wrong road with players
like Stiles and Storey, that the Continent had developed hard
men, powerful in the tackle, who could also play creatively,
such as Bonhof of Germany and Tardelli and Benetti, both in
that Italian team in Rome.

Italy's second goal again stemmed from Causio, who had
drifted over to the left. He sent Benetti away on an overlap, and
his cross from the line was met by Bettega, bursting through
the defence at great speed to take the ball with a waist-high,
full-length dive. England were out, and very much down.
Kevin Beattie, that robust Ipswich defender who, at one time,
had been such a wonderfully athletic and powerful prospect
but whose career was wrecked by injury, was sent out to
replace Clement, but he could do nothing to tip the scales
back England's way. It was another reflection of England's
whole approach to the match that they had begun time-wasting
in the first half!

Revie was left with ten matches in which to find a formula
before the return with Italy at Wembley, plus the slim hope
that Finland might possibly take a point in their home tie with
Italy the following June. Yet, in the next match, Revie got it

badly wrong again, selecting a team with another two centre-backs, Watson and Doyle of Manchester City, both stopper centre-halves, against a Dutch team whom he must have known played without a central-striker! He made no special plan to mark Cruyff, in the way Germany had put Vogts on him in the World Cup Final; and he dropped Channon. Holland duly won with two goals by Jan Peters, and joined Hungary (1953), Sweden (1959), Austria (1965), West Germany (1972) and Italy (1973) as foreign victors at Wembley. As Bearzot, watching from the stands, remarked afterwards: 'In three vital matches, in New York, Rome and London, England have played different teams with a different method!'

And there were more to come. Against Luxembourg at Wembley, back came the touch players, Ray Kennedy and Gordon Hill, with a reversion also to the use of a target-striker, Royle. In the British championship the following spring, for the first time ever, England lost to Wales and Scotland at Wembley and Revie's credibility was rock-bottom. Needing to build a team to score a hat-full of goals away to Luxembourg in the autumn, for the remote chance of qualifying on goal difference, Revie selected a drab, negative team for three defensive draws on tour in Brazil, Argentina and Uruguay—having in the meantime secretly negotiated his deal with the Arabs. It was a shoddy end to an unhappy phase in England's soccer history.

Italy: Zoff; Cuccureddu, Gentile, Facchetti, Tardelli; Causio, Antognoni, Benetti; Capello, Graziani, Bettega

England: Clemence; Clement (Beattie), McFarland, Hughes, Mills; Greenhoff, Cherry, Brooking; Channon, Bowles, Keegan

CHAPTER TWENTY

Liverpool 3

v

Borussia München-Gladbach 1

EUROPEAN CUP FINAL

1977

Borussia, the tacticians of European soccer, decide to play negatively against Liverpool, and pay the price —thanks to a rare, headed goal by Tommy Smith.

Only eleven clubs have won the European Cup in twenty-five years, and England are the only country to produce three different teams to do so: Manchester United, Liverpool and Nottingham Forest. That is something of which we can be proud. Those three can rightly claim that they compare with some of the greatest club sides the game has seen on either side of the Atlantic. Yet in an arbitrary ranking list of the eleven clubs, necessarily reflecting my own personal view and preferences, I would not place any of England's trio in the top three. Moreover, I think that while Liverpool have a unique record in *all* European competitions over a sixteen-year period—twice European Cup winners, twice U.E.F.A. Cup winners, Cup-Winners Cup runners-up—they were somewhat lucky when they took the senior trophy for the first time in Rome.

My ranking list would be: 1. Real Madrid (1956-60, 1966); 2. Ajax (1971, 1973); 3. Benfica (1961-62); 4. Bayern (1974-76); 5. Liverpool (1977-78) and Celtic (1967); 7. Internazionale (1964-65); 8. Milan (1963, 1969); 9. Feyenoord (1970); 10. Manchester United (1968); and 11. Nottingham Forest (1979-80).

Of course, it is always a difficult exercise attempting to compare different eras. All a team can hope to do is be top of the pile at the time they happen to be playing; and who is to say that Nottingham Forest's defensive qualities might not have frustrated the great Real Madrid? All I can say is that, having seen them all, and making my judgement on a basis of team-work *and* individual quality, there is an apparent downward trend if we are to measure the game by its overall appeal to the public. Of course, distance lends enchantment: there is a tendency in all judgements in all walks of life to say that things 'ain't what they used to be'. But it is hard not to argue that this is so in soccer.

The positions from fifth onwards, I accept, can be seen as arbitrary to some extent, but there can be little dispute about the first four. Real, admittedly, extravagantly fortified by the import of Di Stefano, Puskas, Kopa, Santamaria and others, won the title six times in eight finals; Ajax three times in four; Benfica twice in five; Bayern three times in three. We can never know what the fortunes of Manchester United might have been but for the Munich crash and, by the time they eventually won the Cup, their team was a pale shadow of its predecessor.

Liverpool, it will always be argued, were cheated out of a place in the Final in 1965 by a Spanish referee who allowed Inter two most questionable goals, but my opinion would be that it was a superior Liverpool side which faced Borussia in Rome thirteen years later. Yet Kevin Keegan, who was the focal point, indeed the mastermind of a famous victory, now admits: 'Borussia were not what they should have been, definitely not what we expected them to be. If they'd played consistently as they did for a twenty minute spell in the second half, Lord knows which way the result would have gone. It's fair to say we caught them on an off-day, though it's an old adage in the game that you only play as well as you're allowed to.'

In the same way that West Ham had come to be regarded, under Ron Greenwood's direction, as something of an academy in England, a continuing example of how the game should be played—for all their lack of tangible success—so

Borussia in Germany, under the direction of Henness Weisweiler, were the copy-book team over a sustained period. They played in four European finals, twice winning the U.E.F.A. Cup, losing the 1973 final to Liverpool as well as losing in 1977 in Rome.

Helmut Schoen, a dispassionate judge of performance whatever nationality was involved, is informative on the game in Rome:

> 'The Borussia team had too great a respect for Liverpool. The reputation of Liverpool's qualities of endurance and stamina had a great impact on other teams in Europe. On this occasion, the Borussia team was not sure of itself and did not play its natural game, which has always been to attack. But they played slowly, which was not the *real* Borussia. They scored a wonderful goal with Simonsen, but they did not have the personality of former years, there was no Gunter Netzer, and Weisweiler had been gone for almost two years. Liverpool's great strength was their teamwork; the personality of the team was the team itself. They had no single great player in the old traditions of the European Cup. Keegan was the personification of the quality of the team, such a wonderful example of professionalism and effort, and that is why the people of Germany loved him during his three years at Hamburg. He appealed to our national character, and he is always on the move, but he is not really a strategist, he is not a Beckenbauer or a Cruyff, a play-maker. You cannot compare him with Bobby Charlton, yet any team would be delighted to have such a player.'

Liverpool travelled to Italy only forty-eight hours after an emotionally draining reversal at Wembley in the F.A. Cup Final. Wembley, for a change, had been magical on the occasion of this national event. Millions of viewers around the world had witnessed a piece of theatre which was spellbinding. Two of England's three most famous clubs (Arsenal being the third) had staged a Final which put sportsmanship back into football; but grown men had cried as Liverpool surrendered not only their chance of the Treble but the domestic Double in a result as fascinating as it was perverse. Manchester United, outplayed for forty-five minutes, had won when it seemed that Liverpool had blocked every avenue to victory.

Stuart Pearson and Lou Macari shot down the Treble but Liverpool, like modern Corinthians, yielded with a pride and dignity which was matched by their remarkable supporters.

The passion on the terraces could not have been more committed, but there was tolerance and humour from both red armies of followers. The 1977 Final would be remembered for its dignity, for a return to sanity by those for whom the game had supplanted religion. John Mortimer, lawyer and playwright, had written the previous week: 'Sport brings out the very worst in people. I have sympathy for football hooligans because the game is so dull.' Bill Shankly, that fanatical Scot who forged the foundations, and many of the triumphs, of Liverpool's enduring years of success, must accept, besides his share of the praise, a portion of the blame for the degeneration of football ethics. His oft-quoted but mindless remark, 'people say football is a matter of life and death, but it's more important than that', gave impetus to the lunatic fringe. That 1977 Final at Wembley brought out the best in people, in victory and defeat. The lessons of Wembley were the lessons of life: that nothing can be taken for granted.

That must have rested heavily on Liverpool's mind as they set off to Rome. Somehow Bob Paisley, Shankly's lieutenant across the years, and now his able successor, needed to recharge the morale of his beaten troops. Ian Callaghan, veteran of thirteen European seasons, who had only come on as substitute at Wembley, was the man likely to revitalize Liverpool, whose objective in Rome needed to be to control the game, not to gamble.

At Wembley, Liverpool had used a 4-3-3 formation: the return of Callaghan would mean a switch to 4-4-2. Callaghan, at thirty-five, would be the oldest player on the field by three years. In the heat of Rome, Liverpool's policy would have to be one of containment and patience. Borussia, although past their peak, still possessed some formidable players and the sting would need to be drawn from their game. Vogts, Wimmer, and Heynckes might be over thirty, but Bonhof and the brilliant Stielike, shortly to be transferred to Real Madrid, were in their prime. Perhaps not many people in England were fully conscious of the quality of the Germans.

Callaghan, whose career spanned the whole of the Liverpool era in European football, following their promotion from the Second Division in 1962, had played only twice for England, the last time against France in the first round of the 1966 World Cup. Yet he epitomized what football means by 'a players' player', the model professional dedicated to the objectives of the team, and he was the prime exponent of the possession game developed by Liverpool on continental lines. In earlier years, he had been a key figure in the use of John Toshack's skill in the air on crosses from both flanks, with Keegan fastening on to the knock-downs; now Toshack was gone and Keegan's role was radically altered. As Keegan says: 'For us to play four in midfield was not usual; we'd always had three up front, Steve Heighway, Tosh, and myself, and it was only when Tosh became injured that we started to think about playing only two up front.'

Although the pride and the passion which are Liverpool's were instilled by Shankly, it is my belief that Bob Paisley brought a greater balance and *wisdom* to the team. The perfection of Liverpool's possession game took place under Paisley; it was he who made them even better equipped for the European arena. Shankly's Liverpool, such a powerhouse, always had a slightly frenzied air at home, and if one could pinpoint the quality developed by Paisley, it would be patience. It is also a fact that, under Paisley, Liverpool became less physical. Over the years, Shankly had condoned and even encouraged an element of aggression bordering on violence which had helped set the tone in England during the misguided, post-1966 period. When holding court, which he did whenever there was a willing audience of even one, it was well known for Shankly to denigrate some of the more skilful players in other teams who lacked the commitment to withstand the Liverpool softening-up process. Shankly extended the intimidation on the field to television and radio, all part of the process of Anfield propaganda. Paisley talked less but was every bit as shrewd.

Before the game in Rome, Paisley admitted: 'If we hadn't been faced with a possibility of a delayed F.A. Cup Final replay in June, I would have started with this 4-4-2 team at Wembley. But we didn't want to risk wrecking the players' holidays after the stress they've been through this season, so we decided to be marginally more positive—and we lost. But that's life, and now we're in the mood to make up for that disappointment.' Paisley had three strikers on the bench in case Liverpool needed to come from behind—Fairclough,

Johnson and Toshack. Only in a desperate gamble would the less than fit Toshack be used.

Paisley said that he expected to use thirteen men and did not mention an unseen fourteenth—tactical scout Tom Saunders, who had watched Borussia four times, including the 2-2 draw away to Bayern shortly beforehand. Liverpool knew just what they were up against—the team which had just retained the German League title and had defeated both Torino and Bruges in the away leg on the way to Rome. In my preview in the *Express* the morning of the match, I wrote: 'My head tells me Borussia should win by two goals. My heart suggests that Liverpool can just possibly nick it by one goal if they wear the Germans down.'

In the event, Liverpool went out to crown thirteen years' endeavour with a blend of Olympian effort and deadly passing which surpassed anything they had produced before. They paralyzed Borussia, to banish the suggestion that the English had forgotten how to play the game. It was a team performance as good as that with which Celtic became Britain's first winners, ten years before. The team factor was even more important than the story-book goal by the thirty-two-year-old Tommy Smith, Liverpool's second goal and the most critical of the match, in the sixty-fifth minute. It was a fitting climax in his 600th game for the club; he was another survivor from the losing semi-final in 1965. But if Smith's goal was the blow which broke Borussia's resistance, the key which unlocked the door was Keegan's brilliant subjugation of Vogts.

Borussia's manager Udo Lattek's plan was to eliminate Keegan by rigid man-for-man marking in the way that Vogts had subdued Cruyff in the World Cup Final. Yet with a quite exceptional performance, which heralded his emergence as the leading player in Europe, Keegan exploited Vogts' marking to Liverpool's advantage. He dragged him all over the field, yet was always available to receive the ball when Liverpool were ready to push forward from midfield. He was constantly involved in the development of moves, to the exclusion of Vogts who was left trailing some two or three yards adrift. Keegan recalls:

'It wasn't really decided beforehand that I would play this way, but it was no secret that Berti would play on me, and no secret that he was not what he had been two years before. He'd got to the stage where real pace scared him, and sometimes I was able to pull him into really odd positions. But he's a wonderful sportsman. He came round to see me after the match and we had some champagne together. I don't think I could ever have done that if we'd lost. I've talked to Berti several times since I went to Germany about that match, about why they didn't play up to expectations.'

Keegan's performance sealed his £400,000 transfer from Liverpool to Hamburg.

Liverpool began as if Saturday's defeat at Wembley had never happened. Endlessly, they made the Germans cover and run. They totally controlled the game for the first half, except for one breakaway by Bonhof in the twenty-third minute, when he hit the post. Five minutes later, Liverpool were in front. Terry McDermott, who had been sold gladly by Newcastle, had developed from an erratic tearaway into one of the most intelligent and dangerous midfield players in the game with his relentless blind-side runs. It was now one of these runs over all of forty yards which put him precisely on the end of a clever move between Callaghan and Heighway and, with a flourish, he lashed the ball past international goalkeeper Kneib.

But Liverpool's authority stumbled in the fifty-second minute. Jimmy Case misdirected a headed back-pass and Allan Simonsen drove the equalizer past Ray Clemence. For a while, Liverpool were in real trouble: Clemence had to rush off his line to dive at the feet of Stielike when he burst through the middle. But, with twenty-five minutes to go, Heighway took a corner on the left and Smith, thundering in on the near post, headed a rare goal to restore Liverpool's command. From then on, their march was again relentless. Their victory required one more breathtaking save by Clemence at the feet of Heynckes, and then the result was put beyond doubt when a wearying Vogts brought down Keegan and Phil Neal scored from the penalty spot.

It was an inspired performance which demonstrated that England could regain the World Cup if only they could emulate such a combination of skill and teamwork. Skipper Emlyn Hughes said afterwards: 'Kevin Keegan has played all season with his mind elsewhere yet he has still given 110 per cent. The difference now was that Kevin was mentally right with us again; he wanted to play for us more than ever before, as well as for himself, and the result was fantastic.'

What surprised foreign observers from Spain to Sweden was the sophistication of Liverpool's tactics, the use of forward passes by Ray Kennedy, Callaghan and McDermott, as well as by full-backs Neal and Joey Jones, hit so as to turn the German defenders all the time—even if Borussia produced the game's best two moves. What Liverpool had established more than anything was that they possessed the same attitude as the Wales rugby fifteen: that other teams might occasionally score more points, but nobody ever beat them! Paisley, flushed with triumph, said afterwards: 'We slowed the game down to our pace. That allows greater expression of skills, and would be a good thing also for the game at national level. The second goal by Smith was the turning point. It completely put us in command. For the team to come back as it did after the equalizer was tremendous. We had seventeen games in six weeks, so this was a remarkable performance.'

Tommy Smith was so delighted that he even relented on his promise to throw me into the hotel swimming pool and we drank a bottle of champagne instead—the burying of a hatchet which went back three years to the time I had suggested that he was in decline. This was shortly before he was dropped by Shankly for the first time and the *Express* ran the unflattering headline, *Derby Bury Smith Myth*. Smith may have been many things, not all of them virtuous, but myth he was certainly not. Now he had done his team and himself proud, but much of the praise should go to Paisley. As Keegan says: 'After Shankly, Bob let the ship sail on, he didn't want to change things, to make it suddenly "my" team, the way a Docherty or an Allison might have done. Bob let things tick over, the changes were small and the pattern remained the same.'

Liverpool: Clemence; Neal, Smith, Hughes, Jones; Case, Callaghan, McDermott, Kennedy; Keegan, Heighway

Borussia: Kneib; Klinkhammer, Vogts, Wittkamp, Schaffer; Wohlers, Wimmer, Bonhof, Stielike; Simonsen, Heynckes

CHAPTER TWENTY-ONE

4Liverpool 0

v

0Nottingham Forest 1

LEAGUE CUP FINAL

1978

Phil Thompson commits a foul outside the penalty area, the referee judges it inside—and the Brian Clough legend gathers momentum.

Whatever your opinion of Brian Clough—and opinions cover all extremes and many shades in between—there is no denying the phenomenal success of this eccentric manager together with his assistant Peter Taylor. Their record with both Derby and Nottingham Forest allows no room for argument. While Liverpool are indisputably the most successful club of the era, indeed of any English era, what Clough and Taylor have done, twice, is to lift a team of questionable quality out of the Second Division, turn them into League Champions and make them a force in Europe in double quick time. If one is to look for one single achievement which epitomizes their success, it is the lifting of the Football League Cup in the same season that Forest won the League title for the first time in the club's 113-year history, in the first year after promotion.

Many people have attempted to define the Clough formula. What makes it difficult is that in so many ways he is a contradiction of those qualities which he demands from his teams. He is fanatical about discipline and self-discipline, yet over the years his own conspicuous lack of the latter has led him at times into grave difficulties. His indiscretions have been mostly the result of verbal arrogance, but have been nonetheless alarming for that. He expects his players to be dedicated team-men, and is himself immensely loyal to them; yet he is the most notable eccentric individualist in the game. He severely restricts the freedom of his players to talk to the press and television; yet is the most volatile of all talkers, believing implicitly in the absolute freedom of his own speech at all times, a belief which was at the root of his split with, and departure from, Derby. He was an exceptional centre-forward with Middlesbrough and Sunderland, scoring almost a goal a game in 300 League matches before a severe knee injury cut short his career; yet the success of his teams are built on the defensive premise of 'clean sheets', of which he is forever reminding people. That premise was the underlying factor that contributed to the remarkable win over Liverpool in 1978.

Forest had scraped their way out of the Second Division ten months earlier, in third place behind Wolves and Chelsea, one point ahead of Bolton, and conceding only forty-three goals in forty-two games. They had been competent without being particularly impressive, and I had predicted that they would just about hold their own in the First Division. Then Clough and Taylor had pulled off an important coup, buying Peter Shilton from Stoke, further reinforcing the side with dynamic little Archie Gemmill, their original bargain buy from Preston when they were at Derby, and David Needham, the big Q.P.R. defender. They were also reunited with John McGovern and John O'Hare, who had dutifully followed Clough from Hartlepool to Derby and then Leeds and, at the start of the First Division season, they made the bold purchase of Kenny Burns, the wild Scot from Birmingham. Burns at that time was as liable to kick his own colleagues as the opposition, but within months Clough and Taylor not only harnessed his temperament, but converted him from an erratic, attacking player into the most resolute and reliable sweeper in the country. That alone was an exceptional tribute to their man-management. Other than Shilton, a goalkeeper of unrivalled international class, the team consisted of bits-and-pieces until Clough and Taylor welded them into a quite remarkable unit.

Early in January, 1978, with Forest already striding out impressively in the League, Clough had told me:

'I would sacrifice victory tomorrow against Arsenal, or in any two of the three domestic competitions we're still in, if that would guarantee us a place in Europe next season. The challenge of Europe is the most important of all, because I'm sick and tired of being told how good the continentals are. Every manager, every player in England is burdened by the failure to qualify for the last two World Cups, which I believe was Don Revie's fault the last time. Peter Taylor and I believe that we are the best in the business in England, and we'd like to prove that we are the best in Europe. It is another dimension, the next step up. It broadens the players, the management, the administration of any club. It is because of fourteen years' experience in Europe that Liverpool, in my opinion, are our biggest threat in the Championship. They have savoured, survived and conquered—played the Europeans at their own game and won. Peter and I had only one season in Europe with Derby, but I like to think that it is to our credit that we reached the European Cup semi-final. We are confident we can beat Arsenal tomorrow, and go on to win the Championship, but the challenge of Europe must be Forest's biggest objective.'

Here were Forest with visions of the treble—League, League Cup and F.A. Cup—made possible by the corrosive, collective running which epitomized England in 1966, Celtic in 1967 and Liverpool in 1977. Their secret was no real secret at all—just that the same fundamental qualities were possessed by all those three teams: unrelenting work-rate and accuracy. In addition, Forest possessed a tactical sophistication which Alf Ramsey had had when achieving the same double in successive seasons—promotion and the League title. In both cases, that sophistication had been embodied in a shrewd, elusive, deep-lying Scottish left-winger who was the tactical axis of the team: Jimmy Leadbetter for Ramsey, John Robertson for Clough. Forest's running was phenomenal but, as they approached the League Cup semi-final against Leeds, who at that time were playing with conviction, there was doubt about Forest's ability to survive without Shilton, Needham and Gemmill, who were all Cup-tied and ineligible. Yet Forest surged into the Final with a brilliant display at Elland Road which reduced Leeds to rubble.

Liverpool arrived at the Final as European Cup-holders and with an unparalleled record of sustained success. For them, as ever, it had been a heavy season as they pursued Forest in the League, fought their way towards a second consecutive European final and, for the first time, the League Cup Final. They knew that they would have to draw on past experience as much as present strength to overcome upstarts Forest. Ray Kennedy, a veteran of three trophy 'doubles', with Arsenal in 1971 and Liverpool in 1976 and 1977, was well aware that his team had their backs to the wall at Wembley when he told me:

'Wembley always provides its own motivation, and we have no worries that we won't rise to the occasion, even though we failed against Manchester United last season in the F.A. Cup. Whatever Forest have, we have the experience. But it's no secret that the end of the season cannot come soon enough for some of us, especially the international players who regularly clock up over sixty matches a season. Fortunately, there is no England tour this summer so, after the European Cup Final, we hope, we can switch off and have an extended rest for the first time in three years. As Bob Paisley said, we've played at our peak perhaps only half a dozen times this season. Now we've got to raise ourselves for just four more big matches: this Saturday, the two legs of the European semi-final and then, optimistically, the final, back at Wembley again.'

Forest were without a single player with Wembley experience, and much would depend on how they reacted in the first five or six minutes. So many inexperienced teams in the past have 'frozen' when exposed to Wembley's magnifying scrutiny. Liverpool's players had all been through the psychological mangle before and had come through unscathed. But how would Chris Woods, the youngest goalkeeper to play in a Wembley final, react to his surroundings? Only eighteen, he was deputy for Shilton and, though a member of the England Under-21 side, his two semi-finals against Leeds had been his first big-match experiences and his handling at Wembley would be vital. Even Clough, on the face of it, was not particularly optimistic.

Though he was secretly delighted to have thrashed Leeds,

the club which lost its nerve and sacked him after only forty-four days as its manager, he knew that Liverpool was another matter. Not only were Forest denied three ineligible players, but left-back Colin Barrett was injured and there was a serious doubt about the fitness of skipper John McGovern, who had a nagging groin strain.

Clough at this stage seemed more concerned with clinching the League title: no manager since Herbert Chapman in the thirties had achieved this with different clubs. On the eve of the final Clough told me:

'The cash from reaching the Final gives us the chance to compete financially with the Liverpools for the next ten years, the chance to buy another Gemmill, Woodcock, Shilton or Needham. In one fell swoop, we shall nearly clear the cost this season of Burns and Shilton. What we've done at Forest so far is merely to prepare for the time when we can reap the harvest. These are just the first signs, like crocuses in spring.'

Though one may deplore Clough's brashness at times, one has to admire his confidence. Within another year, he was to pay a million for Trevor Francis and win the European Cup. Now he continued:

'Our game against Middlesbrough next Tuesday is more important than Wembley tomorrow. When you look at the two sides, the number of times Liverpool have been at Wembley, at all their experience, then we're wasting our time going down there. We'd like to win, of course, and we think we can. One thing they won't beat us at is application and effort. To achieve the same status as Liverpool, we have to play our first final before the others can follow. It all depends on whether we can get the ball up to our front men, Woodcock and Withe, as regularly as we did in the second leg at Leeds.'

In the event, it all depended on young Woods. The contrast between the old and the new was remarkable: Ray Clemence at one end, with 334 consecutive first-team appearances for Liverpool, and Woods for Forest, never having played a single

First Division match until the previous week. Let off in the opening seconds when Kenny Dalglish delayed critically before pulling a shot wide, Woods proceeded to play the game of his young life. He was as agile and confident in dealing with everything which Liverpool threw at him as Shilton might have been, as sure in extra time as in normal time. Liverpool paid dearly for that error by Dalglish after only twenty seconds; it was a chance squandered—with Terry McDermott screaming at him for the alternative square pass right in front of goal. To some extent, Liverpool limited their own resources going forward by using Jimmy Case to slot in just in front of right-back Phil Neal to confront Robertson with a double obstacle. Without the support of Gemmill and Barrett behind him, Robertson was a shadow of his normal self, and it was this one performance more than any other which misguidedly persuaded the watching Ally MacLeod not to use Robertson in the World Cup finals that summer.

The replay at Old Trafford confronted Liverpool with a serious problem. A week away from their European semi-final first leg, they could not afford to allow the League Cup to go to a third meeting as it had the previous year when Aston Villa ultimately overcame Everton. They did not even want extra-time again, following the goalless draw at Wembley, and, temporarily, they would be obliged to abandon their hallmark: patience. They would need to be more speculative, to sacrifice possession now and again with forward passes. They would have to give Case more freedom to supplement Dalglish and Steve Heighway up front. With McGovern substituted by John O'Hare at Wembley and now out of action, Liverpool could expect to control the middle of the field. The biggest threat to them, it seemed, was mental staleness. The odds, if anything, were more stacked against Forest than they had been —and it took a highly controversial goal to bring about Liverpool's downfall.

Forest's attack was no more effective at Old Trafford than it had been at Wembley, and the burden again fell on young Woods, who was as spectacularly safe as before. He was reinforced this time by a sterling performance in front of him by Kenny Burns which, more than anything, helped earn the defender the Footballer of the Year Award.

For almost the full three-and-a-half hours of the Final,

Forest were outplayed. Yet somehow their team of Central League reserves held out. Their game wasn't scientific, it was arguable whether victory was deserved, but it was gutsy in the extreme. Again, it was in the early part of the game that Woods made his vital saves, from Neal and then Dalglish. It was never really a match as Liverpool constantly poured forward, only for their attacks to break and crumble on Forest's nine- and ten-man defence. It was an experience which Liverpool were to become painfully familiar with in the following two seasons—first in the European Cup and again in the 1980 semi-final of the League Cup.

The critical moment in this historic turning of the tables came seven minutes into the second half. Veteran John O'Hare trundled through the middle, chasing a pass towards the edge of the penalty area with Phil Thompson in desperate pursuit. On and on went O'Hare, almost in slow motion like a man in a sleep walk. As he reached the eighteen-yard line, Thompson, with an ugly lunge, appeared to push and trip him simultaneously. I thought at the time that O'Hare was possibly half a yard inside, but the television evidence suggested that the foul came fractionally outside. Thompson insisted afterwards: 'I knew I was outside when I kicked him. I know it sounds bad but that is the way it was. It was a professional foul.'

If that were the case, then far from winning the sympathy of neutrals, Thompson should consider that justice was done by the decision of referee Pat Partridge, who did not have the benefit of slow-motion television cameras when making the instinctive, split-second judgement which renders any referee's responsibility so onerous. There has long been an argument that such a deliberate foul, if indeed it is inside the area, should be penalized by a penalty goal without a penalty kick even being taken. Partridge himself claimed: 'I'm in no doubt that it was a penalty. Television cameras can be at an angle. I have no doubt.'

John Robertson stepped forward to score from the kick to give Forest and Clough their first trophy in their meteoric three-season climb from the foot of the Second Division. Thompson, so vehemently incensed by the decision, said in a television interview that it was a disgrace—and subsequently found himself fined by the League for his comments. His sense of grievance, and that of all the Liverpool players, had been people of all ages, many of them who had never previously been to a football match in their lives, caught up in that tartan tide.'

Ignorant of international standards and tactics, MacLeod had quickly become intoxicated by his own publicity to the point where, before the World Cup began, he was exhibiting the same extravagant, irrational optimism as the least discerning of the fans. He fanned the flames of a conflagration which ultimately consumed both him and his team. I cannot accept that he was simply 'unlucky'.

He himself quite deliberately polarized reaction to the outcome in advance, claiming that he would return from Argentina 'a millionaire or a condemned man', would be hailed 'a hero or villain'. Such was the height to which his ego climbed that, in an excess of fantasy and bad taste he joked with the Queen, at a dinner after the Ashes had been brought home: 'With a bit of luck in the World Cup in Argentina, I might have been knighted. Instead, it looks as if I may be beheaded.'

MacLeod had taken over midway through Scotland's qualifying campaign. After a two-goal defeat in Prague and victory against Wales at Hampden, when Crystal Palace defender Ian Evans scored an own-goal, Willie Ormond, the manager in the 1974 finals, had resigned, hurt by rumours of approaches made by the Scottish F.A. to Jock Stein of Celtic behind his back. After failing to entice Stein to take over—he was due for a lucrative testimonial—the S.F.A. turned to MacLeod. Following an average career with Blackburn, with whom he had lost to Wolves in the 1960 F.A. Cup Final, MacLeod was for ten years manager of Ayr United, a team of part-timers, and had recently moved to Aberdeen.

His experience of international football was, therefore, non-existent and, even by the time the tournament began in Argentina, he had seen only a handful of international matches. It was like giving command of a Royal Navy aircraft carrier to an Aberdonian trawlerman and, inevitably, some of the blame for the ultimate debacle must lie with the men who made the appointment. However, the truth is that, from the very first moment that he accepted the job, MacLeod was hugely flattered by his unexpected elevation. And he was nothing if not confident for, within weeks of taking over a

squad already selected by Ormond for the British Champion-
ships, MacLeod was talking about 'my' team. When Scotland
beat an uncertain England team 2-1 at Wembley to win the
Championship, the illusion of grandeur had firmly taken root.

A few weeks later, a 4-2 win over a sub-standard Chilean
side when on tour in South America was hailed by MacLeod as
'world class'. Already he was applying the bellows. When
Scotland beat Czechoslovakia at Hampden in the autumn in
the most favourable circumstances—the Czechs were seriously
delayed by an air strike and arrived in Glasgow on the day of
the match by overnight train—the waves of national expectation were already reaching Waikiki proportions. Under the
benevolent eye of the Belgian referee, Rion, Scotland physically
mauled the Czechs; Jordan, Hartford and Dalglish scored the
goals in a 3-1 win, and an 85,000 crowd belligerently chorused:
'Scotland will be there.'

MacLeod continued to ride his surfboard of luck with a
flourish in the decisive qualifying tie with Wales which,
switched to Anfield in Liverpool, was more of a home game
for the Scots than the Welsh. The critical first goal came from
a penalty by Don Masson, an otherwise excellent French
referee, Wurtz, ruling that defender David Jones had handled
when television conclusively proved that it was Jordan. The
kick by Masson took Scotland to Argentina and, within a
short time, MacLeod was proclaiming: 'When we win the
World Cup on 25 June, it should be made a national Ally-
day.'

What was even more alarming than MacLeod's self-
promotion was his evident inability to appreciate the
fluctuations in form among the players available to him. By the
spring it had already become quite clear that Bruce Rioch and
Don Masson at Derby were in sharp decline; but MacLeod,
although it only subsequently became apparent, was gripped
by an unwavering loyalty to the men who had won a place in
the finals. When he announced his squad of twenty-two, Andy
Gray, the Villa striker who had been suspended after being
sent off in the qualifying tie in Prague and had therefore been
unavailable in the remaining matches, was missing, as was
the Leeds goalkeeper, David Harvey. Both would have been
the first choice of many experts. 'These are the twenty-two
who can play tactically the way I want,' insisted MacLeod, but

this confidence should have been quickly dispelled by events in the British Championship, in which Scotland drew with Ireland, then with Wales, and finally lost at home to England. None of this surprised me. I'm not being wise after the event, because I had already said on Scottish television before the England match that I had little confidence in the formation and players MacLeod was persisting with. The performances of Masson and Rioch should now have been cause for real anxiety in MacLeod's mind but, instead, the party departed for South America with a huge, stage-managed, almost hysterical send-off from the public.

Lou Macari, who was a member of the squad but not in the team, was one of those who viewed the prospects with objective misgivings. When Scotland finally fell apart out in Argentina, Macari was one of those who voiced his feelings in a national newspaper, criticism for which he was subsequently 'suspended from consideration for selection in the future'. But Macari had seen the danger signs long before and, as we flew back to England from Glasgow, following victory for Ron Greenwood's team by Steve Coppell's late, sneaked goal, Macari told me: 'If we give away as many free kicks as we did today, we will put tremendous pressure on our defence, because the Latin Americans are so skilful with their free kicks.' What was even more disturbing was Macari's insight into the mentality of the manager. There was much controversy at the time over MacLeod's continuing preference for Joe Jordan, Macari's Manchester United colleague who had scored only a handful of international goals in half a dozen seasons, rather than Derek Johnstone, the big Rangers man who had hit forty goals that season. Macari said unequivocally: 'MacLeod will not select Johnstone because, if Johnstone succeeded, then it would prove that MacLeod had been wrong up to now.' This opinion was to be borne out by events.

MacLeod had not watched Peru, but he had a video-tape of them and abundant second-hand information. He knew, or he should have known, that Peru's wingers Munante and Oblitas were among the most dangerous in the finals. However, when he came to pick his team, MacLeod confronted them with two inexperienced full-backs: young Stuart Kennedy, his own former player from Aberdeen who had only three caps, preferred to Sandy Jardine with thirty-three, and, out of position at left-back and deputizing for the suspended Willie Donachie, Martin Buchan. The choice of Buchan was doubly ill-advised. Not only did it remove Buchan's intelligent reading of the game from the centre of defence, but exposed his lack of speed against the flying Munante.

Inevitably, the midfield was once again Rioch, Masson and Hartford, whilst the men in form with their clubs throughout the season were ignored: Archie Gemmill of League champions Nottingham Forest, Graham Souness of European champions Liverpool, and Lou Macari. Jordan, sure enough, was preferred to Johnstone. On the left flank was Willie Johnston, who was briefed by MacLeod beforehand: 'You are the man we expect to do the business, to get round the back of Peru's defence and supply the ammunition for Jordan and Dalglish.' Yet few professionals in Scotland or England would not have argued that the better man for just that job was John Robertson, the key tactical figure alongside Gemmill in Forest's spectacular triumph. There was a ready-made left-wing partnership, inexplicably ignored. It could be said, without exaggeration, that the only two players who took the field against Peru whose selection was unchallenged were Tom Forsyth, the Rangers' stopper, and Kenny Dalglish. MacLeod could hardly have got it more wrong. It would have made more sense, for example, to have played the versatile sweeper, Burns, at left-back with Buchan in the middle, particularly as MacLeod himself later recalled, discussing Buchan's injury during the second match against Iran: 'As long as Buchan was there marshalling things at the back, we had never really been in any danger.'

The uncertainty of the selection was made no better by a background of controversy during the days of countdown: unsettling rows over money, over the inadequate training camp at Alta Gracia, over an appalling practice pitch. Wild rumours in both the Scottish and foreign press of indiscipline and even drunkenness among the Scottish players, most of it totally untrue, had all added to the mood of instability . . . at the centre of which was the fundamental factor that the bulk of the players had no faith in their manager.

Back home, the nation of five million, with its historical inferiority complex, had pumped itself so full of the adrenalin of expectation that balanced judgement had long gone out of the window. Scotland were the greatest. That was what they wanted to believe; it was what MacLeod had encouraged them to believe. 'We shall finish in at least third place.' Perhaps Alan Sharp, the Scottish novelist, had summed up the link between football and the national character when he had written:

'Against Brazil [in 1974], it was possible to believe that we had taken that step forward beyond our intense infantilism, our terror of being found out. "Found out!" There's an epitaph for you. I have lived all my life waiting for that dread moment when they'll see what I'm really like, not what I claim I'm like. We're all Calvinists, doomed forever to pretend elitism while endlessly dreading discovery of the pretence.'

Once again Scotland were about to discover the pretence.

The game with Peru went well enough at the start. On a warm evening in Cordoba's gleaming new stadium, Scotland played with a degree of cohesion which was encouraging. Early on, Hartford, put through by Dalglish, went close. Masson, played in behind the defence by Jordan's header, shot at goal-keeper Quiroga. Jordan, bustling through on the left, was brought down on the corner of the penalty area by Velasquez. Peru were, if anything, the less at ease. After eight minutes Masson, put through by Hartford and Rioch, again shot at Quiroga from only twelve yards. With a quarter of an hour gone, all the optimism began to crystalize when Jordan gave Scotland the lead. A shot by Rioch was parried, Jordan hustled in the rebound. MacLeod was, no doubt, quietly confident. But the next ten minutes saw an overwhelming transformation, with Peru tearing Scotland's defence to shreds.

Suddenly Kennedy and Buchan were in fearful trouble as Oblitas and Munante began to go past them like the wind. Most sinister of all, the veteran and marvellously skilful Cubillas, survivor of the team in the 1970 finals in Mexico, was destroying Scotland in midfield. In the centre of attack, La Rosa was pulling Forsyth and Burns all over the place. Rough, in the Scotland goal, had to save from La Rosa and Oblitas; Cubillas and Munante singed the fringes of the goal.

On the bench, Gemmill and others were already urging

MacLeod to make changes, even at this early stage of the game, because it was transparently obvious that Rioch and Masson could not cope with the pace of Peru's midfield trio, Cueto, Velasquez and Cubillas. Rioch and Masson were regularly left trailing the wrong side of their men. They were unlikely to reverse the situation. With twenty-seven minutes gone, the unorthodox Quiroga made an exceptional save. Out on the edge of his penalty area, he somehow managed to get his fingertips to a lob from Dalglish: in retrospect it was undoubtedly a turning point. Three minutes before half-time, Peru equalized, Cubillas and Oblitas scorching through on the left, Cueto whipping the ball past Rough from eight yards.

Not only did MacLeod resist the need to change and reorganize the team, but he offered little tactical advice for the second half. His only concession to the gathering crisis was to instruct Rough to make longer clearances to bypass the Peruvian midfield. He seemed not to recognize the fundamental disparity in midfield. In the second half, Peru continued to attack; La Rosa headed close. With an hour gone, Dalglish, taking a headed pass from Jordan on the turn, had his shot deflected over the bar. Two minutes later, Scotland could have grasped a lifeline, but missed it. A questionable penalty was given against Cubillas for bringing down Rioch, but Masson's tame kick, hit without power to a convenient shoulder height, was easily saved by Quiroga. Ten minutes later, Peru were in front.

Munante and Cueto sliced through a hesitant defence and Cubillas struck a tremendous shot to beat Rough from outside the penalty area. Sensing the crisis at last, now that he had actually been overtaken by it, MacLeod sent out Gemmill and Macari to replace Masson and Rioch. But the damage was done and, a few minutes later, Peru were out of reach. Kennedy, all composure gone, flattened Oblitas on the edge of the area. Cubillas, ebony executioner, bent his kick round the end of the defensive wall, just over Macari's shoulder, and into the top left-hand corner of the goal. As Bobby Charlton said afterwards: 'If I could have planned the game for Peru I could not have done it better than Scotland did. Peru wanted two things, to play one-twos going into the penalty area and to win free kicks just outside. To South Americans, a free kick in that position is almost as good as a penalty.'

Extraordinarily, MacLeod compounded his errors the next day—his persistence with Jordan and a fading midfield, the omission of Andy Gray—by blaming his players. 'Eight of the team just didn't play,' he claimed. At the morning press conference out at Alta Gracia, he failed to put forward a single coherent explanation other than the fact that it was simply 'a bad day'. He unwittingly summarized the position when he stated: 'I can't put my finger on it.' He did not, apparently, think his selection was at all at fault, or that he had underestimated Peru's wingers, or that Scotland had been outplayed in midfield. He went so far as to imply that Peru had tactically 'cheated' by not tackling back in midfield when they lost the ball, so that when they regained it they then had more players than Scotland nearer to the Scottish goal! Scotland were almost out of the World Cup at the first hurdle because they had hired the local blacksmith as manager instead of an international architect.

All now depended on the game against Iran but the result of that match proved to be almost as great a disaster as the first. Buchan and Burns were now chosen as central defenders, never having played together before; although Gemmill and Macari kept their places, there was still no room for Souness or Johnstone. Andy Roxburgh, Scotland's director of coaching, had advised MacLeod that Iran used a rigid 4-4-2 formation with only two strikers up front; that MacLeod should play three at the back, two markers either side of Buchan, with four in midfield and three strikers. But MacLeod scorned the advice, persisted with four men at the back, replacing Kennedy with Jardine, who had nobody to mark but seldom provided the extra width in attack which would have been so valuable.

An own goal by Eskandarian gave Scotland a half-time lead. When Buchan had to go off with a cut head, MacLeod replaced him with . . . another defender, Forsyth. This did not prevent Danaie-Fard equalizing shortly afterwards. With a quarter of an hour to go, MacLeod, still ignoring the claims of Derek Johnstone on the bench, sent out Joe Harper; but he joined a team without pattern and, soon, Scotland were out of the World Cup, lacking leadership and tactics. As they sat in their bus afterwards waiting to return to Alta Gracia, they were spat at and jeered by demented Scottish fans chanting: 'You only want the money.'

That was unfair. What the players wanted more than any-thing was a manager. For the third match against Holland, the players virtually took over the running of the team and defeated the Dutch, who could afford to lose, in a belated exposition of the sort of skills which, properly organized, might have made so much more of an impact on a competition decidedly short on great teams. Graham Souness converted them into a slick fighting force two matches too late. Gemmill scored one of the outstanding goals of the competition, but all Scotland were left with was the anguish of knowing what might have been.

Scotland: Rough; Kennedy, Forsyth, Burns, Buchan; Rioch (Macari), Masson (Gemmill), Hartford; Dalglish, Jordon, Johnston

Peru: Quiroga; Duarte, Manzo, Chumpitaz, Diaz; Cueto (Rojas), Velasquez, Cubillas; Munante, La Rosa (Sotil), Oblitas

CHAPTER TWENTY-THREE

Argentina 3
v
Holland 1

WORLD CUP FINAL

1978

Holland plan to go back to the dressing room in a controversial start to the World Cup Final—but Johan Neeskens' ability to speak Spanish gives the game away, perhaps literally.

The 1978 World Cup Final was the climax of a tournament interwoven with more intrigues and downright skulduggery than a Le Carré spy thriller. One almost needed to be George Smiley rather than a football correspondent to follow the plot. Did Peru, for instance, sell themselves for clandestine pesos when they lost to Argentina by six goals in the decisive match which put the hosts in the Final? The rumours raged, but I like to think, possibly naïvely, that Peru were clean. If not, they were most certainly brilliant actors, for they were twice within inches of scoring first in that game in Rosario which gave Argentina goal-difference over Brazil for a place in the Final.

The Thursday before the Sunday final was heavy with drama in the concluding matches of the two second round groups. Holland defeated Italy 2-1 after being behind at half-time, while West Germany suffered their first ever defeat by Austria. But Brazil really put the cat among the pigeons with a 3-1 win over Poland in the afternoon, leaving Argentina needing to win by a four-goal margin in the evening. In Buenos Aires, Holland gave Italy a goal start and then cantered into the Final with more tactical switches than a telephone exchange has lines. Arie Haan hit the winner a quarter of an hour from the end with one of the memorable goals of the finals—a thirty-yard drive which soared past Dino Zoff, in Italy's goal, to end the carefully laid plans of Enzo Bearzot. Holland's young defender from P.S.V., Ernie Brandts, had given Italy the lead with an own-goal, but equalized early in the second half. Italy dominated the first half of an often physical game, Holland the second. The expedient, occasionally ruthless Dutchmen were more than a match for the likes of Italian hardmen Tardelli and Benetti.

At the centre of the smear campaign surrounding Argentina's thrashing of Peru that evening was Peru's goalkeeper, the Argentinian-born Quiroga who, until then, had been one of the competition's most colourful figures with his unconventional style and remarkable saves. I suspect that the Brazilians deliberately began the rumours that Quiroga would leave his door on the latch for Argentina, in an attempt to provoke him to play the game of his life. Quiroga himself professed a desire to excel against the country which had rejected him, even though, he said, 'I know that if I do I will become the most hated man in the country.'

For twenty minutes, Peru attacked with fury; and another factor overlooked by those who claim that the result could have been fixed is that French referee Robert Wurtz had a long-standing friendship with Brazil. Frankly, the eventual landslide, I am convinced, was the outcome of natural forces: the fact that Peru had little to play for and that Argentina had everything.

Of course Argentina were vulnerable. In the first-round matches against Hungary and then France, they had been shamelessly favoured by the referees, Garrido of Portugal and Dubach of Switzerland respectively. Hungary had played superbly for forty-five minutes and, when their marvellous centre-forward Torocsik was sent off, it was for a gesture of retaliation against persistent Argentinian provocation. Dubach gave a penalty against the French centre-back Tresor which was blatantly unjust. When Italy beat Argentina 1-0 in the final game of the first round, they exposed the host's limitations, thanks to some strict refereeing by Abraham Klein of Israel. Without a doubt, Klein should have been given the Final, on account of his resolute impartiality; in the selection meeting, however, Artemio Franchi, U.E.F.A. President and chairman of the referee's committee, gave Gonella the casting vote. In some fierce lobbying, the Argentinians had let it be known that they would protest against the appointment of Klein: not, they claimed, on the grounds of his handling of their earlier game with Italy, but of Holland's political alignment with Israel!

Gonella's feebleness was apparent even before a ball was kicked. With Holland out on the pitch and warming up under the eye of a television audience of some 800 million, Argentina delayed their appearance in front of an ecstatic ticker-tape welcome some eight minutes. Then, following this deliberately calculated piece of provocation aimed at unnerving the opposition, Argentina protested about a bandage-covered plastic splint on the right arm of René Van Der Kerkhof, Holland's right-winger. He had played with this protection for a broken bone in five of Holland's six games, and their skipper, Rudi Krol, says:

'It was unbelievable. An official from F.I.F.A. should have intervened. I'm convinced that both Argentina's late arrival on the pitch, and the protest over René, were carefully planned. We had already warmed up, and where we made a big mistake was in not returning to the dressing room as we intended, even if it meant delaying the World Cup Final by another half-hour. Our manager, Happel, had said when they complained to the referee about René, "we'll go back to the dressing room" but, unfortunately, Neeskens translated his threat to the Argentinian players. And they told the referee. When he realized we were threatening to leave the pitch, he changed his mind and said that René could play. He did not want to take the decision which would have stopped the match, even if only temporarily. He knew the eyes of the world were on him, and he was embarrassed. We were very angry, and that's why we were not concentrating properly in the early part of the match. We should have played them at their own game and returned to the dressing room as we threatened. Neeskens had said to their captain, Passarella, "If that's how you want it, you can play the World Cup Final on your own." It was our mistake.'

The fact is that Argentina were scared, and with good reason. They sensed, correctly, that Holland's collective football was superior, and that if it came to intimidation, Holland had more hard men than they. Out at Argentina's training camp, behind an armada of security guards and police, their left-back Tarantini had voiced the fears among his colleagues when he told me before the Final: 'The gap between European and South American concepts of the game makes me worry. Holland are hard. They are very strong and tackle powerfully. We are worried about what we saw in the Italy-Holland match.'

Cesar Menotti, Argentina's endlessly chain-smoking manager with the austere presence of some religious leader, was unequivocal in his plans for the Final:

'We will attack flat out. Holland have superior physical strength, but we will continue to take the same risks, to go straight for victory. We have achieved more than I dared hope for three months ago. The Final will be decided by possession. Holland's total football is probably unanswerable at its peak, but they have to get the ball first. I'm scared because of the way Holland played against Italy but, in spite of this, we will attack from the start.'

Ernst Happel, in charge of Holland, was one of Europe's mercenaries: a famous Austrian international who had been a trooper in Germany's trenches on the Russian front, he was currently manager of European Cup finalists Bruges of Belgium, and had been offered the startling sum of £50,000 to guide Holland for the duration of the World Cup finals. He talked little to the press, had a tactical attitude which was cynically functional, and said before the Final: 'We are optimistic. We do not know what the word "fear" means. We do not care which team Menotti chooses.' Rudi Krol was more specific when he told me: 'Four years ago in Germany, we played the better football and lost. We are not prepared to accept that again. The emotional crowd factor favours them, the physical factors favour us.' René's brother Willy said: 'Argentina must not be allowed the freedom to flow; our instructions are to lock them up in the middle of the field. They are less strong there and we can make them struggle, and then hit them on the counter-attack.'

Certainly Argentina had no scope for playing a containing game. The only player of their front six who was at all defensive was Gallego in central midfield between Ardiles and Kempes. There was a doubt about Ardiles, who had a damaged ankle. He was the fulcrum of their side and rated by Ron Greenwood, the England manager who was an avid spectator, as possibly the most significant player in the whole competition. Greenwood told me: 'Ardiles does everything right. He's involved all over the pitch and his vision is tremendous.' In an era of tactical sophistication exemplified by Italy, Holland and Brazil, Argentina were almost naïve in having a front line of two wingers, Bertoni and Ortiz, on either side of Luque, with Kempes forging through from midfield on the left side to combine with Luque. Tarantini was defensively suspect at left-back and, indeed, Argentina's capacity to survive against intelligent counter-attack had consistently depended on the consuming ability of their magnificent captain, Passarella, the sweeper alongside centre-half Galvan. Much depended also on the unorthodox brilliance of Fillol in goal.

Holland were far more compact. Krol was at the absolute height of his powers as the 'free' man in defence; Willy Van Der Kerkhof, Neeskens and Haan were the most experienced midfield in the competition; up front, the absence of Cruyff was more a matter of regret for the public than for the Dutch themselves. Cruyff had decided long before the finals that on personal and political grounds—the prospect of being kidnapped on or off the pitch—he did not wish to be there. Johnny Rep therefore switched into the middle to assume Cruyff's role, with René Van Der Kerkhof on the right, and Rensenbrink on the left. Holland still possessed the intellect as well as the muscle.

Looking back now, Krol believes that Holland's chance of winning the title was about as good in 1978 as four years earlier.

'In Germany, we probably had more class players, with Cruyff and Van Hanegem, whereas in Argentina we played a more collective football. Argentina had individuals, but up to a point they were playing collectively. I think maybe we were better prepared mentally in 1974. We had the advantage of having our training camp just over the border from Holland, and we were able to see our wives and families regularly. In Argentina, the early games in Mendoza were bad because the pitch was too soft and, by the time we beat Italy to go into the Final, although we were very happy, we were ready to go home. It was a long tournament and we were tired.'

Neeskens' threat to Passarella as the players stood around the side of the pitch during the row over René Van Der Kerkhof's arm helped to convince the Argentinians and Gonella that Holland would not be messed about any more; and the game started. It was quickly obvious that Holland were looking for some immediate retribution and, in the early minutes, there were crunching fouls by left-back Poortvliet and Haan on Bertoni and Ardiles: exactly what Argentina had feared and, what no doubt, had been partly responsible for their extreme gamesmanship before the kick-off.

Soon, Holland had the first of several openings which, if taken, would have buried the Argentinian dream. Haan was fouled wide of the penalty area on the left, and sent over the free kick himself, Rep climbed above Passarella and Galvan, but his header flew just wide. Holland at this stage were already achieving their objective of slowing the game, with nine or ten men behind the ball immediately Argentina were on the attack. Brandts was having difficulty against the volatile Luque, so sharp on the turn, and this led to Krol being booked after a quarter of an hour for a foul on Bertoni, as the winger exploited an error by Brandts.

However, the inaction of the referee was soon going to bear heavily on the tone of the game. Gonella failed to see, or at least failed to act upon, Bertoni's vicious elbow-jab on Neeskens as the players lined up for a free kick; soon afterwards, no action was taken when Galvan, with total cynicism, deliberately handled a through ball as Haan and Rep counterattacked at speed. At the other end, Passarella forced Jongbloed to save a tremendous shot from outside the penalty area. Jongbloed, the keeper in the Munich Final, was now playing because of an injury to Schrijvers, sustained in a collision with Brandts at the moment of the own goal against Italy.

Kempes and Bertoni were testing Holland's defence, while

the Dutch shook their heads in annoyance at their own lack of coordination when counter-attacking. With twenty-four minutes gone, Passarella, one of the truly great players of the tournament, again missed narrowly with a close-range volley over the bar as he stole in behind the defensive wall to meet Olguin's free kick.

No team since the Second World War has won the World Cup without the help of an outstanding goalkeeper, and now came an example of Fillol's exceptional contribution to Argentina's triumph. Jansen, going through on the right, crossed the ball to the back of the penalty area, Rep let fly a thundering drive and Fillol, to an avalanche of cheers, deflected the shot over the bar.

Seven minutes before half-time, Kempes snatched the first goal which released the crowd, not to say the waiting nation outside, on a tidal wave of excitement. It was Ardiles who set it up: winning a tackle on the left and slipping the ball square to Luque who immediately pushed it on between Brandts and Krol. Kempes had to accelerate past Krol before shooting wide of Jongbloed almost in one movement.

Soon afterwards, Galvan should have been booked for catching a really threatening, chipped through ball by Willy Van Der Kerkhof, but this outrageous foul was passively ignored by Gonella. In the last minute of the first half, Holland should have equalized, but a glorious opening went begging. Willy Van Der Kerkhof crossed from the left, Neeskens beyond the far post climbed up for a tremendous, controlled header back into the goal-mouth. For once Fillol was helpless as the ball arched back towards the left-hand post. Rensenbrink raced forward, lunged with both feet to connect on the half-volley only three yards from the line, but failed to direct properly and somehow Fillol smothered the ball.

If Holland had scored then, I have little doubt that they would have won the Cup. In almost all the individual conflicts on the pitch, except that between Willy Van Der Kerkhof and Kempes, they were holding their own or even had an advantage. Throughout the second half, they were even more in command than they had been against Germany four years previously. Had they drawn level before the eighty-first minute, they would still have won, but the fates and the referee were against them. For the third time, Galvan handled a critical through pass eleven minutes after half-time without so much as a caution, and now Happel sent out Nanninga in place of Rep to apply greater physical force on the centre of Argentina's defence. Twice, within minutes, Nanninga was fouled without a free kick being given. Ardiles, his ankle now giving him trouble, was replaced by Larrosa. As time slipped by, Holland became desperate: Happel replaced Jansen with Suurbier, the right-back in Munich. In the seventy-third minute, Neeskens, stabbing through the middle, was monstrously upended by Galvan a few yards outside the penalty area. Again there was no booking. Holland must have felt like making an appeal to the Geneva Convention, but an equalizer was just round the corner.

René Van Der Kerkhof, put clear by Haan, crossed from the right and the ball was driven home by Nanninga as he outjumped Galvan and Passarella. Now Argentina were panicking; René was streaming past Tarantina and, with almost the last kick of full-time, Rensenbrink, creeping in behind the defence on the left to meet Suurbier's cross, miskicked against the post from an acute angle but no more than a few yards out.

Like England in 1966, Argentina had had victory snatched by a late goal which forced extra-time, the difference being that Holland were convincingly superior during normal time. Now, in extra-time, Holland faded, their energy drained by their ceaseless running off-the-ball in the second half which had so nearly overwhelmed the hosts. In the fourteenth minute, Kempes scored a fine individual goal. Put through by Bertoni on the left, he held off several challenges, had his first shot smothered by Jongbloed, but somehow managed to prod home the rebound as he fell. Neeskens was by now limp with exhaustion, even his remarkable fighting spirit doused and, in the second period of extra-time, Argentina were in full flood. Six minutes from time, Bertoni, Luque and Kempes bore down on the Dutch defence in a line, Bertoni hitting the shot which made Argentina's victory secure. In the remaining minutes, both teams kicked lumps out of each other. As so often during the match, the referee might just as well not have been there.

For the next twelve hours, the streets were jammed yet again as the people celebrated in an orgy of emotion what was regarded as a symbolic 'liberation' of the country. We would never know how many were not celebrating: that was the unseen face of Argentina, the fate of its political prisoners; though it has to be said that the bulk of the population appeared free of repression, and were now briefly and deliriously happy. Not Holland. They knew they had been robbed.

Gonella's handling of the game had been pitifully weak, not to say prejudiced, and it is tantalizing to wonder what might have happened had Klein been in charge. I suspect Argentina would have been denied their celebration though, as Krol admits, 'We did not reach our normal form—and we missed enough chances to have won the match. It is also my opinion that Kempes was lucky with his second goal in extra-time. If we had been drawing at half-time, if Bobby's shot from three metres had gone in, we would have beaten them easily.'

Yet if I felt sick at heart for Holland, it was impossible not to hold admiration and sympathy for the winners. They had waited forty-eight years for this rapturous moment. Since the first World Cup in 1930, they had given more famous players to the game than almost any country including Brazil, and now they had gained their belated reward with style and passion. It was a huge tribute to their manager, Cesar Menotti, who had turned his back on all the traditional post-war brutality of Argentinian football, on the tactical cynicism which had provoked Alf Ramsey's notorious accusation of 'animals', to produce a team bubbling with flamboyance and adventure. Nobody would have believed even a couple of years beforehand that defensive, so-often-villainous Argentina could win a World Cup with open attack. But they had. Menotti had resolutely set himself against the demonic traditions of the infamous Juan Carlos Lorenzo when he stated on accepting the job: 'My country's football needs total reorganization. If we could win the World Cup the way I would like us to, it would inspire others to reassess the way we play the game. Perhaps it will stop us placing such reliance on violence and cynicism, which are the tools of fear. Argentinian football possesses too much skill to need to be afraid.' Few believed that Menotti's resolution would survive. But it had.

Argentina: Fillol; Olguin, Galvan, Passarella, Tarantini; Ardiles (Larrosa), Gallego, Kempes; Bertoni, Luque, Ortiz (Houseman)

Holland: Jongbloed; Jansen (Suurbier), Brandts, Krol, Poortvliet; Van Der Kerkhof W., Neeskens, Haan; Van Der Kerkhof R., Rep (Nanninga), Rensenbrink

CHAPTER TWENTY-FOUR

Arsenal 3

v

Manchester United 2

F.A. CUP FINAL

1979

Arsenal make a controversial substitution, lose a two-goal lead in the F.A. Cup Final with only minutes to go—and still win in one of the most dramatic of all Wembley climaxes. Did the Manchester United goalkeeper blunder?

Many people were leaving their seats at Wembley to avoid the jams on road and rail when, barely five minutes from the end of the 1979 F.A. Cup Final, Arsenal were coasting to victory with a two-goal lead in a match which had only occasionally reached the peaks of excitement which had been expected. As so often with the F.A. show-piece, it had been something of an anti-climax, just 'another' Cup Final. Indeed, a friend of mine for whom I had managed to obtain a ticket for his first-ever Final a few years short of his retirement, was one of those who missed the whole of the last, explosive and remarkable phase.

It was Arsenal's second consecutive final, that of the previous year having been lost to Ipswich by the only goal, and their third outstanding team since the war to have reached two finals. They were hoping to reverse the pattern because, in 1950-52 and 1971-72, they had won the first and lost the second of a 'pair'. How good was the present team compared with the previous two?

Whatever the result of this match most people would reckon that pride of place would have to be given to Bertie Mee's team, which achieved the Cup and League double in 1971. If attempting to make an all-time selection from Arsenal's teams across the post-war span of thirty-five years, Mee's team would claim no less than six of my XI—Pat Rice, Frank McLintock, Bob McNab, John Radford, Ray Kennedy and, from the side which lost to Leeds a year later, Alan Ball. My XI would be: Jennings; Rice, O'Leary, McLintock, McNab; Ball, Brady, Mercer; Radford, Kennedy, Armstrong.

I have to leave out Charlie George, perhaps the most talented of any player on the Highbury books in this time, because he so sadly never fulfilled a throbbing potential for either Arsenal or England. The choice of goalkeeper is a difficult one, because Arsenal have been graced over the years by three marvellous, equally phlegmatic, reliable men: George Swindin, Bob Wilson and Pat Jennings. And that is excluding the exceptional Jack Kelsey, who never played in a Final. Although Jennings only came to Highbury in the evening of his career, when Spurs refused to give him another £5,000 a year at a time when he was still worth £50,000, he must get my vote. His consistency over the years places him above even Gordon Banks.

Arsenal's post-war history has been rich in full-backs, with Scott, Barnes and Smith from the team which beat Liverpool in 1950 and lost to Robledo's late goal for Newcastle two years later. It was Barnes' injury, twisting a knee when trying to pursue Newcastle's elusive winger, Mitchell, which proved the turning point in 1952. But my choice goes to the Double pair, Rice—who survived to captain the 1979 team—and McNab. Masterminding the 1971 team was McLintock, who had been to Wembley so often with Leicester and Arsenal, not to mention Scotland, that he could find his way there blindfold, and there could be no other partner for him than David O'Leary, pillar of the modern side, whatever the claims of dependable Leslie Compton. The brilliant young Irishman was one of the most potent reasons for predicting an Arsenal victory in this match—which I did not.

In midfield, Arsenal have possessed three players whose greatness illuminated not just their own team but the period in which they played—Joe Mercer, Alan Ball and Liam Brady.

Mercer, running himself to a standstill, had almost single-handedly kept Arsenal afloat against Newcastle—in vain. Ball, though he came after the Double and was on the losing side against Leeds, would rate in anybody's team, while Brady, in spite of the severe disappointment of 1978 against Ipswich when only half-fit, was the mainspring of the present side, and possessed a reputation he would confirm to the full against United.

Up front it is a tough choice for the all-time Cup team. Old timers would argue the case for Reg Lewis, who scored both goals in 1950, Doug Lishman and Freddie Cox. Equally strong is the claim of Frank Stapleton, leader of the current team and possibly the most consistent in the British Isles. But, on balance, I must go for the 1971 trio, so well-balanced and knowing each other's movements instinctively.

The Manchester United team which walked out to meet Rice's side was the club's fifth outstanding side since the war. It was their third Final in four seasons, a feat only achieved in recent times by Leeds in 1970-73, and equalled by none of the other Old Trafford teams. Yet in spite of the success achieved by Tommy Docherty and subsequently Dave Sexton, could any team compare with the one which perished at Munich? The comparison needed to be no burden for Martin Buchan when he led out the present side, for Duncan Edwards and that incomparable team of 1957 set the tone and style which for twenty years established Manchester United as something special wherever football is discussed. Standing back from the clamour of the event now at hand, and sifting all those great players who have graced Old Trafford, only Buchan, of the present side, ranks in the all-time Cup XI. There were some excellent men going out to battle with Arsenal: Steve Coppell, Lou Macari, Sammy McIlroy. But if we are looking for the quality which lifts players out of their own generation, then it is fair to say that the sides of 1955-58 and 1966-68 represented the peak—Roger Byrne's tragic team with five of the best XI, the 1968 side with four, Bobby Charlton common to both. Of course, the team which won the European Cup failed in the F.A. Cup through four losing semi-finals, but they, in their spectacular way, came closest to the Munich immortals, with Paddy Crerand, Charlton, George Best and Denis Law, who missed the European Final.

Reaching back into the mists of 1948, the era of Jack Crompton, of Chilton, Aston, Morris and Rowley, I would place in the all-time Manchester United team Johnny Carey at right-back and Charlie Mitten at outside-left from the side which so memorably beat Blackpool 4-2. Moving on to the Busby Babes, Harry Gregg (now an Old Trafford coach), Edwards, Byrne, Viollet and Charlton are automatic selections. That excludes the superb little Eddie Colman, Tommy Taylor and David Pegg, all on the threshold of glittering international careers when they died. Piecing together the broken parts of his club and his own body, Matt Busby took United back to Wembley in 1963 with a new side (if we exclude that remarkable, emotional freak of 1958) with a team including Maurice Setters, Albert Quixall and Johnny Giles. But only Charlton, who spanned three eras, Crerand and Law gain selection for my all-time team. All survived to embellish the fourth great side which earned the ultimate European reward, with support at the back from the veteran Bill Foulkes and controversial Nobby Stiles.

Considering now the present team, with its three or four alterations from that which lost the 1976 Final to Southampton, it was possible they would go on to reach more Wembley finals than any team in history. For the moment, my all-star, post-war team would be: Gregg; Carey, Buchan, Edwards, Byrne; Crerand, Viollet, Charlton; Best, Law, Mitten.

Until Buchan's side matched, and finally beat, Liverpool in two Herculean semi-finals, I would not have given United the flicker of a chance against Arsenal. But now they went into the Final with not a single neutral professional prepared to give odds. Arsenal, I felt, were marginally form favourites with a team which was a blend of craft and true grit and, in Brady, had one of the most gifted players in Europe, who could turn any game. Some of Arsenal's players took the view that for some reason I was down on them, but nothing could have been further from the truth. Certainly I had at times expressed the view that they were unnecessarily defensive, but this was because I recognized in them the talents which could be more expressive. As some of Europe's great clubs decline—Real, Ajax, Benfica, Inter—it is more than ever desirable for English clubs not just to be successful abroad, but to set standards. I had played some part, before Terry Neill's appointment, in trying to help Arsenal secure one of the world's best managers, Miljan Miljanic. It is almost an axiom that if English soccer is to be strong, then Arsenal must be strong. I was as ready as anybody to welcome a spectacle worthy of the historic setting. We see too few. But if Arsenal interpreted their responsibility as whacking their opponent instead of the ball, or dropping their shorts, as had recently happened at Highbury, then they must expect the condemnation of millions. What we got was beyond expectation.

There were so many battles in prospect which could tip the result within the main battle. Buchan's ability to control the immensely mobile Alan Sunderland would be as vital as his marking of Kenny Dalglish in the semi-final. Both he and Gordon McQueen would have to be alert for Stapleton's blind-side runs to meet crosses from the opposite flank—something Arsenal had been busy working on in training in the week leading up to Wembley. In the other penalty area, O'Leary and Willie Young would have to win the battle in the sky with Joe Jordan, while simultaneously facing the thorny problem of whether to follow Jimmy Greenhoff when he wandered, or guard the middle. On a true, fast surface, Young, such a favourite at Highbury, could be in difficulties on the big day. In goal, Jennings the immovable had in fact been strangely at fault on his last visit to Wembley with Northern Ireland, while the twenty-year-old Gary Bailey might find his precocious self-confidence either an armour or his downfall.

In midfield there would be the tussle of will-power between Lou Macari and Brady, Sammy McIlroy and Brian Talbot. Who would dictate to whom? Any marked advantage here would probably be decisive, and Arsenal had again laid careful plans. Yet for me, beforehand, the key seemed to lie down the flanks of the Arsenal defence, where Coppell and Mickey Thomas could prove too swift, too insistent for the veteran Rice and Sammy Nelson. In the *Express* I wrote: 'Frankly, there isn't a whisker in it, and we may well see extra-time or a replay. If pushed for a verdict I would say that, because fortune favours the brave, Manchester United's greater persistence in attack and resourcefulness on the wings will edge it.' It nearly did.

My feelings about the need to entertain echoed those of Dave Sexton, who told me on the eve of the Final:

'Throughout my football life I've always had one ideal: that is to have a team which plays eleven-man soccer, in which every player is in tune with the others. It is when this happens that you get a great spectacle for the public, and it would be marvellous if this could happen tomorrow, a Final for people to remember whether we win or lose. As coach and manager with both a top club and the national squad under Ron Greenwood, I have a big responsibility for the shape of the game as it is played in England. Although we tend to be highly self-critical, the game here is strong. Teams like Liverpool, Forest, Arsenal and, I hope, United are proving this continually in Europe. But the sort of things we need to improve are mostly technical, above all in variations of movement. Particularly crossing, because this is a special skill which has been allowed to lapse during a period in which wingers went out of fashion. Some years ago when I was a player, I sat down to make a note of the things I most wanted from football and it was: 1. To play well myself; 2. For my team mates to think I was a good player; 3. For the opposition to think I was a good player; 4. For the opposition to think my team was a good team; 5. For it to be a good game for the spectators; 6. For my team to win. That's not to say I lacked the will to win. That's something I take for granted, but it is important that we should play in such a way that everyone, not just our own supporters, admires our performance.'

You could not find a better platform on which to approach a Wembley final.

Don Howe, Arsenal's coach, has always been essentially pragmatic, a student of the art of the possible rather than the ideal. In the build-up that week, his instructions to his side had been:

'United hustle and bustle, their midfield men are here, there and everywhere, they're always wanting to get forward. How can we turn this to our advantage? If they throw men forward, we must get behind them and attack their back four, get Liam in to the dead-ball line. We have Talbot, Price and Rix who we can pull back to defend, which leaves Brady free. If we do get in behind them we must get over the crosses, because our spies, Wilf Dixon and George Male, have seen that they're vulnerable on the far post, because the opposite full-back tucks in too far, both Nicholl and Albiston over-cover on McQueen, almost as far as the penalty spot.'

It was to prove a critically accurate assessment.

When the match began it was soon evident that Macari was intent on keeping a close check on Brady but, after only twelve minutes, Brady rippled through on the right to set up the opening goal. Going past Thomas, he sent Stapleton clear. Stapleton's sharp near-post cross found Price, who had quickly pushed forward, and, with the help of a lucky bounce, he evaded a tackle and pulled the ball back into the path of Sunderland. Talbot was also moving in fast, the two went for the ball together, and it was Talbot—on the winning side for Ipswich the previous year—who got the touch. Yet for the next half hour it was United, unshaken, who had most of the game. Arsenal conceded a succession of corners, Rice was booked for repeated robust challenges, and Jennings dealt competently with shots from Thomas, who was finding a lot of space, and Jordan. Greenhoff made an opening for himself with a fine diagonal run but snatched at his shot; Macari headed at Jennings from close in. Certainly, United were making the running now, but there was something lacking from their game; they were not really solid. And now came a masterstroke from Arsenal's pre-match planning. A cross by Thomas was intercepted, United's defence were caught four against five on the break . . . and the man in possession was Brady.

Weaving through on the right, Brady reached the edge of the penalty area and there, sure enough, over on the left was Stapleton, stealing round the back of the defence. Brady's right-foot cross flew straight to Stapleton's forehead, level with the far post, and United, having been the more positive of the two teams, went in for half-time two down.

Marginally United continued to have the edge afterwards, but their game lacked sparkle and bite. McQueen went close with a header over the bar; another chance came and went for Macari. Arsenal were clearly more intent on controlling the game now than embroidering it, and it had every appearance of fading away into disappointment.

It was then, with only five minutes to go, that Arsenal's manager, Terry Neill, decided to send on his substitute, Steve Walford, in place of Price. The game was seemingly won, and there were two instant opinions of Neill's move: that, reasonably enough, he was giving a young player at least a few minutes of Cup Final football which he might never again experience, or that he was tampering unnecessarily with a balanced side. Howe was to tell me later:

'United had been having a lot of the ball, but without giving us too many problems. On the other hand, Price was clearly tired, he'd been filling a double role, checking both their left-back Albiston, when he came forward, and Thomas. We put on Walford to help cope with the work load, after discussion on the bench for ten minutes or so beforehand. The only slight reservation was that Walford was a left-sided player, not right, but Price had increasingly been getting caught out through fatigue. There was no way that Walford was to blame for what happened—it was our left side which crumbled, which was where we'd been strong.'

What did happen will be remembered for a long time. Suddenly, Arsenal lost their composure. Coppell took a free kick, Jordan moved away to the left of the penalty area, swivelled and centred, and McQueen, taking a big, swinging, hopeful swipe with one of his long legs, drove the ball past a crowd of legs and wide of Jennings. There were four minutes to go. Now there was clear evidence of panic in Arsenal's defence, and it must be said, contrary to Howe's opinion, that the goal had come down Arsenal's right flank.

With only two minutes remaining, with the United thousands on the terraces wild with sudden hope, United unbelievably scored again. McIlroy, receiving from Coppell, set off on a dribble down the right. He went past O'Leary, then by-passed Walford, who had frantically come across to cover, and drove the ball firmly inside the post to put United level. There was pandemonium on the terraces and on the pitch. Arsenal, almost transfixed where they stood, could not for the moment comprehend what had happened. United, almost hysterical with relief and excitement, had to be prised apart like sticky boiled sweets to restart the game. Clearly, United now believed that victory was theirs in extra-time. There could not be another goal now: they still had their substitute to bring on, while Arsenal were already committed. And did not the team coming from behind, never more dramatically than now, traditionally have the ascendancy in morale and physical uplift? Brian Greenhoff, United's substitute, began warming up on the touchline for extra-time as United, after a protracted, premature celebration eventually lined up again to allow Arsenal to kick off.

There can be no doubt whatever that United now temporarily relaxed, just at the moment when they should have been moving towards what had seemed an impossible victory. With Sexton anxiously signalling that only two minutes of full-time remained, Arsenal kicked off and immediately attacked down the left. Brady, as mesmerizing as a poised cobra, swayed towards the United defence, drew two men and slipped the ball out to Graham Rix, who was racing clear down the line. Cutting in, Rix pitched across the perfect centre, close to the goal but fractionally too far for Bailey, sufficient to tempt him fatally. In these few split seconds which made soccer history, United sealed their fate with two errors.

As Rix's cross swung away from Bailey's vain, groping arms at the near corner of the six-yard area, Sunderland was sprinting in on the far post, where Albiston, as Howe had predicted, was too far in behind his centre-backs. As the ball dropped, Sunderland lunged forward and scooped it across the line. Howe said: 'If Sunderland had missed, there was Walford coming in behind him. We had got four men forward very quickly. I know a lot of people blame Bailey, but just look at the quality of Rix's cross. They had relaxed, even on the bench next to us.'

But for this unforgettable, second turn-about, Arsenal would indeed have been in serious trouble, because Sunderland, in spite of managing to stretch for the winner, was suffering from a painful knee and would have had to come off, leaving Arsenal with ten men. Buchan, too, was injured, but United still had Greenhoff in reserve. The climax, rivalling the finish of the 'Matthews' final, will be attributed as much to Bailey's blunder as Brady's nerveless eye for the kill. The British invented team games because they are character-forming, and Arsenal's triumph overflowed with the pain and joy of life's always uncertain river. With that same dead-pan, destructive

instinct with which the immortal Matthews buried Bolton a
quarter of a century before, Brady had now floored United with
passing as deadly as poison darts.

Yet the Final had illustrated one of the most pressing
anomalies of British soccer: had the most valuable factor of
Arsenal's victory been Brady's skill, or Talbot's consuming
running? There would be many claims that Talbot, who had
played five times for England under Revie, should now be
recalled by Greenwood. His energy a year before for Ipswich
had sapped Arsenal then as much as it now drained United.
Yet in the final analysis I believe that, as the professionals will
always tell you, football is about passing. Brady is a passer, and
Talbot is not.

Perhaps the most impressive of all was Dave Sexton's
magnanimity in defeat, when he said:

'I'm proud we were part of something as dramatic as this.
It was very cruel for us, having to run uphill for almost all
the game, reaching the top and then falling off. I don't blame
our boys, it wasn't that we relaxed but that Arsenal caught
us on the counter-punch. The fact that we came back to
make such an historic finish typifies the character that has
developed in the United team. Arsenal's three goals were
very similar, one of their players getting through to the line.
That's ideal: the goalkeeper has to come to the near post and,
from that moment, you just sit and pray. They were three
good crosses and three good goals, though Price was lucky
when the ball bounced right for him for the first goal. Of
course I'm unhappy that we gave away three goals, when you
consider the amount of play we had, but it's our responsibility to prove that the way we play is superior to the
way, say, Arsenal play. I do not believe that the way United
play makes it any more difficult to win the League, because
the public demand entertainment in conjunction with
success, and I agree with that.'

In defeat, Sexton's honour and pride were still intact—which is
how it should be.

Arsenal: Jennings; Rice, O'Leary, Young, Nel-
                        son; Price (Walford), Talbot, Brady,
                        Rix; Sunderland, Stapleton
Manchester United: Bailey; Nicholl, Buchan, McQueen,
                        Albiston; Coppell, Macari, McIlroy,
                        ~~Thomas~~; Jordan, Greenhoff J.

Bibliography

Banks, Gordon, *Banks of England*, Arthur Barker, 1980
Busby, Matt, *Soccer at the Top*, Weidenfeld and Nicolson, 1973
Crerand, Pat, *On Top with United*, Stanley Paul, 1969
Green, Geoffrey, *History of the F.A. Cup*, Naldrett Press, 1953
    Soccer in the Fifties, Allan, 1974
Gutteridge, Reg and Greaves, Jimmy, *Let's Be Honest*, Pelham Books, 1972
Kelly, Sir Robert, *History of Celtic*, Hay Nisbet and Miller Ltd, 1971
Law, Denis, *Denis Law: An Autobiography*, Queen Anne Press, 1979
MacLeod, Ally, *The Ally MacLeod Story*, Stanley Paul, 1979
Matthews, Stanley, *Feet First Again*, Transworld Publishers, 1955
Meisl, Willy, *Soccer Revolution*, Phoenix Sports Books, 1955
Miller, David, *Father of Football: The Story of Matt Busby*, Stanley Paul, 1970
Murphy, Jimmy, *Matt, United, and Me*, Souvenir Press, 1968
Pawson, Tony, *100 Years of the F.A. Cup*, Heinemann, 1972
Peebles, Ian, *Celtic Triumphant*, Stanley Paul, 1967
Powell, Jeff, *Bobby Moore*, Everest, 1976
    Sixty Memorable Matches, The, Marshall Cavendish, 1973
Stepney, Alex, *In Safe Keeping*, Pelham Books, 1969
Wright, Billy, *One Hundred Caps and All That*, Robert Hale, 1962

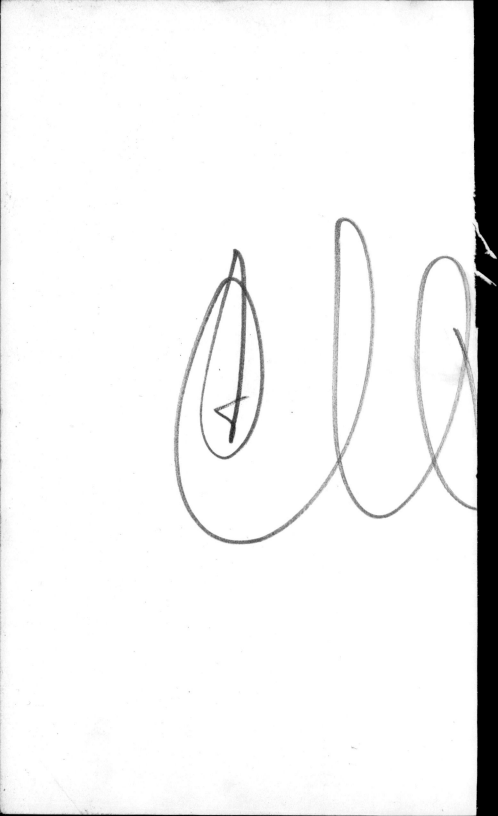